How to Read *an* Oral *Poem*

How to Read *an* Oral *Poem*

John Miles Foley

University of Illinois Press
Urbana and Chicago

∞ This book is printed on acid-free paper.

Library of Congress Cataloging-in-Publication Data
Foley, John Miles.
How to read an oral poem / John Miles Foley.
p.   cm.
Includes bibliographical references and index.
ISBN 0-252-02770-1 (cloth : alk. paper)
ISBN 0-252-07082-8 (pbk. : alk. paper)
1. Folk poetry. I. Title.
PN1341.F65   2002
398.2'09—dc21   2002002329

For Anne-Marie, Isaac, John Jr., Liz, and Hannah Frances

Moji dragi, ćemo svi zajedno,
u ovome mestu i svakome.

Contents

Prologue

You've opened this book; now how should you proceed? There are two choices, it seems to me, and either of them will prove quite viable. You can continue reading this prologue to learn more about the book's upcoming contents, or you can simply have a good look at the cover photograph and then plunge right into the "Four Scenarios" that begin the discussion. Some fair warning: there are a few surprises waiting for you in that first scenario, whenever you get to it.

* * *

How to Read an Oral Poem starts from square one. Above all, it's intended as a reader-friendly invitation to think about oral poetry on its own terms. Too many books about oral poetry assume that their readers have some prior experience or training in the subject, making it difficult or impossible for the nonspecialist to enter the conversation. *HROP* attempts to speak to the nonspecialist in a straightforward, uncomplicated way. Plain talk, plain style, and a cornucopia of examples are its mainstays. If in championing the cause of the nonspecialist this book errs on the side of simplicity and availability, then so be it.[1]

I've long felt that such a book was needed, and have wanted to write it for years. But there was always some built-in hesitation. What got in the way wasn't the material itself, but rather the challenge of explaining the structural and artistic dimensions of oral poetry clearly and directly enough to reach the audience I most wanted to reach. What came to the rescue was the continuing challenge of teaching and lecturing, which has spurred me to formulate basic ideas and premises in new ways, to find strategies for communicating complex and sometimes difficult observations in easily apprehensible form. In an important sense oral communication has provided the arena for evolving many of the strategies employed in this book.

Let me explain. In university classes and in lectures around the world I've seen time and again how the phenomenon of oral poetry captures the imagination of people from very different areas and backgrounds. I've watched them get excited about a field (and a technology of communication) that lies mostly outside modern Western experience, that causes them to reshuffle their cognitive categories and think about verbal art in new and different ways. Oral poetry often seems like a breath of fresh air for people who know verbal art only as literature. But there's another side to things as well. My own prior writings—as opposed to those classes and lectures and discussions—have always assumed a specialist readership, most often of scholars with expertise in ancient Greek, Old English, or South Slavic traditions. While these books and articles may have served certain purposes, they have not addressed the audience that in many ways most deserves attention. *HROP* is for that audience.

So precisely who are they? While I'd prefer not to set boundaries (since this book is all about getting beyond boundaries), I'd start by mentioning general readers above all. No prerequisite other than interest in verbal art and human nature is necessary to understand this book; it aspires to be a "good read" for anyone in search of learning more about the human expressive arts. As for disciplines, studies in oral poetry draw from and speak to literature, anthropology, music, folklore, religious studies, linguistics, history, theater, and many other well-defined areas. It's simply impossible to overstate the importance of oral poetry across the disciplinary spectrum, primarily because on available evidence it appears to be a universal human enterprise. Because oral poetry dwarfs written literature in size and variety, it should be everyone's concern.

Naturally enough, such an enormous and complex subject is daunting. It calls for more than any single book could ever provide. To meet that complexity I advocate two extensions or prostheses that, materially speaking, aren't part of this book. Nonetheless, they're freely available to all interested parties. First, I've established a Web site, <http://www.oraltradition.org>, that will host an electronic companion to this volume. At that address the reader will find such aids as an annotated bibliography, audio and video examples of oral poetry, and other opportunities to deepen and enrich the ideas presented in this book. I urge readers of *HROP* to visit this site, preferably with the book in one hand and a mouse in the other. Second, let me also encourage the extension of these ideas beyond the stage of theory, even beyond the examples given here as illustrations, to the oral poetries with which individual readers are most acquainted and most comfortable. Only through your ownership and personal application of these methods in your home area(s) will they take on a level of meaning with which you'll be satisfied and fulfilled.

Because no prologue should upstage the story it introduces, I'll be content with offering a brief map for our journey and leave you—like the audiences for oral poetry—to fill in the details as we proceed together. "Four Scenarios" is the jumping-off spot for our trek: it offers you the chance to become an audience for a Tibetan paper-singer, a North American slam poet, a South African praise-poet, and Homer. Oral performers are still in charge in the next section, "What the Oral Poets Say," where South Slavic *guslari* discuss such fundamental questions as what a "word" is. The answers they give are surprising and instructive.

After these initial sections comes a series of chapters, which I choose to call "words" for reasons that are explained in "What the Oral Poets Say." In the First and Second Words I concentrate on explaining the book's intentionally provocative title, *How to Read an Oral Poem*. Toward that end I pose four questions: (1) What is oral poetry? (2) What is reading? (3) What is *an oral poem* (as opposed to the collective phrase, "oral poetry")? and (4) What do we mean by "how"? The last of these questions then leads to descriptions of three well-developed methods: Performance Theory (the Third Word), Ethnopoetics (the Fourth Word), and Immanent Art (the Fifth Word). This menu of approaches proceeds from the conviction that the innate diversity of oral poetry requires multiple perspectives. Together they constitute a sort of interpretive tool kit for reading oral poetry.

The final four units in *HROP* complement what precedes them. The Sixth Word consists of a "Poor Reader's Almanac" of ten homemade *proverbs*, each of them constructed to capture the essence of an important idea in a memorable nutshell.[2] For example, in order to stress the contribution of idiomatic as well as literal meaning, one of the *proverbs* will maintain that "Oral poetry works like language, only more so." Another pseudo-maxim will hold that "True diversity demands diversity in frame of reference," advocating a pluralism of approach to match the natural pluralism of oral poetry. The Seventh Word applies our menu of reading methods to six oral poetries: Zuni and Kaqchikel (Mayan) storytelling, North American slam poetry, the south Indian *Siri Epic*, Homer's *Odyssey*, and the Old French *Song of Roland*. In the Eighth Word the focus narrows to the single, ethnically complex area of South Slavic oral poetry, viewing the genres of metrical charms, genealogies, funeral laments, and various strains of epic as an ecology of forms that interact with their traditional environment. The book closes with a brief Post-Script, which identifies dynamic similarities between oral poetry and the Internet and probes the advantages presented by the new electronic media for more faithful and useful editions of oral poetry.

* * *

Because of the genesis and development of *HROP,* I start my catalogue of thank-yous by remembering the many incarnations of classes in Oral Tradition at the University of Missouri-Columbia. More than anyone else, it was these students who helped me translate ideas about oral poetry into a language suitable for general discussion. I have profited far more than they did from our joint work. Conversations that arose during and in connection with lectures at various colleges, universities, and other institutions have also been extremely important to the formulation of this book. Let me remember with special gratitude colleagues' and students' comments and contributions during recent visits to Amherst College, the Universität Bonn, Bradley University, the Université de Caen, the University of California Los Angeles, the Chinese Academy of Social Sciences, the Universität Düsseldorf, the Folklore Fellows Summer Schools (at Mekrijaervi, Lammi, and Turku), the University of Helsinki, the University of Iowa, the Université de Lausanne, the Université de Lille, the University of Natal–Durban, Northwestern University, Odense University, Ohio State University, the Université Stendhal (Grenoble), Vassar College, and the University of Washington. Very much in the same vein, the six highly motivated groups of postdoctoral scholar-teachers who came to Missouri for eight-week seminars on "The Oral Tradition in Literature," under the auspices of the National Endowment for the Humanities, were highly instrumental in helping me work through the ideas presented here.

A list of individual heroes and heroines is harder to compose, since unlike an oral poet I can't lean on traditional implications in singing my catalogue. They all have to be credited explicitly in this single, textualized performance. Although I despair of faithfully recalling all friends and colleagues who in one way or another helped me make this book, let me offer my best recollection: Mark Amodio, Flemming Andersen, Pertti Anttonen, Egbert Bakker, Richard Bauman, Felice Belle, Mark Bender, Roger Bonair-Agard, David Bouvier, Susan Berry Brill de Ramírez, Wilhelm Busse, Jesse Byock, Chogjin, Carol Clover, Robert Payson Creed, Georg Danek, Robert Doran, Thomas DuBois, Joseph Duggan, Ruth Finnegan, John García, Scott Garner, Lauri Harvilahti, Jan Helldén, Ingrid Holmberg, Lauri Honko, Daniel Hooley, Richard Horsley, Dell Hymes, Bonnie Irwin, Martin Jaffee, Minna Skafte Jensen, Ahuvia Kahane, Russell Kaschula, Werner Kelber, Svetozar Koljević, Michelle Lacore, Anne Lebeck (*in memoriam*), Françoise Létoublon, Albert Bates Lord (*in memoriam*), Mary Louise Lord, Anne Mackay, Richard Martin, Catharine Mason, William B. McCarthy, Marty McConnell, John McDowell, Nada Milošević-

Djordjević, Jane Frances Morrissey, Gregory Nagy, Joseph Nagy, Susan Niditch, Walter Ong, Svetozar Petrović, Thomas Pettitt, William Plumstead, Michael Reichel, Karl Reichl, Alain Renoir, Philippe Rousseau, Mary Sale, David Schenker, Amy Shuman, Anna-Leena Siikala, Dennis Tedlock, Barre Toelken, Barbara Wallach, Phil West, Steve Zeitlin, John Zemke, and Russell Zguta. I trust those unintentionally omitted won't take offense at this poor bard's faulty memory.

Special thanks go to Barbara Kerewsky-Halpern and Joel Halpern, longtime mentors and generous co-fieldworkers and co-authors; to Stephen Mitchell, Gregory Nagy, Matthew Kay, and David Elmer, who helped so much with access to materials from the Milman Parry Collection of Oral Literature at Harvard University; to Nancy Mason Bradbury, who tried out some of the strategies presented here in her classes at Smith College; and to Lori Peterson Garner and Dale Smith, who read the manuscript in its entirety and offered many suggestions for its improvement.

Let me also register my gratitude to the University of Illinois Press, especially to Joan Catapano, editor-in-chief, and the three readers engaged by the press as reviewers.

Closer to the homefront, the University of Missouri–Columbia sponsored a 2000–2001 Provost's Research Leave that gave me the time and the space to conceive and complete this book. Its roots are also traceable to a 1995–96 fellowship from the American Council of Learned Societies, which has continued to provide unforeseen benefits and for which I remain very grateful. My two departments at Missouri, Classical Studies and English, have in various ways supported this project (never more enjoyably than in the latter-day oral epic performances known as the Homerathon and the Beowulfathon). Colleagues and assistants at the Center for Studies in Oral Tradition have often served as sounding boards for freshly minted ideas, and I appreciate their patience and their responses. Most recently, this *comitatus* has included Michael Barnes, Adam Dubé, Kristin Funk, Heather Hignite, Heather Maring, Marjorie Rubright, Aaron Tate, and John Zemke. Nor should I forget Darwin Hindman, mayor of Columbia, Missouri, who more than anyone else is responsible for the miles of local running and biking trails and the wetlands and bird sanctuaries they encircle. Whether he's aware of it or not, a great many problems in oral poetry studies have been solved while plodding along those trails.

Finally, I dedicate *How to Read an Oral Poem* to my beloved family, who enrich my life every day and "make my circle just."

Center for Studies in Oral Tradition
University of Missouri–Columbia

Notes

1. *HROP* is meant to stand on its own as a "way into" the subject of reading oral poetry. For detailed background information, which supports *HROP* in a number of different ways, let me cite a few of my prior, more specialized works: *The Theory of Oral Composition* (1988; history of Oral-Formulaic Theory), *Traditional Oral Epic* (1990; comparative structural analysis), *Immanent Art* (1991; the implications of structure for aesthetics), *The Singer of Tales in Performance* (1995a; comparative approaches to oral traditions), and *Homer's Traditional Art* (1999; guidelines for reading Homer as oral poetry). More background on various areas and approaches is available in *Teaching Oral Traditions* (Foley 1998a), a collection of thirty-seven essays by specialists in various fields; as well as in the journal *Oral Tradition* (1986–). Let me make explicit my admiration for three books that have in their very different ways succeeded brilliantly in reaching a wide and general audience: Albert Lord's *The Singer of Tales* (1960), Ruth Finnegan's *Oral Poetry* (1977), and Walter Ong's *Orality and Literacy* (1982). While I don't agree with everything these authors have to say, and while *HROP* takes a very different tack, I have nothing but respect for their achievements.

2. Because these aren't real proverbs in origin, dynamics, or reference, I will be using the convention of *proverb* (with an asterisk on either side) to name them.

Pronunciation Key

To make the experience of South Slavic words more realistic, I offer the following brief pronunciation key, intended for the nonspecialist. The reader may use it to approximate the sound of singers' and characters' names, for example, or of various traditional phrases in the original language; these occur chiefly in the Third and Eighth Words. All instances of South Slavic language in this book are set in the Latin alphabet, with the customary diacritics, rather than in the Cyrillic alphabet, regardless of which system was used for initial publication (if any). Both of these alphabets, regularized by the great collector and linguist Vuk Karadžić in the mid-nineteenth century, are entirely phonetic. For more specific information, see Magner 1972.

Consonants pronounced approximately like their English counterparts:
  b, d, f, g (hard, as in "get"), k, l, m, n, p, s, t, v, z

Consonants without direct English counterparts:

c	[ts], as in ra**ts**
ć	[tch], **ch** pronounced at the front of the mouth, as in **itch**
č	[ch], **ch** pronounced further back in the mouth, as in **ch**air
j	[y], as in to**y** or **y**es
dj	[dy], as in the phrase an**d y**ou
lj	[ly], as in mi**lli**on
nj	[ny], as in the phrase o**n y**our
h	similar to English, but rougher, more aspirated (like German ch)
š	[sh], as in **sh**ow
ž	[zh], as in a**z**ure
dž	[j], as in **j**udge
r	trilled or rolled sound, as in th**r**ee in some British dialects; often in Spanish

Vowels

a	[a], as in m**a**ntra
e	[ɛ], as in s**e**t
i	[ee], as in tr**ee**
o	[o], as in f**o**r
u	[oo], as in m**oo**n
r	trilled or rolled vocalic sound

Vowels can be temporally long or short; vowel sound does not vary with duration. For present purposes, I omit all tonal and accentual qualities because tone and accent are well beyond the scope of analysis in this book. On the role of these features in the structure of the South Slavic decasyllabic line, see Foley 1990: chap. 5.

How to Read *an* Oral *Poem*

Four Scenarios

Oral poetry requires an audience. It isn't complete without one. So we begin by offering four opportunities to join an audience listening to an oral poet. Drawn from four different continents over a time span of three millennia, these performances collectively illustrate the natural diversity of oral poetry as well as some features and strategies that tend to be shared, even among traditions widely separated in space or time. Here, then, is your invitation to participate in the four performances. Just one word of caution: you may be in for a few surprises.

#1. A Tibetan Paper-Singer

Before you sits Grags-pa seng-ge, a 47-year-old oral epic singer from the Chabmdo area of the Tibetan Autonomous Region in China. He specializes in tales of King Gesar, an enormous cycle of stories told in a wealth of Indian, Turkic, and Sino-Tibetan languages across the broad face of central and northeastern Asia. Such epics routinely reach tens of thousands of lines, surpassing and sometimes dwarfing the Homeric poems and other European narratives in length and elaboration. The Gesar stories have proliferated over time as well as deeply permeated the dozens of societies that tell and preserve them. Officially sponsored projects now aim at collecting all extant versions of the Gesar cycle within China, a Herculean task, even as the orally transmitted tales find their way into "high-culture" media like the Tibetan national opera.

Learned academic fieldworkers encountering a scene like the one captured here will automatically fall back on their own cultural predispositions. They'll quickly notice that, whatever else may be going on, the performer is staring intently at a sheet of white paper in his hand as he chants. Armed with the usual presumptions, such investigators are sure to conclude that—"oral poet" or not—Grags-pa seng-ge is leaning heavily on the technology of literacy to sup-

Grags-pa seng-ge, a Tibetan paper-singer, "reading" an oral poem. Photo by Yang Enhong.

port his performance. His visual aid may turn out to be scribbled notes, a few key lines, a list of scenes, or perhaps some more detailed *aide-mémoire*, but one fact will seem inescapable: his oral performance rests on a foundation of reading and writing. Discovering that this kind of bard is called a "paper-singer" within his culture will only confirm this logical hypothesis.

But viewing the paper-singer's performance in this way, obvious as it might seem, proves dead wrong. Grags-pa seng-ge is in fact completely illiterate, and therefore entirely unable to utilize the technology that we text-consumers would so insistently force upon him through our misreading of the situation. To put it much more accurately, he is skilled in using an alternate technology that is very powerful in its own right and on its own terms: the language and craft of oral poetry.

So back to the drawing board we go. Reframing the scene as oral poetry may seem counterintuitive for those of us who celebrate and depend upon the written and printed word, and on (the myth of) its fixity and permanence, in virtually every aspect of our daily lives. However, Grags-pa seng-ge depends not on our chosen medium but on an ancient way of speaking he has inherited from the poetic tradition and continues to practice. The white sheet of paper does serve a purpose, the poet explains; when he keeps his eyes fastened on it, the story of King Gesar appears in his mind and he is able to compose the stories fluently. But, the paper-singer adds, on those occasions when no white sheet is available, mere newsprint—which he can't read, of course—suits him just fine. In other words, what is a text for us is for him a talisman, a symbolic piece of his singing equipment. In no way does it literally encode or represent the tale he tells; in no way does it take up the slack of oral performance. On closer examination, then, the unexpected truth comes out: in spite of our initial assumptions, Grags-pa seng-ge is an oral poet.

#2. A North American Slam Poet

You walk into a dimly lit, smoky coffeehouse. It could be the Green Mill in Chicago, the Met Café in Providence, the Nuyorican Poets Café in New York City, or a club in any one of dozens more urban centers. The particular geographical spot is irrelevant; it's what happens there that defines the place. A modest-sized stage with one or a couple of microphones stands bare under hazy illumination, remarkable more for what seems to be missing than for anything on it. There are no musical instruments, amplifiers, or even stools— maybe you spot a posterboard with scrawled numbers to one side of the stage, but there's no clue as to what the numerical code means, or even whether it's actually linked to what goes on here.

The audience is buzzing with talk. Expectant smiles glisten in the near-darkness as people mix happily in anticipation, apparently well aware of whatever it is that's about to happen. A census of performers and audience members would doubtless surprise you: those taking the stage might range in age from about fifteen to sixty; those who have come to watch span a wider spectrum. Performers include elementary school teachers and waiters, government employees and actors, students and professors; a few have had enough success— and made enough of a commitment—to forgo their day jobs altogether. They are of African American, Hispanic, Caribbean, Asian, Native American, and pan-European backgrounds, and their audience reflects a cognate diversity. In fact, a more diverse collection of people, no matter what the site or event, would be difficult to find. And why have they all assembled here? The answers are many: to entertain one another (but far from gently; harsh realities are the common coin of this exchange), to shout encouragement (at the top of their lungs and smack in the middle of things, without waiting politely until the performance has finished), and, perhaps most importantly, to teach and to learn (in a "classroom" where almost all the lessons are hard but also urgent and moving).

Aya DeLeon slams at the Nuyorican Poets Café. Photo by J. M. Foley.

You have just walked in on an emerging form of oral poetry in North America, a self-proclaimed performance poetry called *slam*. Once the action resumes, you see the way things set up. Contestants mount the stage in a series, one by one or in groups, to speak their poetry aloud, to give it living voice with all of the power and bravado they can muster. What's at stake is a competition, in some venues even a national title, trophy, and prize. Judges, chosen from and energetically applauded or dissed by the audience, will decide whose making of reality is most persuasive, most forceful, most irresistible as performance art situated in contemporary life. This isn't an open mike for stand-up comics, nor is it the narcissistic ritual of lip-synching or karaoke; no one here's prepping for some future gig. What it is is a serious, full-throated, up-from-the-belly wail about what it means to live in America after the year 2000: the social injustice visited upon women and minorities, the meaning of ethnic heritage, the fight for gun control, the rage of the oppressed, the challenge of public education, the dark insides of the city, the ever-present specter of police brutality, and dozens of other crippling human problems that customarily enter the staid, circumscribed arena of elite poetry only under contract with literary traditions. This is a sophisticated performance art that makes brilliant use of the acoustic and expressive effects that define oral poetries worldwide: complex arrays of rhyme, alliteration, and other sound-play; formulaic patterns of speech and intonation; coded gestures of all sorts; electric and continuous exchange between poet and audience; and not least the withering force of silence. But it also gets up in your face, hits you right between the eyes, demands that you listen and react—in a word, that you participate. Why?—because, as slammer Marty McConnell puts it, "metaphor is hard-wired truth."

#3. A South African Praise-Poet

Early descriptions and fieldwork indicate that the Xhosa *imbongi* or praise-poet (plural, *iimbongi*) has long held the responsibility of creating and maintaining the reputation of the tribal chief via the medium of oral poetry. Within a society that "publishes" such résumés orally rather than committing them to paper or electronic circulation, these poets have occupied a uniquely powerful position for many generations. While they can eulogize the subject of their performances as a peerless hero and leader, they can also criticize his shortcomings and thereby qualify or diminish the chief's stature. As far back as the evidence goes, scholars agree, the *imbongi* has always played a strongly political role, commenting on an individual's virtues and vices without fear of reprisal. Such is the immunity of his station. This is one of the most significant aspects of the praise-poet's social identity: people expect and accept his frank pronouncements, always couched in the familiar, idiomatic language of traditional *izibongo* (praise-poetry).

In modern South Africa the *imbongi*'s responsibilities have shifted. Providing oral résumés has mostly given way to various brands of social activism and ceremonial functions with new and wider audiences, contexts, and implications. *Izibongo* became a vehicle for public criticism of governmental leaders well before the fall of apartheid, for instance. As long as such verbal attacks remained unwritten they also remained untreasonous; as long as they existed solely as oral performances rather than documentary records, their "authors" enjoyed freedom from censure. Just as in contemporary folk dramas that

Bongani Sithole, a South African *imbongi*. Photo by Russell Kaschula.

chronicled the evolving oral history of those shut out of official print media, or the musical *Township Fever* that criticized and even ridiculed the tactics of the white establishment from the safe space of a performed play, the praise-poet used his oral poetry as an unassailable platform for free speech. *Izibongo* came to serve as a dedicated channel for no-holds-barred political commentary, and the *imbongi*—always highly political—discovered new ways to mine its special advantages. His oral poetry often became a vehicle for social protest, not unlike slam poetry.

Just how secure the modern *imbongi* continued to feel is illustrated by a famous incident that occurred during the installation of the new chancellor at Fort Hare University in the 1980s.[1] During a well-scripted and extremely polite European-style ceremony marking the administrative transition, a praise-poet rose, walked uninvited to center stage, and began spontaneously to eulogize the new chancellor. Anyone who has experienced the stentorian delivery style associated with this oral poetry will realize how impossible it was to ignore such a riveting performance. Helpless to intervene, the interrupted speaker promptly broke off his formal address and stepped aside, yielding the floor (and the ceremony) to the oral poet. When his poem and its praise were finished, the *imbongi* returned to his seat, the honored speaker resumed his script, and the prevailing cultural gears slipped back into place.

Very much within this tradition of politically charged oral poetry, *iimbongi* like Bongani Sithole also sing praises to the single most prominent figure in South Africa in recent years—Nelson Mandela. When President Mandela first returned home to his birthplace Umtata in April, 1990, after finally having been released from prison earlier that year, his appearance sparked a new and fascinating species of *izibongo*. Modern *iimbongi*, who emulate the intratribal poets in dress, method of delivery, stylistic techniques, societal role, and overall themes, used this uniquely powerful and effective vehicle to celebrate his visit and to ponder his and their future. By contextualizing this greatest of chiefs in the idiom of praise-poetry, they made his return meaningful in a way that could be managed in no other medium. Gesturing and energetically declaiming in the traditional manner of the social and political commentator, one poet appealed to Mandela to take strong measures to unify black South African peoples:

> We will never change,
> Tshangaans, Sothos, Malawians, Xhosas, Vendas, Tawanas,
> And Zulus as well,
> We are black people.
> Please!
> Please, son of Mandela,
> Please go and fetch Gatsha Buthelezi and arrest him,
> The problem is there,
> Take Gatsha Buthelezi,
> Put him in jail,
> He is the one who is connected with the poor whites and Boers,
> Which results in the death of our people.
> That must be done.

The oral poetry of *izibongo,* always a partner to social life and an ongoing digest of people's history, attitudes, and hopes, was here serving as a harbinger of new realities in post-apartheid South Africa.

#4. An Ancient Greek Bard

Realizing that our *Iliad* and *Odyssey* stem from a long-standing tradition of oral poetry, you wish to join the ranks of Homer's audience. Significant obstacles arise, of course, not least the two and one-half millennia that stand between the performances of these epic poems and the present day. And then you have to face the grand, immutable silence of the texts. In contrast to the three scenarios presented above, there's no opportunity for the hands-on experience that fieldwork brings, no chance to participate in a live performance, not even a report from the field. Under such handicaps, reading Homer as oral poetry may seem a categorical impossibility.

But all is not lost. Even if all we have left are manuscripts, we can at least begin to piece together the missing context and in the process understand the art of the *Iliad* and *Odyssey* a little more thoroughly. Texts don't represent a total impasse if our aims are realistic and measured, based on the belief that a partially reconstructed frame of reference is surely better than misreading this oral-derived poetry as unilaterally textual. We can proceed in two steps. First let's examine Homer's description of an ancient Greek singer, or *aoidos,* from the *Odyssey.* Then we'll ask what other clues the poetry offers to help explain itself.

Consider Homer's portrait of the Ithacan court bard Phemios and the situation in which the Odyssean singer finds himself early in the poem (Book I, 150–55, 325–59). Phemios's performance comes on the heels of the feast, according to custom, and his subject is the Greeks' homecoming from Troy after the great war. He apparently wins and holds the attention of his audience; they listen, engaged, to a kind of story that seems to have been popular throughout Europe and parts of Asia from the ancient world onward—the story of the returning hero. But soon Penelope intervenes and pleads with Phemios to choose another song from his repertoire, since this one reminds her too cruelly of the only Greek who hasn't returned, namely her long-lost husband Odysseus. Telemachos, however, vetoes his mother's request and ascribes the blame for any woes associated with Troy not to the singer but to Zeus. In this cameo, then, we glimpse the centrality of epic storytelling as a ritual, the power of the bard to move his audience, and the blameless nature of his craft. Clearly, even this brief description hints at the special place of oral poetry in the *Odyssey* and the society it reflects.

But Phemios's performance is not entirely representative. Homer makes the point that he sings against his will, at the demand of predatory suitors who have usurped the long-absent Odysseus's home and possessions, holding his family hostage to their lawless takeover. Even the highly ritualized feast scene

An ancient Greek *aoidos* sings oral poetry to the accompaniment of a *kithara.* From a red-figure amphora by the Berlin Painter. The Metropolitan Museum of Art, Fletcher Fund, 1956. (56.171.38)

that immediately precedes the bard's performance offers evidence of their perfidy: Telemachos shamefacedly greets the disguised Athena while the suitors carouse noisily, casting dice on the hides of slaughtered bulls. Their raucous behavior amounts to an inversion of the classic guest-host relationship, just as threatening to Odysseus's family as another such inversion—Cyclops's cannibalism—will later be to the hero and his comrades. And yet even against this abnormal, topsy-turvy background Phemios prevails. His performance holds the suitors rapt and moves Penelope to tears. Such is the power of his oral poetry.

But of course Phemios is not Homer. This portrait is a poetic description, not an on-site ethnographic report, and we must distinguish between its idealized reflection and the three real-life scenarios presented above from modern-day Tibet, North America, and South Africa. For the first three we have the hard evidence of recordings and firsthand witness, including photographs like those included here and on the *HROP* Web site; for the ancient Greek *aoidos* we have only poetic reports and latter-day texts, with illustrations limited to similarly idealized vase-paintings like the one presented here. Such reflections provide a starting point, but only that.

Thanks to the modern rediscovery of long-dead oral traditions, however, we have other tools to reconstruct the context of Homer's oral-derived poetry, and here is where the second step comes in. Simply put, through patient analysis of now-silent texts we can start to learn the bard's specialized language, or register. And once we have some idea of how that language works, we can discover how it means. Instead of misunderstanding Homer's words as wooden and conventional, we can begin to hear their implications. Instead of regretting how often he repeats himself, we can start to interpret his recurrent phrases and patterns as the idioms they really are. We can even learn a great deal about ancient Greek oral poetry by comparing and contrasting it to living oral poetries from our own time. Twenty-five hundred years and more after the fact of the *Iliad* and *Odyssey*, we can still join Homer's audience.

Note

1. I was shown a videotape of this incident while visiting Fort Hare University in 1989.

Further Reading

Homer and oral tradition: Foley 1990, 1999; R. Martin 1989, 1998; G. Nagy 1996a, b; the unit on Homer's *Odyssey* in the Seventh Word below

Slam poetry: Bonair-Agard et al. n.d.; Glazner 2000; Poetry Slam International and National Poetry Slam Web site (<http://www.poetryslam.com>); the Slam News Web site (<http://www.slamnews.com>); two recent videos (Devlin 1998 and Hemstreet et al. 2000); the units on slam poetry in the Fourth and Seventh Words below

South African praise-poetry: Kaschula 1995, 2000; Opland 1983, 1998; Gunner forthcoming; on Mandela, cp. Nixon 1994: 175–92

Tibetan paper-singer: Yang Enhong 1998

What the Oral Poets Say (in Their Own "Words")

The essential goal of *How to Read an Oral Poem* is to expose its readership to different ways of composing and "reading" poetry. We seek to become a better audience by broadening the range of possibilities, diversifying the menu of verbal art, and rethinking some of our most basic assumptions about poetic communication. Part of this rethinking will involve nothing less than reshuffling our cognitive categories, a process that can be both exhilarating and unsettling. The common phenomenon of "culture shock" offers a rough analogy. Just as we initially experience both fascination and anxiety on entering or reentering foreign societies and attempting to cope with different sets of rules and demands, so our study of oral poetry is likely to run head-on into conflict with some firmly held beliefs. We may even tend to resist the new perspectives because they undermine entrenched (and unexamined) principles. But *HROP* encourages neither a desperate advocacy nor a wholesale abandonment of any particular theories about verbal art—established or "new." Rather it calls for a healthy pluralism in approaching oral poetry, and that means genuine open-mindedness. We must use what we can of literary, textual approaches while enlarging our interpretive tool kit to include methods discovered through responsible study of nonliterary, nontextual forms.

In that spirit I chose to begin the book by opening four windows on oral poetry: scenarios from four continents (Asia, North America, Africa, and Europe) dating from before 600 B.C.E. to the present day. From the perspective afforded by these scenarios, we can see that oral poetry is an international medium, and that it has been and continues to be a vital cultural activity from the ancient world on into the twenty-first century. At the same time, these four scenarios collectively demonstrate a striking variety and warn against a monolithic model. Such extraordinary universality of occurrence paired with thoroughgoing variety is the essence of oral poetry.

Now, for a second step, let's consult some true experts. In what follows I yield the floor to some actual singers of tales, oral epic bards or *guslari* from the former Yugoslavia. In doing so I seek to start with an "inside" perspective on the art of oral poetry, to complement what will be offered later from an outsider's perspective. As with any such inquiry, the poets' observations will apply most accurately and specifically to their own tradition, in this case South Slavic oral epic from the former Yugoslavia. But their remarks will also have at least two further applications. For one, the *guslar*'s "take" on his own oral poetry will prove illuminating for oral poems from other traditions as well. More generally, and in the end most importantly, the *guslar*'s working assumptions—in some ways so fundamentally different from ours as we silently read literary, written poetry in texts—make an urgent case for examining our own unexamined assumptions. The disparity they highlight indicates that we must begin by reconsidering the most basic premises of verbal art, by asking not *what* but *how* a poem means.

Toward that end I present below a digest of South Slavic oral poets' responses to a very simple question: "What is a *word* in oral poetry?" The poets who provided answers were interviewed by Milman Parry and Albert Lord in the central Hercegovinian region of Stolac in the former Yugoslavia during the mid-1930s. They responded directly if (from our point of view) quite surprisingly to this question as it was put to them by Parry's and Lord's native assistant Nikola Vujnović.

Mujo Kukuruzović

The first *guslar* to speak here will be Mujo Kukuruzović, a preliterate bard who was forty-three years old at the time of his interview on June 11, 1935. He earned his living by farming inherited land and, like his Stolac colleagues, specialized in the Moslem tradition of epic songs, the longer species of songs that evolved under the sponsorship of the Ottoman court and afterwards continued in coffeehouses. Kukuruzović claimed a repertoire of thirty-eight epic tales, which he tells Nikola Vujnović he learned from eleven different singers. He was proud of his ability to pick up new material, as the following exchange testifies:

> MK: So now, brother, you go ahead and find some song I don't know. Then, brother, read it to me twice and then give me the *gusle* [the musical instrument used for accompaniment], brother. If I make a mistake, I'll give you a finger off my hand.
> NV: And with everything just so?
> MK: Just so; I'll repeat every single *reč*.

I intentionally leave *reč* (plural, *reči*) untranslated at this point. A quick glance at any standard Serbo-Croatian–English dictionary will turn up the translation "word," but as we shall see that is hardly the end of the story.

Somewhat later in the same conversation the interviewer Vujnović poses the crucial question directly:

> NV: This *reč* in a song, what is it?
>
> MK: Well, here, it's this—"miserable captive" ("sužanj nevoljnik"), as they say, or this—"Ograšćić Alija" [proper name], or, as they say, "He was crying out in the ice-cold prison" ("Pocmilijo u lednu zindanu").
>
> NV: Is this a *reč?*
>
> MK: This is a *reč.*

It seems that a *word in a song* is something quite different from what we mean by the everyday term "word," and Kukuruzović goes on to be quite explicit about that difference:

> NV: Let's consider this: "Mustajbey of the Lika was drinking wine" ("Vino pije lički Mustajbeže"). Is this a single *reč?*
>
> MK: Yes.
>
> NV: But how? It can't be *one:* "Mustajbey of the Lika was drinking wine."
>
> MK: In writing it can't be one.
>
> NV: There are four *reči* here.
>
> MK: It can't be one in writing. But here, let's say we're at my house and I pick up the *gusle*—"Mustajbey of the Lika was drinking wine"—that's a single *reč* on the *gusle* for me.
>
> NV: And the second *reč?*
>
> MK: And the second *reč*—"At Ribnik in a drinking tavern" ("Na Ribniku u pjanoj mehani")—there.
>
> NV: And the third *reč?*
>
> MK: Eh, here it is: "Around him thirty chieftains, / All the comrades beamed at one another" ("Oko njega trides' agalara, / Sve je sijo jaran do jarana").
>
> NV: Aha, good.

Let's step back a moment and assess just what Kukuruzović is telling his interviewer. For the *guslar* a *reč* in a song is clearly not the same thing as a textual word, defined like those you're reading now by the convention of white space on either side. Nor is it a lexical word certified by inclusion in a dictionary, nor some abstraction defined in linguistic terms. For Kukuruzović a word in oral poetry is a unit of utterance, an irreducible atom of performance, a speech-act. It may be as short as a phrase but no shorter, as his examples of "miserable captive" and the hero's name "Ograšćić Alija" testify. Or it may be a whole line in length, as in the verse "Mustajbey of the Lika was drinking wine." Or a single *reč* may even be some multiple of a line, such as the couplet "Around him thirty chieftains, / All the comrades beamed at one another." Were we to listen to the whole of his conversation with Vujnović, we would learn that Kukuruzović also thinks of scenes and motifs—such as traveling to a destination, arming the hero, marshaling troops, and the like—as single *reči*. As a first approximation, then, the *guslar*'s words are larger, more extensive units than ours. He simply uses bigger words.

Bigger, yes, but not just any size at all. A closer look at his examples reveals that each one answers another requirement; each is a sound-byte, a distinct and integral unit of expression within the *guslar*'s special way of speaking. That is, whether phrases, lines, multiple lines, or scenes, these *reči* function like whole integers—rather than fractions—in a verbal mathematics. The line-long examples have exactly ten syllables, matching the decasyllabic meter of the heroic epic, and the phrases always occupy some regular subdivision of the line, either four or six syllables long. The scenes and motifs, with their narrative rather than metrical boundaries, are also whole units and not fractions; partial journeys or arming scenes have no usefulness or meaning for poet or audience. The structural logic of this special language is plain to hear and to see. Just as we cannot subdivide any of our words and maintain its meaning ("bird" is more than the sum of its individual sounds, and none of them can be deleted without losing the whole), so the *guslar* cannot afford to dismember any of his *reči*.

What is more, these phrases, lines, and scenes are *traditional*. That is, they are not created by any one *guslar* but transmitted from one bard to the next over time, learned like any other kind of language. To that extent all such sound-bytes are discrete and recurrent units with lives of their own outside the confines of any particular song or performance. To put it plainly, *reči* for Kukuruzović are the "bigger words" that constitute his shared epic vocabulary, the phrases and narrative patterns through which he and other singers tell their tales, the idiomatic expressions that convey their poetic tradition. He uses "our words" to respond to most of the questions posed by Vujnović, or to bargain at the market, or to converse with friends. But for performing epic he switches the code—only the "bigger words" will do.

And herein lies the danger for us textually conditioned readers as we face the challenge of South Slavic oral epic. If we insist on reducing the singer's *reči* to our words, if we "murder to dissect," we will blunt a finely honed instrument of expression that has long served as the prescribed channel for communication. Imposing our assumptions will prevent truly fluent communication, since in effect we will be misreading or mistranslating the poem. Culture shock or not, we must make the effort to hear the *guslar*'s performances in their original language. We must be willing to acknowledge the difference that the preliterate singer Kukuruzović himself acknowledges in reference to "Mustajbey of the Lika was drinking wine," a whole decasyllabic verse. It can't be a single word in writing, he admits, but it remains a single *reč* on the *gusle* for him.

Salko Morić

Another *guslar* from roughly the same geographical region makes precisely the same point. Salko Morić, also forty-three years old when he was interviewed on June 9, 1935, near his home village of Rotimlje on the border between the Mostar and Stolac areas, freely admitted his ignorance of what a poetic line (*stih*) might be. Yet he readily used *stihovi* in composing oral epics and was able to distinguish perceptively among various species of words. His exchange with Vujnović, which proceeds out of their discussion of the feasibility of "word-for-word" (*reč za reč*) reperformance, is intriguing:

> NV: But let's say . . . tell us a single word, so I can see what it is. What's a word so I can hear it? For example, "He/she was drinking wine" ("Pije vino")—is that a *reč*?
> SM: Yes.
> NV: This is also a *reč*?
> SM: Yes.
> NV: So then is "Salko," "Salko," is that a *reč*?
> SM: Yes.
> NV: It too?
> SM: Uh-huh.
> NV: But what would this be?—"At Udbina in a drinking tavern / Sat the agas, they were drinking wine one after another" ("Na *h*Udbini u pjanoj mehani / Sjede age, redom piju vino"). What's that?
> SM: "All together they were drinking wine one after another" ("Svi ukupno redom piju vino").
> NV: So you're saying it's a *reč*, then?
> SM: It's also a *reč*, yes.

Vujnović starts the exchange by asking the singer whether "He/she was drinking wine," an extremely common phrase shared among many *guslari* over centuries and repeated often, is a single word. Morić, echoing Kukuruzović in the earlier excerpt, affirms that it is. So far, so expectable: the phrase occupies a regular subdivision of the epic line and thus answers the definition of a *reč* as a unified sound-byte—two words in everyday speech ("Pije vino"), but only one within the special language of South Slavic oral epic. Then, however, the conversation takes another turn, as Vujnović asks whether "Salko," his interviewee's first or given name, is also a word. Yes, he's told, although we should note that the target has shifted: the implied context is now everyday communication rather than the epic way of speaking. On these grounds "Salko" of course qualifies as a unit of utterance, an atom of speech. Once again we have a preliterate singer making a sophisticated distinction between two varieties or registers of language.

Finally, Vujnović poses what for us must stand as his most interesting question. He recites two common lines from the epic and asks Morić whether this
entire couplet—fully two decasyllables and ten of our words in the original
language—is also a single *reč*. Morić responds in a fascinating way. Rather
than simply confirm or deny that the two poetic lines do in fact amount to
a single "word" or speech-act, he goes a step further, remaking Vujnović's
couplet into a single decasyllable and roughly equivalent "word" of his own.
This affirmation is more striking than a simple "yes" could ever be. Morić
is memorably illustrating the rule-governed but plastic nature of his poetic
language by remaking one "bigger word" into another. In doing so he's following the same guidelines for poetic composition employed by other *guslari*, but in the present case what results is a different phrase at half the length
of the original. What better proof could we obtain of the singer's fluency in
the special language of *reči*?

Ibro Bašić

The same fluency is shared by a third *guslar* from the Stolac region, Ibro Bašić, who was seventy years old when Vujnović interviewed him at considerable
length on June 7, 1935. About halfway through a conversation that lasted more
than two hours, Vujnović posed the familiar question and elicited an enlightening response:

> NV: But what is a *reč?* What is a *reč?* Tell me.
> IB: An utterance.
> NV: An utterance?
> IB: Yes, an utterance; that's a *reč*, just like when I say to you now, "Is that
> a book, Nikola?" "Is that a coffeepot, Nikola?" There you go, that's a
> *reč*.
> NV: What is, let's say, a single *reč* in a song? Tell me a single *reč* from a
> song.
> IB: This is one, like this, let's say; this is a *reč:* "Mujo of Kladuša arose
> early, / At the top of the slender, well-built tower" ("Podranijo od
> Kladuše Mujo, / Na vrh tanke načinjene kule").
> NV: But these are poetic lines (*stihovi*).
> IB: Eh, yes, that's how it goes with us; it's otherwise with you, but that's
> how it's said with us.
> NV: Aha!

Bašić begins explaining *reč* by offering a synonym, *besjeda,* which I translate here as "utterance." In using the term *besjeda,* which various lexicons gloss
as "speech," "oration," or even "sermon," the singer is stressing at least two

aspects of the epic "word": its oral nature and its force as a speech-act. He's telling us that a *reč* is spoken and has power. All well and good, and thus far he echoes the remarks of Kukuruzović and Morić. But now look at his first set of examples. Instead of the phrases and lines cited by the other *guslari*, Bašić offers two rather ordinary questions as illustrations—"Is that a book, Nikola?" and "Is that a coffeepot, Nikola?" While such examples may initially seem irrelevant or confusing, note that they share some basic features with poetic *reči*. Both the questions and the lines of poetry are complete and idiomatic units. They depend for their meaning on higher-level wholes that are greater than the sum of their parts, and both kinds of utterances stand to lose their effectiveness as phrases if we choose to fracture the wholes in favor of focusing on the parts. Indeed, Bašić's analogy shows that he is a fine linguist; when it comes to words versus "words," he knows what he's talking about. Just as Morić recognized both "He/she was drinking wine" and "Salko" as *reči*, so Bašić compares the "bigger words" of epic storytelling to "bigger words" in everyday conversation, characterizing them both as "utterances." His comparison reveals a great deal about how the *guslar* composes oral poetry and just as much about how it means.

When Vujnović goes on to ask specifically about a single *reč* in a song, the singer responds with the sort of "bigger word" we've come to expect: multiple lines of poetry. The interviewer then attempts to force his hand by commenting—correctly, from our point of view—that "Mujo of Kladuša arose early, / At the top of the slender, well-built tower" is not a single word but rather two lines of poetry (*stihovi*). And once again the preliterate singer shows more linguistic savvy than many professional scholars by making an even-handed and fundamental distinction. They may be poetic lines within your frame of reference, he counters, with a respectful nod toward the highly trained specialists from the world of writing and texts. But "with us," and by this attribution he designates the singers' own frame of reference, the entire couplet is a single *reč*.

What's in a "Word"?

Nikola Vujnović's interviews with Mujo Kukuruzović, Salko Morić, and Ibro Bašić establish a clear and categorical difference between the "bigger words" they employ for epic singing and our words. For the three *guslari* a *reč* is not a string of black letters bounded by white spaces or something enshrined in a dictionary, but rather a unified utterance—never as small and partial as what we mean by a word but large and complete enough to have idiomatic force as a speech-act. Thus a phrase that occupies a regular section of the ten-syllable line, like "He/she was drinking wine," qualifies as a functional vocabulary item within the language of epic singing. So too do larger phrases of a line, two lines, or more in length. Beyond the level of lines or line-parts and determined not by metrical but by narrative patterns, *reči* can also take the form of unified scenes and motifs such as assemblies, journeys, and arming episodes. The common thread that runs through the singers' conception of their craft is the existence of a specialized epic language, a way of speaking, that depends upon "bigger words."

But what importance does that fact have for us as we seek to learn how to read an oral poem? First, the demonstration that *guslari* think and compose with these "bigger words" offers deeper insight into their process of composition. This phenomenon is inherently interesting in itself, of course, but there are practical ramifications as well. When a singer claims "word for word" accuracy in reproducing a song he has heard from another bard or in reperforming a song he himself sang earlier, we need to interpret his claim realistically. Does he mean "printed character for printed character"? Obviously not. Is he suggesting that no part-lines or lines will be added, substituted, or left out? Not likely, especially if the *reči* involved are whole scenes, which can vary significantly from one instance to the next, even if the same singer is performing the same epic story. When we add the demonstrated fact that "bigger words" at every level can show an internal flexibility in their construction, the defining feature of this and many other oral poetries emerges: variation within limits, flexibility within rules.

Second, if the *guslar* thinks and composes with *reči,* then we must strive to listen and read in terms of *reči.* Our responsibility, after all, as with any act of communication, is to understand the medium fluently. What's more, the stakes are particularly high in this medium. These "bigger words" often bear additional meanings larger and more complex than the literal sum of their parts, meanings that enrich the story being performed by reference to the implied poetic tradition. For instance, calling a woman a "black cuckoo" in South Slavic epic identifies her as a particular character-type: an imperiled figure who either has lost or stands to lose her husband and, according to the way this fictive world works, her entire social existence. Proverbs and proverbial expressions like "There is no summer without St. George's Day, / Nor a brother without a mother giving birth" lend a special inevitability to a wide range of actions and initiatives in the epic universe. Actions to which this proverb is attached, no matter how unlikely in themselves, are as good as realized. At the narrative level, an opening scene involving a hero shouting in prison guarantees a sequel in which this long-absent hero will bargain with his captor, return home in disguise, and confront rival suitors who are striving to win his wife's hand. Like a trusty map, this initial *reč* points unerringly toward a South Slavic *Odyssey*. In short, then, the "bigger words" engage a traditional frame of reference, a naturally resonant context larger and deeper than any individual situation or story. If we don't know the code the singer is using, if we can't read the *reči* idiomatically, then we'll inevitably miss something of the poetry. That's why the stakes are so high. "Words" are as crucial for listeners and readers as for the South Slavic oral epic poets who speak them.

But our small tutorial in *reči* shouldn't end there. In addition to other oral and oral-connected poetries that depend upon "bigger words," notably the ancient Greek *Iliad*, the Old English *Beowulf*, and poems from dozens of other traditions,[1] there's a more fundamental reason to pay attention to what the *guslari* are telling us. Specific traditions and particular features aside, the South Slavic singers' perspective teaches us a more general lesson: that we can't afford to take things for granted, that we can't assume "poetics as usual," that we can't presume that even so basic a "given" as a word will stand as a universal throughout the world of verbal art. What we see and hear will always depend on what we bring to an experience; that much is inarguable. And if we don't know the rules that frame an experience, what will our default response be? In nearly every case, we'll automatically impose our own rules, our own frame of reference; in the case of verbal art, that will mean rules that we use every day to compose, transmit, and interpret written and printed words. In the particular case of the *reč*, we scholars have often stumbled badly by naively ignoring this kind of difference. Sometimes we've even accused singers of not knowing what they were talking about, in effect criticizing them for failing to use our words. We'd do well to aspire to the open-mindedness and linguistic sophistication that the *guslari* have shown us.

Consider the case of the Tibetan paper-singer. Our initial assumption that he is depending on a source-text for his performance couldn't be more mistaken. For slam poets, live performance before an audience is the goal and the lifeblood of their art, not to mention the name of the game; words on paper simply aren't the poem. The South African *imbongi* wields power unknown to masters of mainstream media, and committing his words to texts only saps their natural strength. And Homer's beloved Phemios prevails even amid the lawless usurpation of Ithaca by Odysseus's deadly rivals. All of our customary assumptions to the contrary, spoken words have power that even the most finely crafted manuscripts and most accessible mass-market paperbacks can't match.

Most profoundly, then, the three *guslari* have alerted us to the need to examine our unexamined assumptions about poetry. In many cases what we know about (written) poetry will carry over, with minimal translation, to the much broader spectrum of oral poetry. All poetry begins with oral tradition, so we should expect a continuity between oral and written expression. But there are also many features and strategies—like the "bigger words" of South Slavic epic and other traditions—that work somewhat differently, or with different emphases and associations, than the poetic features and strategies to which most of us reading this book are accustomed. Such differences are hard to keep in mind, not least because so many of our waking hours are spent immersed in textual media (though the Internet is changing some of that, as we shall see later on). Nonetheless, as we begin our study of oral poetry we need to make the effort to speak and hear the right language as fluently as we can manage, even if that effort entails a degree of culture shock. The challenge is substantial, but the process is intriguing and the rewards are great.

*   *   *

Now, because *HROP* also has a responsibility to communicate within our way of speaking, via our own cherished medium of books and pages, I turn away from scenarios and interviews with poets toward the kind of description and explanation we text-consumers expect. Throughout what follows, however, I'll attempt to bridge the gap between words and "words," between page and performance, between the relative comfort of our familiar book-idiom and the relatively less comfortable ways of thinking and understanding introduced above.

If the "insider's" view must now largely shift to an "outsider's" perspective, I'll try for a change of key rather than a wholly new melody. The oral poet's stock-in-trade—voice, performance, audience, tradition, special ways of speaking, shared implications, and not least "words"—will continue to be our subject. To emphasize that continuity, we'll blaze a path not through chapters (or book-bytes) but rather through thought-bytes called the First Word, Second Word, and so forth. I transfer the South Slavic singers' terminology of "words," shared as we noted across many other traditions, for two related reasons: it will remind us of oral poetry's organization via nontextual units and of the danger inherent in failing to examine our assumptions. In the same spirit, I'll depend centrally on the traditional strategy of (homemade) *proverbs*, as introduced in the Sixth Word (a.k.a. the sixth "chapter"). One of them holds that "Composition and reception are two sides of the same coin," for instance, emphasizing how performers and their audiences need to play by the same rules. Operating as a pseudo-traditional way of speaking, these facsimile *proverbs* will offer nuggetlike indexes for the major ideas presented in the First and Second Words, the menu of theoretical approaches explored in the Third through Fifth Words, and the array of actual oral poetries sampled in the Seventh and Eighth Words. To the extent that such a process can be initiated and maintained in this inescapably bookish medium, then, we aim at a hybrid experience in studying oral poetry. As the title explicitly states, we seek to learn *How to Read an Oral Poem.* To the unpacking of that intentionally loaded title we now turn.

Note

1. On the ancient Greek *muthos* ("word") as a performance by a speaker, see R. Martin 1989: esp. 1–42; on the Old English *word* ("word") as an expressive unit of utterance, see Foley 1990: 219, 223. Cp. Dennis Tedlock's discussion of the Quiché Mayan term *tzih,* as in the opening sentence of the *Popol Vuh:* "This is the beginning of the Ancient Word," where it means "a 'Word' that was spoken with the intention that it be preserved and that its provisions be carried out" (1983: 272–73).

Further Reading

South Slavic oral epic poetry: *SCHS,* vols. 1–2 (Novi Pazar songs), 3–4 (Avdo Medjedović, *The Wedding of Smailagić Meho*), 6 (Medjedović, other songs), 8 (Bihaćka Krajina); Foley 2003

South Slavic oral epic, background and analysis: Lord 1960 (2000), 1991, 1995; Foley 1990, 1991, 1999, 2002; Kay 1995; Erdely 1995; the section on epic in the Eighth Word below

First Word:
What Is Oral Poetry?

The four scenarios sketched earlier in this volume hint at the broad spectrum of verbal art outside the familiar arena of the text. Oral poetry lives throughout history and around the world, dwarfing written poetry in size and variety. More specifically, the South Slavic epic singers' remarks on the nature of a "word"—something it's only too easy to take for granted—suggest that we need to revisit unexamined assumptions of all sorts. We can't afford to let cultural reflexes get in the way of exploring how to read an oral poem.

Let's begin by facing some stubborn realities rooted deep in our contemporary culture and everyday life. Say *text* and *writing*, and a very particular set of associations comes flooding in. Texts-as-things have enjoyed a long and privileged reign in modern Western culture as the medium of choice, with their monolithic dependability only recently challenged by philosophers and literary critics. And writing? Well, that's the way literature gets made, by authors with pen or mouse in hand. Say *poem*, and a similarly predetermined montage of images appears. We imagine great individuals wrestling mightily with their muses, their predecessors, their contemporaries, and themselves to fashion something unique, something timeless that will outlast the lesser, perishable artifacts that surround us. And how do we recognize poems? Often the answer is by probing what we take to be their linguistic physiology: by counting their feet and measuring their rhythm, by ferreting out their rhymes and other "poetic" devices, even by tracing the telltale ragged right-hand margin on the altar of the page. Say *read*, and most of us holding this book in our hands have somewhat the same vision: a silent, lonely decoding of inscribed symbols.[1]

But just because a culture awash in texts and increasingly wired for cybercommunication has certain predispositions doesn't make them universally and eternally so. Consider a few seldom asked and potentially unsettling questions. Just what are "oral poetry" and "reading" across the historical and multicultural waterfront? What varieties of medium and message do we conceal by celebrating the fixity of print as the best of all possible vehicles for thinking, expression, and learning? What if inscription in its many forms—the ideographic sign, the alphabet, the manuscript, the printed page, the electronic text file—were not the evolutionary apex of human communication? What if an unbiased look revealed writing and texts as merely one extremely useful and powerful communicative technology among other recent or longstanding alternatives?

Poised as we presently are on the cusp of the age of the electronic word, we're in an excellent position to answer questions such as these. Citizens of today's Western world, who must be "bilingual readers" of written-text and e-text alike, are becoming aware of the advantages and disadvantages of both media. If we conclude (as we must) that neither is perfect in every respect, it will also be easier to give nonwritten, nonelectronic media their due. The connection may seem counterintuitive at first, but the ongoing cyber-revolution can open up precious insights into manuscripts, print, and most of all oral poetry.[2]

Media Technologies and Our Species-Year

A rough outline of media history can provide a start. For instance, notwithstanding its centrality and crucial importance in today's Western world, writing technology is a relatively recent invention. If we superimpose the history of homo sapiens onto an annual calendar, writing turns up only midway through December, more than eleven-twelfths of the way through our species-year, and is for many centuries employed only for record-keeping. As the table below indicates,[3] numeracy, the fluent reading and writing of numbers or their symbolic equivalents, precedes literacy chronologically, but even it appears no earlier than late November, about the time of the Thanksgiving holiday.

Media Events in Homo Sapiens' Species-Year

Invention	Date		Day	Species-date
Numeracy (Middle Eastern tokens)	8000	B.C.E.	328	November 22
Pre-writing (Vinča signs, Balkans)	5300	B.C.E.	338	December 2
Egyptian script traditions	3200	B.C.E.	346	December 10
Mesopotamian cuneiform	3100	B.C.E.	346	December 10
Indus script	2500	B.C.E.	348	December 12
Semitic scripts	2000	B.C.E.	350	December 14
Minoan Linear A	1800	B.C.E.	351	December 15
Linear B	1550	B.C.E..	352	December 16
Phoenician script	1200	B.C.E.	353	December 17

Media Events (*Cont.*)

Invention	Date		Day	Species-date
Greek alphabet	775	B.C.E.	355	December 19
Mayan and Mesoamerican scripts	500	B.C.E.	356	December 20
Alexandrian Library	fl. 250	B.C.E.	357	December 21
Chinese printing technology	750	C.E.	360	December 24
Gutenberg's printing press	1450	C.E.	363	December 27
Cherokee script (Sequoyah)	1821	C.E.	365	New Years Eve, 8 A.M.
Typewriter (C. L. Scholes)	1867	C.E.	365	New Years Eve, noon
Current IPA alphabet	1993	C.E.	365	New Years Eve, 11:24 P.M.
Internet	fl. 1997	C.E.	365	New Years Eve, 11:44 P.M.

The earliest true writing systems arose in Egypt, Mesopotamia, and the Indus valley during the second week of December, with the Phoenician script, parent to our alphabet, emerging about the 17th of that month. Mesoamerican scripts were not invented until December 20, the day before the Alexandrian Library. Gutenberg's printing press begins churning out its pages only four days before the end of the year; although the Chinese beat him to the technological punch by seven hundred years or three species-days, it's striking how recently homo sapiens entered the age of print. Many scripts have come on the scene less than a species-week ago, like the Cherokee syllabary invented by Sequoyah and the latest version of the International Phonetic Alphabet (IPA), which appear only on New Year's Eve. And the Internet—the now-central medium that has become so much a part of everyday life, especially for Western societies but increasingly the world over—does not come into play until a mere sixteen minutes remain in our species-year. How were we functioning, how were we making and preserving our societies, from January through November without access to the technology of letters and texts we now consider so essential? Like it or not, for most of our existence as a species, "cultural literacy" didn't involve literacy.

What about "literature," which owes its very name to the classical Latin *littera* ("letter") and medieval Latin *litteratus* ("lettered man")? As much as we prize the textual phenomenon of literature, and as firmly ensconced as it is in both our academic institutions and our everyday lives, this letter-based species of verbal art proves statistically the rarest of cultural phenomena. Despite its prevalence in modern Western societies, we human beings have produced only about one hundred true literatures over the entire course of our history, anywhere on the planet. That is, as a species homo sapiens has created only about one hundred situations in which a literary tradition of individual authors, the craft of text-making and -reproduction, and a mass readership have combined to support an ongoing, self-sustaining literature. Of languages spoken today, the count is even lower: seventy-eight living literatures, by one estimate.[4]

If we are surprised at the nonuniversality of a phenomenon that seems so common to us, a few seconds' reflection will expose the discrepancy as one of our own making. By telescoping events according to a modern model, we fall victim to a kind of "slippery slope" thinking: if letters, then *littera*-ture. But the invention of literacy is only the first step in a multidimensional process, and the mere existence of writing technology may have little or no impact on broad segments of a society, and especially on certain sorts of verbal transactions, for a long time if ever. Inscription may in fact never lead down our imagined one-way street toward libraries full of books. In order to gain a foothold, the new technology must develop a capacity for generating multiple, user-friendly texts, which will in turn make possible authorship and mass readership as we know them. A literature may then take shape over time. Once we jettison our culture-specific presumptions and realize that true literature can evolve only when these rare ingredients combine, its scarcity becomes less startling. Even by default, the role of oral tradition looms ever larger.

Oral Tradition and the Present Day

So writing is recent and literature is rare. On the other hand, as far as we know all peoples have composed and transmitted oral traditions, an alternate verbal technology that has shown itself not only far more widespread than texts but also much more adaptable and durable. Even today the majority of the planet's inhabitants use oral traditions as their primary communicative medium, a fact obscured by modern Western egocentrism. Virtually every single one of the fifty-five officially recognized national minorities in the People's Republic of China, for example, possesses a thriving oral poetry.[5] Rich traditions of oral composition and performance are alive in all regions in Africa, from the praise-poetry of the Xhosa and Zulu to the West African epics of the Banyanga and Mande.[6] Notwithstanding the suffering and tragedy that has marked much of their history (indeed, often in response to such crises), the Balkan peoples still nurture traditions of oral poetry in some regions.[7] And the catalogue could go on indefinitely: oral poetry is a major presence in today's world, not just an antique from the past but a living part of the contemporary scene, despite what we text-consumers might unwittingly suppose.

Nor does the story end there. Recent research has shown conclusively that the once-attractive binary notion of "oral" versus "written" cultures—or even "oral" versus "written" individuals—proves in most cases much too crude a distinction.[8] Rather than reduce human behavior to this Great Divide model, we would do better to apply what physicists call a finer-grained analysis—a more exacting, truly diagnostic distinction at an appropriately realistic level. It proves closer to the mark to speak of a culture's or an individual's diverse repertoire of expressive strategies, to imagine a pull-down menu for various possible modes of communication. Anthropologists call these different modes "registers" of language, ways of speaking or writing that are linked to specific social situations. As we'll see in the Second Word, cultures and individuals learn to manage whole repertoires of registers. Rather than view communication as limited to a binary, on-off switch that selects either oral tradition or texts, we'd do much better to conceive of an integrated, well-made kit of verbal tools, each tool fashioned for a particular communicative job.

This finer-grained analysis takes us beyond the Great Divide of oral versus written and provides some perspective on what research has uncovered about the mix-and-match character of verbal art from one time and place to another. Some expressive strategies are oral, some are textual, and some, as we'll glimpse in a moment, draw from both modes of expression. The fact is that oral and written just aren't segregated absolutely. And not only can oral and written appear in the same society, they can and do appear in the very same individual. And why not? Multilingual speakers of French and English are not uncommon; effective writers glibly choose from a smorgasbord of styles to suit their artistic goals; even everyday people adroitly handle multiple registers, multiple ways of communicating.

Practice bears out this common-sense model everywhere we look. The North Carolina Ph.D. lays aside his reference books and switches off his word-processor to serve as a leading informant for the oral tradition of Jack tales.[9] Literate Balinese bards create and re-create oral poetry in both texts and oral performances.[10] A Serbian peasant woman with sufficient schooling to maintain an exchange of letters with kinfolk serving as guest-workers in Switzerland composes and chants an oral lament for her departed son.[11] The North American slam poet writes out a poem with one aim in mind—to perform before an audience—and hears it evolve from one performance to another once it escapes the prisonhouse of the page.[12] Whatever the particular complexities of the given situation, the lesson is simple and basic. Oral poetry cannot be reduced to a single pristine form that arises strictly in letterless societies and out of the mouths of certifiably preliterate speakers. Human nature—and oral poetry—are much more diverse, complex, and interesting than that.

Media Bias

Awareness of the prevalence of oral traditions, of both their fundamental role throughout human history and their remarkable persistence on the contemporary scene, has been slow to develop in our text-centered environment. It's not difficult to see why. We "document" the rites of passage in our lives, "jot down" ideas before they escape us, "take notes" in high school and university classes, even go so far as to "write a book" to explain oral poetry! At every turn contemporary Western society asks us to conduct a healthy percentage of our daily cultural business by manipulating visual signs, by exchanging voice and face-to-face communication for the silence and distance of paper-based or electronic print. Such is the largely unchallenged priority of the written word that most of us manage to ignore oral traditions that continue to survive right around us, or to discount their value because they don't meet the mythical standard of textual fixity or attain what we think of as completeness, real accuracy, or suitable formality. How many of us pay serious attention to living performances of folk sermons, rap music, slam poetry, or folktales as verbal art? How often do these forms find their way into the publication network, or into college and university curricula? Given the built-in bias in favor of the technology of writing and printing, is it any wonder that oral poetry is implicitly ranked as a second-class citizen among the verbal arts—if, indeed, it is ranked at all? We have much to learn on that score, many layers of media prejudice to peel away.

One of these layers is epitomized in the frequently used term "oral literature," which proves even more problematic than "oral poetry." As noted above, the word *literature* describes works composed in letters by a lettered person. To prefix the adjective "oral" to this core idea may be an admirable and well-intentioned attempt to cancel out that etymology, but the result is nonsensical. What "oral literature" really boils down to is a name for "letterless verbal art in letters" or "letterless verbal art composed by a lettered person." You can see how even our terminology reveals its bias. Down deep, we've been scrambling rather desperately to carve out a place for nonwritten forms within the conventional world of literature. What we haven't been doing is recognizing that our familiar world is actually only one part of an immensely larger and—for many of us—largely unexplored universe of verbal art.

Another reason for our failure to understand the role and importance of oral poetry is the narrowness with which we define the role of verbal art in society. While modern preconceptions turn on aesthetic, formal, literary-critical, poststructural, new historicist, and other approved criteria—all of them mainstays of the study of literature in our time—oral poetry has long served a much more extensive list of cultural needs. Across the span of human societies, oral poetic traditions encode what we call history, anthropology, folklore, mythology, law, philosophy, medicine, and numerous other disciplines. Indeed, perhaps counterintuitively for the modern reader of texts, art and social function often share the limelight. Because oral poetry has always been an essential technology for the transmission and expression of ideas of all kinds, it does not divorce entertainment from instruction, artistic craft from cultural work. The Old English poet who composed *Widsith* was making oral history as well as oral poetry. Slam poets aim at striking, memorable verse, a fit vehicle for their continuing project of social criticism. The Yurok, Hupa, and Karok peoples of northwestern California use traditional songs to gain power over physiology and social activities. Serbian peasants marshal the poetic forces of octosyllabic and decasyllabic poetry to preserve their genealogies and administer their medical remedies. The south Indian (Tulu) epic singer is also a possession priest whose knowledge and performance of the *Siri Epic* has ritual implications shared with his followers in everyday life.[13] Oral poetry is a people's poetry serving a wide spectrum of people's needs.

For such reasons, looking at oral poetry through the lens of literature—our ever-present if usually unnoticed filter—is much like peering through the wrong end of a telescope. Instead of enlarging the object or process on which the instrument is trained, this "backwards" perspective graphically diminishes it. (And yes, the pun on "graphically" is intended.) We are in the habit of understanding poetry as a species of written poetry, not the other way around. We see this bias at work even in the selection of poetic genres collected, studied, and described by fieldworkers: epic very often enjoys pride of place, along with other narrative or story-based forms, because of their prominence in the realm of literature. Lyric verse from oral traditions also readily wins attention on the basis of our familiarity with lyric poetry in written traditions worldwide. But charms, recipes, proverbs, genealogies, funeral laments, and the like are apt to be dismissed as "minor genres," if dealt with at all. And why? Because they have been denied admission by the gatekeepers of the literary arts; they just don't appear on the literary menu.

Such neglect of poetic genres that do not survive into literature has an unintended but crippling consequence: it defines a great percentage of oral poetry out of existence. Since we obviously can't appreciate what we don't know, our perspective is fatally skewed from the very start. The model we unconsciously apply to verbal art thus has a built-in blind spot, and a sizeable one. And the excuse that this misapprehension stems from a sin of omission rather than commission doesn't make the result any more justifiable or any less disabling. The fact remains that unexamined assumptions about collection, analysis, and representation have long kept us from a fair understanding of what oral poetry is and how it figures within the genus of verbal art. Viewed fairly—through the right end of the telescope—verbal art turns out to be much more extensive, more diverse, and more fascinating than we customarily presume, and our practice of "reading oral poetry" must respond to that challenging diversity.

Explaining the Title: Four Questions

Toward that end I now turn to the title of this book—*How to Read an Oral Poem.* As noted in the Prologue, this phrase is intentionally provocative, coded for controversy, meant to inspire the reader to move beyond the unconscious prejudices imposed by the reigning cultural context of books and printed pages. At the top of our agenda, then, must be an explanation of the major components of the title, a task I will undertake by posing a series of four questions: (1) What is *oral poetry?* (2) What is *an oral poem?* (3) What is *reading?* and (4) What do we mean by *how?* Number one is the most demanding, and will require the most attention; we'll devote the remainder of the First Word to answering it. To one extent or another, the remaining three answers will flow from the first; they will be the subjects of the Second and Third Words.

But why adopt this strategy? Initially, all four questions may seem as simplistic as worrying over what a word is—after all, don't we already know the answers, more or less? Can't we move on to tackle some deeper, more meaningful inquiries? However, as the South Slavic *guslari* taught us, it is precisely the simplistic, obvious questions that most need our attention. We can't afford to settle for the conventional wisdom on such matters exactly because it's too conventional, because it takes its cue from assumptions based on texts. As we have seen, textual assumptions artificially limit our horizons. Hopefully, by addressing these four questions—by peeling back accumulated layers of faulty presumptions—we can open up our investigation and work toward an understanding of verbal art that gives oral poetry a full hearing and due process.

What Is *Oral Poetry?*

Most of us think we have a fair idea of what poetry is, and many of us feel we know what the term "oral poetry" designates. But consider the scale of our parochialism. For anyone trained in North American or European academic institutions, poetry is and has long been almost exclusively the kind of poetry composed and consumed via texts. It does not include oral composition and performance or aural reception except as something additional, something nonfundamental. For us poetry's etymological sense of something made or created (from ancient Greek *poièsis*) is a casualty of history; the default designation of poetry has become written poetry. That's why we have to prefix the adjective "oral," because the unmodified noun no longer covers anything but written poetry. That's also why we resort to other unwieldy phrases to pigeonhole events and phenomena that our cultural proclivities have silently eliminated from consideration. Thus a "poetry reading" describes a performance (from a published text, of course) before a well-behaved, often academic audience. Thus "spoken-word poetry"—so redundant from a historical perspective—identifies voiced verbal art, verse that is lifted off the page and into the world of presence and experience.

So what is oral poetry? Rather than campaign uselessly for a return to an inclusive sense of poetry or impose a series of unlikely compound labels, I propose an exercise in reality-based pluralism. By concentrating on four aspects of poetry that we customarily take for granted, I will aim at illustrating the radical difference and diversity of oral poetry, as well as how we need to revise our working assumptions to take account of that difference and diversity. Here, then, are our targets for the exercise, four areas where default presumptions need some rethinking: (1) the poetic line, (2) the genre or poetic type, (3) the oral versus written dichotomy, and (4) the media dynamics of oral poetry. Some of these aspects are self-evident once we step outside of textuality, and can therefore be treated briskly. Others, especially the last one, will require closer scrutiny. As noted above, we're dealing with a species of verbal art that dwarfs literature in both size and variety, so we must be willing to start at the most elementary level and remain open to very basic distinctions.

Step 1. Opening Up the Poetic Line

In English and American literature, most poems trace their ultimate heritage to Greek and Roman antiquity by one genealogical route or another. The family connection may be distant, with myriad other influences impinging, but a high percentage of English-language verse bears the primary genetic trait of a syllable-counting meter as the underpinning of the poetic line. The gene may have been transmitted indirectly through Romance traditions like French, but much English poetry still carries it as a telltale, dominant factor. If poets choose iambic pentameter or even blank verse, for example, they are selecting a familiar, time-honored vehicle for their art, whether they are conscious of a debt to antiquity or not. There can be no doubt of the power exerted by the classical heritage in this regard: Greco-Roman meters have marked English poetic lines for many centuries, deepening the resonance of more modern poems and attaching new members to a very sturdy family tree. Academic institutions teach a classical poetics, and many poets practice it.

For all its positive aspects this lineage has also blinded us to other possibilities, some of them right under our noses in the English tradition. Old English poetry, an oral-connected tradition that dates from before the Battle of Hastings in 1066 C.E., well illustrates what havoc the tyranny of a narrow definition can wreak. Scholars seeking to understand the poetic line of *Beowulf* have spent many decades and pages trying to force the square peg of Old English meter into the round hole of Greco-Roman models. But the prolonged search for the expected syllable-counting meter could never succeed, as the following four lines from *Beowulf* (51–54) exemplify in their variation from eight to thirteen syllables:[14]

sécgan to sóðe, sélerǽden*de*,	10
hæleð under heofenum, hwa þæm hlæste onfeng.	13
Ða wæs on burgum Beowulf Scyldinga,	10
leof leodcyning longe þrage.	8

to say in truth, hall-counselors,
heroes under the heavens, who received the burden.
    Then in the strongholds was Beowulf of the Scyldings,
beloved nation-king, for a long time.

Searching for syllabic regularity as a defining feature of these poetic lines amounts to using the wrong symptom to diagnose the "disease" of poetry in Old English. It's doomed to failure.

What then are the real symptoms, the characteristics genuinely indicative of poetry in *Beowulf* and other poems from this tradition? As the **boldfaced** letters suggest, the feature of alliteration or matched initial sounds is a significant one. It binds together the two half-lines or verses (indicated by the extra space at mid-line in the original Old English). One alliterating partner per half-line is the minimal complement to make a poetic line metrical; thus, for instance, *hæleð* (heroes) and *hlæste* (burden) would have been enough to satisfy the rule in the second line. The other chief criterion is stress, and most metrists agree that four major stresses define the Old English poetic line. I have marked the four most heavily stressed syllables with acute accents in the first line above. Third, and here more disputes arise, the Old English poets seem to have favored certain patterns or sequences of stresses as organizing frames for the poetic line.

Simply put, then, syllables and classical meters lead us down a blind alley in Old English poetry. What matters in this Germanic meter and verse-form is primarily the linked features of alliteration and stress, and secondarily adherence to stress-patterns. What are the lessons learned from this small exercise in diversity? At a specific level, if we do not "read" *Beowulf* and other Old English works on their own terms, we simply can't call them poetry. This potential shortfall is more than a bump in the road: the very idea of poetry in Old English—and in English as a whole—hangs in the balance. More broadly, if such a fundamental "disconnect" can occur within the orbit of English poetry, which we too easily see as the recognizable offspring of classical verse, imagine how cautious we must be as we move outside that relatively familiar, well-mapped universe. The concept and function of the poetic line just can't survive if we define it too narrowly. Nor can the idea of poetry.

To continue the journey outward, let's examine the case of the poetic line in South Slavic epic, a major site for the rediscovery of oral poetry in the twentieth century.[15] The intricacies of the ten-syllable meter are beyond our interests here, but it should be acknowledged in passing that it too has suffered under the tyranny of Greco-Roman archetypes. Pronounced a trochaic pentameter in the early going, it was later shown to be nothing of the sort. Too easy an analogy to a widely distributed kind of poetic line not only resulted in misclassification but also obscured the way poets made their poetry. True enough, the analogy seemed logical: the South Slavic epic line has ten syllables, and some of the odd-numbered syllables are accented regularly. But a dolphin is not a fish, and an eel is not a reptile, despite obvious resemblances in gross anatomy. Any conclusion based on incorrect assumptions, no matter how meticulously the investigation is conducted, must fall victim to error. That's how the "epic decasyllable" sung by the *guslari* got into trouble with Western-trained scholars. They settled too easily for something it wasn't.[16]

But with South Slavic oral epic the disparity between reality and our assumptions is much greater than the faulty hypothesis of a trochaic pentameter. Indeed, the problem goes directly to the core question of what a poetic line is. The story begins as I was listening to and transcribing the *guslar* Halil Bajgorić's performance of *The Wedding of Mustajbey's Son Bećirbey* in preparation for paper and electronic editions described in the Post-Script to this book. In the process I met with quite a few lines that seemed to be metrically deficient. Some were too short or hypometric (nine syllables) and others were too long or hypermetric (eleven syllables). Here's an example of each type:

hI junačka ga sreća nanijela   "too long": 11 syllables

And a hero's good fortune guided him

[ ] Počeše vadati dorina   "too short": 9 syllables

[ ] They began to lead the red-brown horse

The question then arose: how can we explain these apparent flaws in line-making? Do we attribute them generally to the rigorous demands of composition in oral performance, where poets have no opportunity to ponder possibilities or to revise (a dangerously global and sometimes condescending explanation)? Do we seek a cause for the supposed defects in nearby lines? And what if anything should we do to correct the perceived problems? The burden weighs heavy on the editor to account for such blemishes and deal with them effectively.

However, after listening carefully to the *guslar*'s vocal melody and his own instrumental accompaniment on the *gusle*, I realized that I was the one making the mistake, and a very basic one at that. If understood on their own terms, these lines and others like them were neither too long nor too short. The "extra" syllables were actually sung *before* the usual starting-point in the vocal and instrumental melodies, outside the ten-syllable increment as defined musically and rhythmically—and not just syllabically and textually. Likewise, the "missing" syllables actually coincided with vocal rests, and those rests were full partners inside the ten-syllable increment. The *guslar* started singing the nine-syllable lines one syllable *after* the usual melodic starting point. From a multimedia point of view, nothing was superfluous or lacking. Music and silence weren't adjunct phenomena; they were part of the line.

Stepping back from the textual perspective, I was able to see that (along with everyone else) I had been defining an oral poetic line much too textually, transcribing its syllables out of performance and onto the page for visual consumption, deforming the true shape of the poetic line by stripping away crucial aspects of its self-definition. The translation from voiced reality to the straitjacket of the page, supported of course by the technology and mind-set that govern our presumptions about verbal art, had induced a disfiguring parallax. The most fundamental unit of South Slavic epic poetry—the poetic line—needed radical redefinition. It was a unit of utterance, a byte of oral poetry, and should be treated as such.

Similar stories can be told about many other poetic lines that diverge from the default model of syllables and feet and put the lie to our customary assumptions. One of the more striking stems from Native American oral poetries, which have proven different enough from Western forms to have prompted the establishment of a new approach to verbal art. Called Ethnopoetics, this method insists on making every effort to discover and portray the structures that really exist in the given tradition. Ethnopoetics rests on a simple but far-reaching principle to which we will return in the Fourth Word: given the choice, we should "read" according to the poet's and tradition's "way of speaking" rather than our own. Of course, the more a poetry departs from our default conception of a poetic line, the more important this principle becomes. Thus

Dennis Tedlock reports that a line of Zuni verse can reach as many as seventy syllables,[17] marked—like the *guslar*'s "word" or *reč*, we might add—as a unit of utterance rather than a numerically measured string. For the same reason Dell Hymes restores the units of verses, lines, stanzas, scenes, and acts to foreground a meaningful set of structural patterns in the verbal art of Northwest Coast tribes that prior editions had obscured.[18] In such cases queries about the nature of the poetic line become more than theoretical inquiries, more even than creditable attempts to "get it right." If we don't know what a line is in the Zuni and Northwest Coast oral performances, we can't really "read" them. We can't even identify them as poetry.

Step 2. Opening Up the Poetic Genre

Once again we start with a narrow focus—first the limited arena of written poetry, and within that culturally sanctioned space the English literary tradition. But even within this relatively small and homogeneous sample, we meet with a large family of genres or types of poetry, many of them quite unlike their siblings. What do the epic, the sonnet, and the ode have in common, for example? How about the ballad, the elegy, and the romance? We wouldn't make the mistake of turning as a model for Shakespeare's "Shall I compare thee to a summer's day" to Milton's *Paradise Lost*. And we wouldn't rely on Chaucer's *Troilus and Criseyde* to provide much direct insight on Frost's "Mending Wall." All of these works fall under the heading of English (written) poetry, but generically they have very little in common. In order to read them effectively, we have to pay attention to the idiosyncrasies of their specific poetic types.

Now shift your focus back to the much larger and much more diverse arena of oral poetry, and notice the result: a geometric increase in the inventory and variety of genres. For one thing, the broader view brings into focus all of those verse-forms that for whatever reason didn't persist into texts. Collections of maxims or proverbs, a staple of many oral poetic repertoires, present themselves for inspection. So too do the highly stylized verbal dueling performances from a wide variety of cultures such as African American, Turkish, Mayan, ancient Greek, and medieval Germanic, to name only a few.[19] For another thing, oral poetry admits the functional genres to which the modern Western canon has denied admission. Thus the healing charms practiced by numerous societies, the speechmaking report of a curing specialist among the Kuna in San Blas, or even the counting rhymes used to organize children's games take their rightful place alongside more "elevated" poetry.[20]

Then, too, we can't forget two sobering facts that stand as the chief roadblock to our appreciation of generic diversity in oral poetry. First, only a tiny fraction of the world's oral poetry has ever been collected, at any time or place in history. For example, until its recent recording specialists in comparative oral epic had no way to study the *guritan* of Radin Suane, a living epic from South Sumatra in the Sumatran-Malay language of Besemah.[21] The neglect of this striking analogue to other oral epic poems has nothing to do with its quality and everything to do with its invisibility. Second, of those forms actually collected a much smaller fraction have so far reached publication in a distributable format. The scarcity of Native American poetic forms offers mute testimony to our failings in this regard, and even the better-collected genres—South Slavic women's songs, for example, or the rich field of central Asian epic—have long languished in archives without much prospect of gaining the wider audience that extensive publication and contextualization bring.[22] In comparison to the audience generated for any ode written by John Keats, or any sonnet penned by William Shakespeare, most species of oral poetry remain well-kept secrets.

But beyond important matters like these lies perhaps the most basic problem of all: the oral poem versus its representation, the stark discrepancy between the performance of an oral poetic genre and its partial reincarnation in published format. What if this or that type of oral poetry depends for its identity on modulations of voice, for example, or on vocal or instrumental music, or on dance or other physical, gestural features? What if the performer uses loudness, pitch, or pause to signal the audience according to the rules of a particular genre? How do we preserve even an echo of such activity in a published text? Don't we stand the chance of misrepresenting the genre by failing to include crucial audience cues? We'll consider such intriguing problems carefully in the Second and Fourth Words, as we examine how the textual representation of an oral poem can and cannot imitate the experience it seeks to codify and transmit. We'll also make some proposals to improve the transition from performance to text in the Post-Script.

For now, let me suggest just one measure of how important it is to approach oral poetry with a wide-open, pluralistic concept of genre. It was the so-called Oral-Formulaic Theory that first offered solid evidence that Homer's *Iliad* and *Odyssey* were at some point oral poetry, and it did so by comparing those ancient, manuscript-prisoned epics to living, collectable oral epics from the former Yugoslavia. The idea was to use the known to explain the unknown, to conduct research in a living laboratory and then transfer the results of the lab analysis back to the *Iliad* and *Odyssey*. As that approach developed, it continued to model every other oral (or oral-connected) poetry—whatever its genre—to that one living epic witness. All types were modeled on a single type, without regard for inevitable, built-in discrepancies. In fact, the basis for comparison was even weaker than a single genre, since the lone witness was actually only one particular subgenre of South Slavic epic, the Moslem variety.

And what was the result? As things turned out, the comparison that began Oral-Formulaic Theory worked reasonably well for the Homeric poems, which resemble the Moslem epic in numerous ways. But it worked very inadequately for many of the more than one hundred other traditions and poetic genres to which it was subsequently applied. Oral poetry—much more diverse than written poetry, we must remember—was poorly served by offering it only a single subgeneric slot. Would we insist on comparing Spenser's *Faerie Queene*, Yeats's "A Prayer for My Daughter," and Ginsberg's "Howl" to a single subspecies of sonnet? Comparison without due attention to generic contrasts cannot yield sustainable results for written poetry, never mind oral poetry.

What's the lesson here? Simply put, when dealing with the genres of oral poetry, expect a cornucopia. Don't model everything on any single genre any more than you would fixate on one kind of poetic line. Examine all defining features of each oral poem according to its idiosyncrasies rather than according to a prepackaged set of expectations. It may be that productive comparisons can be made across genres or traditions once due calibration is made, but care must be exercised to "read" each oral genre on its own terms first. Oral poetry adopts different guises by genre as well as by tradition.

Step 3. Opening Up the Oral versus Written Dichotomy

With the rediscovery of oral poetry and attempts to evaluate the "new" medium, many questions have arisen. Eager to make a useful distinction, many scholars tended at first toward a binary, black-and-white contrast. What was oral poetry? Well, it must be everything written poetry wasn't. It didn't use writing technology, it existed outside of texts, and its performers were better understood as transmitters than the literary artists we celebrate. This "strong thesis," which aimed at driving a wedge between oral and written, led to hypotheses of *oral cultures* in which letters were either nonexistent or of little importance (no matter that such societies were much rarer than societies in which oral poetry was actually collected). It also led to the notion of *oral individuals* who practiced the letterless technology exclusively (no matter that it was surprisingly hard to find such untainted, monodimensional individuals). Scholars even devised *quantitative tests for orality,* procedures designed to determine which manuscript poems from the ancient and medieval periods must have been written down from oral performance and which were composed in writing (no matter that such litmus tests produced irregular results and failed to divine much about the process behind the product).[23] All these misconceptions stemmed from insisting on a Great Divide model, from setting oral versus written.

Reaction to such overstatement is not hard to imagine. Most damaging to the romantic thesis about oral cultures and individuals—but in the end most salutary for understanding oral poetry—has been the continuous stream of reports from fieldwork on living oral traditions. Folklorists and anthropologists have shown unambiguously how cultures that use writing for some of their social transactions still resort to oral tradition for numerous other purposes and activities. The same proves true for individuals, who have no problem juggling the two technologies according to applicable social demands.[24] The scientific-seeming tests for orality met with the same fate. Specialists in various areas seized on this or that written poem and demonstrated that, lo and behold, it showed many of the same features as supposedly oral verse. Old English poetry was one such case. If we find similar features in *Beowulf* and in Old English poems we know to be translated pen in hand from Latin, so one argument went, then how can we pronounce *Beowulf* oral?[25] Of course, we can't. Indeed, pronouncing a manuscript oral is a problematic act, anyway; we may try to establish it as a transcription or libretto to be performed, but how is a text *itself* oral?

But if the real message in all of this is that the two-part typology of oral versus written can't be maintained, we need not conclude that dichotomous thinking was an empty gesture or a dead end. It served an important purpose in the overall evolution of our ideas about how to read oral poetry. Seeing the rediscovered medium as "other"—carving out some space and definition for oral poetry—helped to pave the way for a more nuanced view of verbal art as a whole.

Much water has passed under the bridge, and we no longer need to resort to binary models to make a place for oral poetry. We can now squarely confront questions that once threatened to undo hard-won distinctions, to collapse voice into silence, performance into text, aural audience into readership. Here are some versions of the same basic query: Isn't oral poetry very much like written poetry? Isn't it true that we really don't need to "do anything differently" with oral poetry? Can't we continue to treat all verbal art in pretty much the same way no matter what its ultimate source or its present medium? Isn't verbal art all of a piece?

We start with a carefully qualified "yes, to a degree." Oral and written poetry are certainly alike in some dimensions. Indeed, how else could it be? To the best of our knowledge, all cultures that eventually developed written literatures were using the technology of oral tradition much earlier and for a much longer time. Written expressive strategies take great advantage of the fixity and spatialization that are the stock-in-trade of the textual medium, but these strategies did not spring full-grown from the first literate author's head. There remains a genetic relationship between the kinds of verbal art we find in texts and those we encounter in performance. Given this reality, it would be foolish to argue against broad similarities between two kinds of poetry that are historically and genetically related.

On the other hand, for reasons discussed above and illustrated throughout this book, oral poetries are also quite different from poetries that come into being under textual rules and live out their lives solely as texts. Oral poetries are different, as we shall see, in three fundamental ways—in their *composition, performance,* and *reception.* That doesn't mean we should expect any facile uniformity, any more than we would expect the complex riches of world literature to answer a lockstep definition or characterization. One size just won't fit all: oral poetry involves too many traditions, genres, and individuals for that. In fact, as uncomfortable or as downright messy as it may seem, the truth about oral poetry lies somewhere between the Great Divide and the telephone directory, between the false dichotomy and the never-ending laundry list. Our challenge is to fashion a model for oral poetry that realistically portrays both its unity and its diversity, a kind of biology that allows for species differentiation within the composite genus. To that challenge I now turn.

Step 4. Opening Up Media Dynamics

Oral poetry actually reaches us through a diverse array of media. Let's follow one possible sequence. As fieldworkers we may experience various oral genres firsthand, as temporary members of a society during an extended on-site investigation in which we record on audio or video the events we were a part of. After we return to our own society, others may then listen to and view our recordings, appreciating them as best they can. An edition may then be formulated by the original fieldworkers, who had the advantage of having been present during the original performances, or by others with varying degrees of expertise and experience. Eventually this edition, at most a textual shadow of the original event, can be made available to a much wider audience using the print network established, approved, and maintained by text-consumers. The oral poem has become a book. Whether that book ever wins inclusion in an academic curriculum or in a culture's canon depends on myriad factors. Some of these include the form in which the editions are circulated, the mindset of the readers who encounter them, and the relationship of this "other" material to the existing curriculum or canon. If it makes the transition, the book becomes an item in the Museum of Verbal Art, a lofty achievement that is nonetheless a far cry from the performance from which it stems.

Not only is oral poetry itself remarkably diverse, then, but the media through which it evolves are many and various. Indeed, the path we chose to follow for this example—from live oral performance to museum exhibit—is only one of several possible routes for oral poetry. There are many more paths, and each of them bristles with alternate possibilities all along the way. Does the performer play an instrument or sing? Is there a text involved at any stage in the process, either read to or read by the composer? Are the composer and performer the same person? What role does the audience play? All of these questions (and many more) warn us that, as mentioned above, we need to find the most useful level for our inquiry. Too broad and typological, and we condemn ourselves to over-generalized models like the Great Divide. Too narrow and case-study-oriented, and we miss the forest for the trees. The trick is to find a level that is just fine-grained enough to be diagnostic, just comprehensive enough to demonstrate some overall unities and offer some practical bases for comparison, and just flexible enough to accommodate the natural diversity of human expression.

With this goal in mind, I sketch below four generalized but fact-based situations for the composition, performance, and reception of oral poetry. Settling on these four patterns naturally requires some simplification, some sacrifice of individual details to principles of explanation. For our purposes, however, this is as it must be. As indicated above, we seek a reasonable middle ground: a set of models that together offer a rough outline of various media possibilities, a flexible taxonomy that can boost our understanding by organizing myriad individual cases under a few meaningful headings. If configured with due attention to features that truly matter, such a model can serve as a sort of filing system for the diverse collection of oral poetries from around the world and from ancient times to the present.

Here, then, is a proposed system of media categories, each illustrated by a single example:

	Composition	Performance	Reception	Example
1. Oral Performance	Oral	Oral	Aural	Tibetan paper-singer
2. Voiced Texts	Written	Oral	Aural	Slam poetry
3. Voices from the Past	O/W	O/W	A/W	Homer's *Odyssey*
4. Written Oral Poems	Written	Written	Written	Bishop Njegoš

Our categories begin, expectably, with *Oral Performance,* which entails oral composition, oral performance, and aural reception; they end, perhaps not so expectably, with *Written Oral Poems,* that is, with texts composed in writing and meant for individual readers. Oral poetry can be detected across this entire spectrum of media, even when camouflaged in textual form, and we need to be aware of its many guises.

Let me prefix two cautionary statements to our discussion. First, as explained above, I intend no hierarchy among the four categories. *Oral Performance* describes one situation in which we discover oral poetry; it is not necessarily the "finest" or the purest or the most valuable. Correspondingly, as written technology enters the picture in various ways, it doesn't degrade or pollute or diminish something pristine any more than it moves poetry forward in quality or complexity; it simply makes for other brands or types of oral poetry. Media combine and interact in interesting ways.

Second, and this goes to the heart of our book-long campaign to examine unexamined assumptions, I offer this four-part system as a wide-open spectrum without any ancient-to-modern or primitive-to-sophisticated axis. Nor is it meant as a series of discrete, self-contained categories. In other words, I've plotted these four points to map the breadth of the spectrum and to suggest some organizational benchmarks, but the most faithful representation of oral poetry will also be the least categorical. Systems of analysis are necessarily imposed from outside, not generated from the inside; they can make no claim to universal, archetypal solutions. We need to grant every culture, tradition, genre, poem, and individual poet and audience the license to complicate the system, to add their own qualifications and footnotes to whatever assertion we make in the spirit of overall explanation. With these flexible and nonhierarchical categories in mind, then, let's see how each of them works.

#1. Oral Performance — For many people, the designation "oral poetry" means only one thing: verse composed and performed orally in front of a listening audience. In this first category the processes of composition and performance are usually simultaneous, as in South Slavic epic or Xhosa praise-poetry. When these paired processes are separated, we're usually dealing with a memorized text for later performance (sometimes by a different person), a situation that falls into our second category of Voiced Texts. In Oral Performance, however, reception is customarily live and immediate. Poet and audience participate together, and everything takes place in present time and experience. This is the easiest kind of oral poetry for us text-consumers to grasp, chiefly because it's so opposite to literature in every respect. Indeed, for some of us Oral Performance is the only scenario that qualifies. Change any part of the equation— composition, performance, or reception—and it no longer adds up; we no longer have oral poetry. But as the opening scenarios in this book indicated, and as common sense would argue, this kind of fundamentalism isn't defensible. It disenfranchises a great many oral poems that have also involved writing and texts as part of their history.

Of course, there can be little question that Oral Performance is by far the most widespread and copious of our four patterns, with scores of examples from six of the seven continents. Alongside Jack tales and folk sermons from North America and the *romances* of Spain and its diaspora stand, for example, the traditional songs of the Maori from Australia, Basotho migrant songs from Africa, the *Pabuji Epic* from southern India, and Sibundoy oral sayings from Colombia, South America.[26] Even a selective catalogue would soon reach heroic proportions. And this is to say nothing of the myriad instances of Oral Performance that have been lost simply because they were never documented, indeed couldn't be *document*-ed because they flowered and expired before the invention of writing in mid-December of our species-year. Even in our own time, however, a relatively small percentage of such oral/aural performances are ever collected, and fewer still ever reach publication, broad dissemination, and either the academic or the general reader. On theoretical grounds alone, the case for limiting oral poetry to category #1 is critically weak; what do we do with poems that weave in and out of performance, that are composed in writing but performed aurally, that audiences may experience only via books, and so forth? Categories #2–4 will cover these and other possibilities. Practically, the case is just as weak; there simply aren't many opportunities for most of us to experience Oral Performance firsthand or even secondhand.[27]

Indeed, it's impossible to overemphasize the fact that most of us get to know Oral Performance only in a textual format, whether in manuscripts or books or perhaps via audio or video facsimiles (which are still texts). We aren't part of the Tibetan paper-singer's audience, the Xhosa praise-poet's constituency, or the rapt participant-audience of Mexican folk-drama.[28] Rather we're restricted to reading frozen, carefully configured editions of these real-life events, full of contextualizing information and analysis but by no stretch of the imagination equivalent to actual experience of the events themselves. That's a natural sort of thing, of course; relatively few of us do original fieldwork, and even those who do limit their activities to one or a couple of cultures and languages. But let's be absolutely clear—our treasured editions, piled high with versions, notes, and context, are not themselves Oral Performance. Why not? Simply because another medium has intervened. Nonetheless, as flawed and partial as such editions endemically are, I'd staunchly maintain that what they (re)present is oral poetry.

Take a related if not identical case. Suppose someone shoots a multimedia video of an Oral Performance, encoding not just the words we enshrine in texts with whatever accompanying textual information can be tacked on, but also the visual images, sounds, audience involvement, and so forth. This still isn't Oral Performance. Although the video preserves more of the original performance dynamics than the printed page, it's still a text, fixed and unchanging no matter who views it, no matter when or where they "read" it. In place of the poet's creation in the here-and-now we experience a distanced, cinematographic refraction of the performance, shot with certain equipment from a certain point of view under certain assumptions and qualified by whatever film-editing occurs from the moment of recording onward. Even if we think of playing the video as something approaching Oral Performance and watching it as something akin to aural reception, the basis of the experience is still a text. Book, acoustic tape, and film may represent Oral Performance, but strictly speaking they're not equivalent to it.

An anecdote may help explain things from an alternate perspective by showing how the translation of Oral Performance into texts can be positively undesirable and even dangerous. During a 1989 visit to South Africa, well before the dissolution of apartheid, I was sponsored by the University of the Western Cape, very much an anti-apartheid institution, as a speaker at various other universities. After a lecture at a historically conservative university, I was asked by the African Languages department head to meet privately with a younger African colleague who wished to discuss his research. The department head didn't know what the specific subject would be. After some preliminaries it became apparent that the young man had a question to pose about his fieldwork with Xhosa praise-poets, in particular with *iimbongi* who were composing poems that sharply criticized the government. He needed to record their poems acoustically, he explained, in order to study them carefully. But if he went ahead and made what amounted to texts of any of these performances, he ran the risk of opening up the poets to severe political reprisal. What did I think he should do? This difficult question—impossible to answer except on ethical and humanitarian grounds—crystallized the issue of Oral Performance versus its textual record: the event that took place in the performance arena could become treasonous once it was "document"-ed.

Then too, other research has unearthed examples of what is called "oralizing" or "reoralizing." Such discoveries productively put the lie to the evolutionary paradigm of oral-to-written, turning the imagined one-way street leading from oral poetry to literary texts into a broader thoroughfare that permits and even fosters two-way traffic. The Anglo-American folk ballad is a striking example of this natural volatility, circulating back and forth among tradition-bearers, collectors, printed broadsides, and the like. Pushkin's *Eugene Onegin*, originally a highly literary document, has entered Russian oral tradition as dramatic poetry in its own right and earned a place in category #1. Balinese poetry in oral tradition interacts in substantive ways with the textual culture and record, not only exposing the deficiencies of the Great Divide model but giving clear evidence of two-way migration across the imagined gap.[29] These and other such cases illustrate why a doctrinaire, purist conception of oral poetry as restricted to Oral Performance cannot work. What we need is a more complete and sensitive system of media dynamics that makes room for the innate diversity of human expressive arts.

#2. Voiced Texts — Real-life observations, as distinct from mere theorizing, can help us toward this kind of pluralism. There's another type of oral poetry that begins life as a written composition only to modulate to oral performance before a live audience. For poems that cluster around this node in the spectrum I suggest the designation of Voiced Texts. What separates this kind of verbal art from contemporary written poetry enshrined in literary reviews, chapbooks, and anthologies is precisely its intended medium of publication, the means by which it reaches its audience. Voiced Texts aim solely at oral performance and are by definition incomplete without that performance. Compare this trajectory with the more usual and familiar kind of written poetry, which aims primarily at transmission through print to an audience of silent, individual readers. Of course, poets of any sort may read their poetry aloud and often choose to do so, but only in the case of Voiced Texts is the spoken word the necessary and defining outcome of the composition-performance-reception process.

Slam poetry offers us a ready example of Voiced Texts that can be experienced in urban centers across the United States and increasingly in Western Europe. While it customarily begins life as a penned or word-processed composition, slam doesn't really live until it is orally performed before a live audience. It may reach publication later on, but that's secondary. This species of oral poetry is not as widespread internationally as Oral Performance, but its easy accessibility in contemporary Western cultures makes it an attractive opportunity for anyone reading this book who might be interested in directly experiencing oral poetry. Unfortunately, however, slam poetry and other Voiced Texts suffer from some of the same media prejudice as does Oral Performance. Because it doesn't usually intersect with the print network that supports documentation and literature, oral poetry in this second category has usually met with one of two equally discouraging outcomes. Either it's been judged unworthy of comparison with elite, mainstream poetry or simply ignored or gone unnoticed because it operates below the literary radar. Now, with more venues and the increased visibility they bring, as well as print collections like *Burning Down the House* and *Poetry Slam,* video recordings like *Slamnation* and *nycSLAMS,* and dedicated Web sites,[30] slam poetry is beginning to make a substantial inroad and gain a wider, even more diverse audience.

Audience is hardly a problem for most contemporary popular music, some of which also belongs in the Voiced Texts category of oral poetry. Although a fixed, written text lies at the basis of most rock songs, for example, musicians like Sting and Dave Matthews regularly speak of how a song evolves as a band works with it over the succession of live performances that make up a tour. The instrumentation may change, a harmony may be deleted or added, various members of the band may experiment with rhythms or insert instrumental solos (leading to extended versions), the lead singer can modify phrasing or even lyrics. A particular song usually begins life as the fixed text copyrighted with a record company and burned onto a mass-market CD—essentially providing an identical "book" for everyone to "read." But by the time the tour is finished, that same tune may have evolved quite a distance from the original text, taking on a new shape each time it's performed and reperformed for live audiences. Indeed, "live" albums of well-known songs make their mark by taking advantage of the distance between "canned" versions and fresh reinterpretations of what is recognizably the same song, but with a difference.

Blues, an African American genre in origin, is perhaps most profitably understood as straddling the Oral Performance and Voiced Texts categories.[31] At one end of the spectrum, many blues songs are traditional; we can no more say who "wrote" them than we can attribute this or that South Slavic epic or Hispanic ballad to a single creator. What is more, blues is more often than not learned and transmitted wholly without texts—written or acoustic—via face-to-face transmission from one player to another. That's not to say that texts don't enter the mix in some situations: a musician may learn from a recording or, more rarely, from sheet music or written-down verses. And we must make room for the blues songs whose lyrics are in fact penned by one individual, though characteristically within the melodic, verbal, and instrumental idiom of the blues tradition. Regular melodies and guitar licks, always varying within limits, are part of the cueing mechanism that identifies a blues song as what it is.

Voiced Texts can also be performed orally by someone other than the person who composed them in writing. Our team's fieldwork in the former Yugoslavia turned up the interesting case of a *guslar* who did just that: Živomir Milojević, a singer of epic songs from the Christian tradition of Serbia who preferred to be known as "Čika Žika," or "Uncle Žika." But he didn't voice (or wholly remake) a text-story that was read aloud to him, as in the famous instance involving the preliterate Parry-Lord *guslar* Avdo Medjedović and his *Odyssey*-length version of *The Wedding of Smailagić Meho,* a feat we'd have to call Oral Performance. No, Čika Žika proudly informed us that he had learned his best song by reading it himself from a songbook or *pjesmarica.* Intrigued over his boast of having personally consulted a written medium as his source, we asked to see the songbook and were presented with a brief pamphlet that did indeed house the song in question, attributed to a *guslar* from the nearby market-town of Arandjelovac.

It was true, then: Čika Žika had apparently learned his favorite song from this small text by reading it himself. Using literacy skills gained during his six years of formal schooling, he had crossed out a line here or there and scrawled a few words on some of the pages. But when he began to play "live"—and this was confirmed more precisely via later analysis of his text and the tape of his performance—the source quickly faded into the background. Notwithstanding his claims and our expectations, there was very little to compare in the text and his performance. Lines corresponded here and there, while parallel sequences of ideas rolled along without much overlap in actual expression. The text had started the process, there was no denying that. But in voicing it Čika Žika's own traditional competence had taken over, molding the song to his personal idiomatic shape. In terms of what the South Slavic singers taught us about units of utterance, he had put it in his own "words."[32] His song existed on the cusp of Voiced Text and Oral Performance.

In a sense, Voiced Texts are the opposite of what happens when Oral Performance gets recorded and distributed as a print, audio, or video edition. In both cases we're still dealing with oral poetry, only now mediated through a text that becomes the newly created source for everything that follows. But there's also a difference. In Oral Performance that text comes into play as the medium for those not present at the performance, while with Voiced Texts the fixed form exerts its influence—whatever that influence may be—at the beginning of the whole process. In the one case the oral poem is frozen and distributed to audiences as a fossil; in the other the text initiates a sequence that leads to aural reception. Voiced Texts live only in, and solely for, oral performance (with the exception of documentary videos of slam poetry and the like), and their audience knows them only as oral poems.

#3. Voices from the Past — Suppose we're no longer able to hear the voice of oral poetry, at least not firsthand, no matter how hard we try? Here's the problem in a nutshell. The poetic tradition we wish to understand has died many decades or centuries or millennia before, leaving us with textual shards of a once-living work of verbal art. Direct experience of that oral poetry lies forever beyond our reach. Under such conditions attending a performance, watching a video, even listening to an acoustic tape are of course all out of the question. Do we then collapse all distinctions between oral and written poetry? Do we stop trying to listen? Do we settle for the usual routines of textual gymnastics? Do we default to *littera*-ture?

As a first principle, I would argue that we can't afford to ignore oral poetry simply because its original form flourished too early in our species-year for it to be studied and recorded as such. Especially when various kinds of witnesses offer evidence that poems like the Old English *Beowulf* or the ancient Greek *Odyssey* or the Indian *Mahabharata* or the Persian *Shâhnâma* existed first in oral tradition and were only later written down, how can we ignore a formative chapter in their biography? If we feel comfortable extrapolating from Hubbell telescope photographs of deep space to the Big Bang or from measurements of collisions between high-energy particles to theories of elemental matter, we should be able to see beyond textual products to the oral poetic processes that produced them. As a practical matter, we can't allow mere chronology and the historical accident of available technologies to diminish or delimit our awareness of oral poetry. As an artistic matter, we can't hope to read ancient, medieval, and other manuscript-based but oral-connected poetry without considering its true dynamics. Much is at stake here.

For these reasons I propose a third category of oral poetry: Voices from the Past. What does it include? Simply put, it offers a slot for those oral poetic traditions that time has eclipsed and which we can now consult only in textual form. Built into that capsule definition is a necessary flexibility. Any given poem's original composition may have been oral or written; in many cases we just can't tell whether the document we hold in our hands is a direct transcription of an oral performance or an artifact some generations of editing and recopying removed from performance. The particular version that survives to us may even have been composed as a text, written down by a poet adhering to the rules of Oral Performance. All of these possibilities must be kept open or we run the risk of claiming more than we really know and as a result falsifying any conclusions we may try to draw.

Beowulf from medieval England and the *Iliad* and *Odyssey* from ancient Greece are two renowned examples of Voices from the Past. So too are the Mayan *Popol Vuh*, the Old French *Song of Roland* and medieval Spanish *Poem of the Cid*, the Persian *Shâhnâma*, the medieval Welsh *Mabinogion*, and numerous more poems that we can know only as texts. If we take a broad view of what we call poetry, we'll need to include parts of the Hebrew Bible and the New Testament as well.[33] Just how many scribes and editors stand between the last oral performances and these surviving documents—and what sorts of influence such intermediaries exerted—is for the most part beyond our ability to determine. Indeed, we can't absolutely rule out a Homer who had enough literacy to write down his epics himself (though most would argue against that position), or a *Beowulf*-poet who memorized great chunks of his poem, partially fixing it in rote memory even before it was written down. Of course, flexibility and latitude are prime attributes of our model of media dynamics: all four categories of oral poetry readily accommodate the natural variety of individual circumstances and help forestall preemptive judgments. But with Voices from the Past, when so many of the facts surrounding the history of performances and traditions are lost to us, it's particularly important to keep an open mind. We must be willing to accept some blind spots in our knowledge of these works as we try to "hear" oral poetries exclusively through the texts they have left behind.

At first encounter, Voices from the Past may resemble the infamous "wastebasket" or "trapdoor" that some theories use to dispose of troublesome, awkward phenomena that don't quite fit the hypothesis. But that's not the case here. This category renders a crucial service by helping us face up to the real-world challenge of fundamental diversity in human expressive forms—the inescapable fact that "*Oralpoetry* is a very plural noun," as one of our *proverbs* will put it in the Sixth Word. It also allows us to build a sensible agnosticism into the overall explanation, to admit forthrightly that we lack final answers to some questions. If we attempt to force too much order on such diversity, if we try to impose too much from the outside by making assertions we can't substantiate, any system of media dynamics will be compromised. At that point it will be only too easy to collapse all verbal art back into our default category of text-bound literature. The baby will have gone the way of the bathwater.

What we can say—and here is the crucial point—is that all of the poems in this category were composed according to the rules of the given oral poetry. They bear a telltale compositional stamp. Whatever the exact scenario of their commission to textual form and their history since that moment, they remain oral poetry. As we'll see in the Second and Seventh Words, this has important implications for how we hear these Voices from the Past.

The evidence for calling them "oral poetry" is of two sorts—direct accounts of how they were composed and performed on the one hand, and structural symptoms of oral composition and performance on the other. The direct accounts are self-explanatory: the famous portraits of Hrothgar's singer (*scop*) in *Beowulf,* or of the Ithacan bard (*aoidos*) Phemios or his Phaeacian counterpart Demodokos in the *Odyssey.* Of course, we must be very careful not to overestimate the ethnographic reliability of this kind of information, which is not at all the same thing as an anthropological analysis or a field report. Poetic depictions of oral performance, as idealizations with primary loyalty to their poetic traditions, cannot be taken as on-site ethnography. Indeed, even fieldwork can produce stories of transparently legendary singers who serve as anthropomorphic images of the poetic tradition rather than "real people."[34] But in combination with references from other contemporary sources (Plato's *Republic* or *Ion,* for example, for ancient Greek oral epic) or histories close to the period and place,[35] poetic accounts give us confidence in what amounts to an Oral Performance background for Voices from the Past.

The evidence of telltale symptoms is less direct, but no less dependable as long as we don't press it too hard. Research has isolated key features, somewhat different for each tradition and genre of course, that mark a poem's media heritage. These features are the residue of oral performance; they constitute "what's left" when an oral poem is reduced to a text. Recurrent phrases and scenes are a few of the more widely observed characteristics of Voices from the Past. Thus the celebrated formulaic phrases in Homer, with "swift-footed Achilles" and "rosy-fingered dawn" recurring again and again; thus the formulas in Coptic hymns from before the year 1000, in the Persian *Shânâhma* of the eleventh century, and in the Latvian *dainas* of the nineteenth, as also in the living tradition of African American rap music.[36] Homeric epic features a number of pliable recurrent scenes, such as the "Assembly" or "Feast," that vary within limits to suit the particular situation or story. Typical scenes like these also populate the Old Norse sagas, and once again the living traditions such as central Asian epic and the Mongolian *Jangar* cycle as well.[37]

But phrases and scenes hardly exhaust the inventory of expressive signs in oral poetry. Northwest Coast Native American peoples frame their oral stories in a complex, recognizable series of structures as small as the verse and as large as story-sections. These keys to organization and meaning have been recovered by analyzing texts written down from dictation in the early and mid-twentieth century, and they make a substantial difference in how we read the stories. Given the diversity of oral poetry in this third category, we cannot expect archetypal features across its wide expanse. But if the particular shape and texture of signals and structures is always idiosyncratic, the plain fact of patterning and of variation within limits is not. Voices from the Past reveal their status as oral poetry through their recurrency and multiformity of language, however their special poetic language may happen to work. Oral poetry has left behind recognizable footprints in these silent texts.

In the early going some specialists believed that the mere density of such patterning could serve as a litmus test, that it constituted "proof" of the actual orality or writtenness of a manuscript poem—whether the text in hand was originally an oral performance or not. We now claim much less, but at the same time something much more fundamental: that these features signal a background in oral poetry, though they don't magically reveal the precise story behind any given text. In the case of Voices from the Past, we usually can't say whether this or that poem was actually an oral performance. We just can't confidently stretch things that far. But, on the basis of these two kinds of evi-

dence—direct accounts and structural symptoms—we can confidently pronounce *Beowulf,* the *Odyssey,* the *Shâhnâma,* the *Mahabharata,* the *Roland,* the
Mabinogion, the *Cid,* and many other manuscript works "oral poetry." As we
shall see later on, that identification carries with it a wealth of important implications for reading.

So much for composition. How were these Voices from the Past performed
and received? Ascribing either oral or written performance and reception may
seem like hedging, but it's a realistic representation of what we know and can
figure out. In the ancient and medieval traditions cited above and many more
poetries worldwide, there is every reason to conclude that both kinds of performance took place, sometimes side by side in the same era. Performers composed without texts in front of audiences and they read aloud from texts for
others; probably less frequently they read to themselves, whether aloud or silently.[38] Consider the real-life situations in the ancient and medieval periods.
Few people controlled the arts of literacy, and what literacy there was enjoyed
a limited range of applications. Few copies of oral poems existed in any user-
friendly format, and mass readership had not yet been invented. Under such
conditions the last thing we should expect is tidily organized modes of performance. *Beowulf* may well have been performed in Anglo-Saxon England both
without a text and by voicing a text. Homer's oral poems seem to have been
performed in numerous different venues, perhaps voiced from rote memory
or from texts by rhapsodes (*rhapsôidoi*) as well as composed and recomposed
by oral bards (*aoidoi*).[39] Artificially compressing such natural variability for the
sake of a well-ordered model can only cloud our perspective, not only on the
oral poems in question but on Voices from the Past more generally.

As with composition and performance, so with reception. If anything, the
spectrum of possible scenarios broadens even further at the far end of the chain
of communication. We can imagine—and we have believable evidence for
imagining—an oral poet performing before an audience. This is essentially
Oral Performance as reflected in the versions of these poems that survive to
us, though of course we can never personally verify that reflection. We also
know that Voiced Texts were widely in play in the ancient and medieval periods, with a fixed version serving as the basis for the performance.[40] As we have
learned, the Voiced Text scenario demands that we allow for departures from
that fixed version, in effect for recomposition during performance. It also requires that we allow for the composer and performer to be different people.
Indeed, in a manuscript tradition like the Old English, where even writing
scribes recomposed formulaically as they copied, variable performance from
manuscripts by a range of people seems a foregone conclusion.[41] Finally, the
existence of a manuscript text, whether from ancient or medieval Europe, Asia,

or the Americas, means that we can't afford to deny the possibility of readers who read only to themselves. This is liable to be a very small group, given literacy rates, the uses to which writing is put, and contemporary textual technologies. But Voices from the Past must include all feasible scenarios, forthrightly acknowledging what we don't know as well as recognizing the combination of media in play.

With what does this category of oral poetry finally present us? What's the underlying logic that sorts its various manifestations? We need to be clear and realistic in answering such questions: Voices from the Past are not—and can never be—as economically defined and delimited as Oral Performance or Voiced Texts. Too much remains either unknown or dependent on composite media to settle unambiguously on single options for composition, performance, and reception. But beyond an admittedly messy spectrum of possibilities lies a saving grace—the rationalizing fact that, whatever guise they may take in their various histories and manuscript forms, Voices from the Past are still oral poetry. By allowing for the uncertainties generated by centuries of distance and by different mixes of performance and text across different cultures, we can focus on what really matters: namely, that the verbal art of *Gilgamesh,* the *Shâhnâma,* the *Mahabharata,* the Hebrew Bible, *Beowulf,* the New Testament, the *Odyssey,* and other such works springs from an oral tradition. Whether they reach us on clay tablets, papyrus rolls, vellum codexes, or printed pages, these works are also oral poems.

#4. Written Oral Poems — How can oral poetry exist as written verse silently read from texts meant for individual readers? What's oral about a process that begins and ends with writing technology and entirely lacks living voice and aural reception?[42] Isn't a Written Oral Poem a contradiction in terms?

Although this may well be one of the smaller of our four categories, it's just as important as the others—not only for what it contains but also for what it reveals about what really constitutes oral poetry. Poets who write oral poetry are composing according to certain rules, just like readers who read oral poetry. Thus a learned figure from nineteenth-century Yugoslavia, Bishop Petar II Petrović Njegoš, accomplished what conventional wisdom once pronounced impossible: he composed oral poetry pen-in-hand for consumption by literate, reading audiences. Some investigators have termed his works "imitation oral," a designation that seems to question their quality or genuineness, but the fact is that Njegoš "sang" on the page. He wrote oral poetry.[43]

How he managed this apparent miracle is an important consideration for us as we try to learn how to read an oral poem. Born Rade Petrović in 1813 in a Montenegrin village, Njegoš was eventually to succeed his uncle as bishop of Montenegro in 1833. His biography thus begins with early immersion in the South Slavic oral tradition of heroic stories, apparently both the Moslem and the Christian varieties. He even learned to sing the songs to the *gusle* himself, under the tutelage of his father and uncle. As for the "other world" of letters, as Albert Lord puts it, Njegoš received lessons in reading and writing in the monastery at Cetinje starting at age twelve. The trajectory of his own life mirrors the mixed context of orality and literacy that characterized nineteenth-century Montenegro.

Straddling these two worlds with a bilingual familiarity, Njegoš was able to use the traditional oral style at the same time that he could also stand outside it. We can see his multiple-media fluency in his early collection, *Pjevannija* (2d ed., 1837), which runs the gamut of expressive forms. Some poems are reperformances of well-known traditional stories, some are "new" songs, and still others begin to introduce literary conventions into traditional song-making. These "new" poems are topical and locally situated but composed in the formulaic, decasyllabic idiom; their language and style come from one world and their subjects from another. Throughout this collection Njegoš displays a repertoire of registers or expressive strategies, the result of his dual competence in oral tradition and literary texts. In sum, his example shows us the importance of grasping the diversity of oral poetry across traditions, genres, and especially across media. Njegoš probably composed entirely in writing (some say oral dictation may have figured into his work, but there's no evidence for that); he "performed" the poems in a published text, and readers came to know them exclusively from that textual source. Nonetheless, there's no question that what the bishop wrote was oral poetry.

A few easily accessible additional examples may help to establish the breadth of the Written Oral Poetry category. Consider the intriguing case of the Finnish *Kalevala* (1835–62), which derives from orally performed poems but reached composite epic form only through the active intervention of Elias Lönnrot, a physician-folklorist whom some would call a ghost-writer and others would call a singer.[44] Lönnrot wore a number of hats: he was a collector of Oral Performance, an arranger of these living specimens, and a creative author. Drawing his building blocks primarily from a series of field trips, he fashioned a long, continuous story by employing two main strategies: sequencing the parts he collected into a grand master-story and filling out individual passages with lines borrowed from other versions and performances. On the one hand, there can be little doubt that Lönnrot was using "real" oral poetry in this project; only about 3 percent of the lines in the *Kalevala* are of his invention, and even these coinages proceed in strict accordance with relevant rules. But there is also no doubt that what he fashioned was a Written Oral Poem, since nothing remotely like it in length or elaboration was to be located anywhere in the Finn-ish-Karelian region. As Lauri Honko puts it, "the patches may be identical with oral poems but the patchwork as a whole is Lönnrot's vision of a long epic" (1998: 176). Was Lönnrot an author driven by the nineteenth-century passion to discover his culture's ethnic roots in folk narrative or was he in effect a tra-ditional singer who had so thoroughly learned the poetic register that he could "sing on the page"? Reading the *Kalevala* as Written Oral Poetry allows us to avoid that false dichotomy and answer yes to both sides of the question.

About one hundred years earlier the same passion for folk-poetic roots had led James Macpherson down a road to both worldwide acclaim and interna-tional infamy.[45] In publications that first appeared between 1760 and 1763 and in many editions thereafter, Macpherson claimed to be presenting translations of Gaelic epic from the Scottish highlands, sung, so he affirmed, by a gifted poet named Ossian. It soon became apparent, however, that Macpherson had himself composed these poems via clever management of three kinds of re-sources: actual Oral Performance written down from dictation during field-work, verses and poems copied from existing manuscripts, and his own per-sonal creation. For this he's been praised to the skies by some (including Thomas Jefferson), branded an outright fraud by others, and sympathetically reinterpreted as responding to political and historical realities by more recent readers. Is his achievement—or rather that of Ossian—less genuine than the *Kalevala?* Probably so, since he seems to have filtered the collected poetry to a greater degree and added far more to the field transcriptions than did Lönn-rot. But is it still Written Oral Poetry? I believe that not only does it fall com-fortably into that flexible category, but that placing it there helps us to better grasp its meaning and significance. Macpherson was harnessing the cultural power and political momentum of an oral tradition to speak through his own textual voice; he wasn't so much penning inauthentic folklore as translating between media. And that's precisely what a Writing Oral Poet does.

Looking ahead now to the next stage of our inquiry in the Second Word, we'll continue to explore the ramifications of this volume's title: *How to Read an Oral Poem.* Our discussion will begin with the question of "What is *an oral poem?"*—not at all the same question, as we shall see, as "What is *oral poet-ry?"* Building on those observations, we'll then ask "What is *reading?"* and, as the basis for the Third through Fifth Words, "What do we mean by *how?"* Overall, our chief aim in the Second Word will be to explain why we must "read" oral poetry differently from written literature, no matter what medi-um it happens to appear in. From that point it's but a small step to introduc-ing some of the most popular and well-developed approaches to reading oral poetry (Third through Fifth Words), as well as to offering some examples of how to apply these approaches (Seventh and Eighth Words).

Notes

1. The meanings we assign to these terms are of course latter-day developments from often quite different original meanings. *Text* derives from Latin *texere* ("to weave"); *write* comes from Old English *wrītan* ("to cut or incise," usually in stone); *poem* stems from ancient Greek *poiein* ("to make, create"); and *read* derives from Old English *rǣdan* ("to offer advice or counsel," originally in an oral context). For more on these terms, see esp. Howe 1993 and G. Nagy 1996b: 64–66.

2. See further Foley 1998b and the Post-Script to this volume.

3. The table assumes the age of homo sapiens to be approximately 100,000 years. This is a conservative estimate; according to some anthropologists, the species may be much older (see <http://www.britannica.com/bcom/eb/article/printable/0/ 0,5722,127620,00.html>), pushing all of these dates of invention even later into the species-year. The dates for scripts are based on the earliest tangible evidence and therefore reflect the time by which the script was in use rather than the moment of actual inception (which by definition is lost); for the sake of uniformity, they are all taken from Daniels and Bright 1996. The date for Chinese printing technology reflects "the earliest printed text in the world . . . a Buddhist Charm scroll printed in China and preserved in the Pulguk-sa Temple in Kyongju, south-east Korea" (Temple 1986: 111). The two dates marked with "fl." (*floruit*, or flourished) indicate the approximate time by which the institutions in question were reaching a position of importance and influence: the Alexandrian Library under the leadership of Zenodotus of Ephesus in the mid-third century B.C.E. (see Foley 1990: 23–24) and the Internet as correlated with the first skirmishes in the Netscape-Microsoft browser wars (ca. 1997).

4. These figures derive from Ong 1982: 7. Absolute accuracy is unattainable here, and probably unimportant; for our purposes, the extreme lateness of writing and the extreme rarity of literature are the crucial points.

5. Personal communication, Chao Gejin, Institute of Minority Literatures, Chinese Academy of Social Sciences, Beijing.

6. See Opland 1983 and 1998, Kaschula 1995 and 2000 on praise-poetry; Biebuyck and Mateene 1969, Johnson 1992, Johnson et al. 1997 on epic.

7. See further the Eighth Word below.

8. Recent studies illustrate clearly that neither orality nor literacy is the monolith we once imagined. On the complexity of literacy, see, e.g., Street 1984, 1993; on the complexity of reading, see the Second Word.

9. See "What Jack Learned at School: Leonard Roberts," in McCarthy 1994: chap. 7. In fact, four of the eight oral storytellers who contributed to this book were teachers, and a fifth was a Methodist minister.

10. de Vet 1996: esp. 65–66.

11. See further the Eighth Word.

12. As Roger Bonair-Agard put it (personal interview, 9/21/00), "the poem itself morphs over time." As for the process, he stipulated that "memorizing leads to the poem becoming a more mutable thing in performance."

13. On the history behind *Widsith*, see Malone 1962: esp. 105–12; on its oral poetry, Creed 1975. For examples of slam poetry, see note 30 below as well as the Fourth and Seventh Words. On oral poetry among the Yurok, Hupa, and Karok peoples, see Keeling 1992. On Gopala Naika's performance of the *Siri Epic*, see Honko et al. 1998a, b and Honko 1998. On Serbian genealogies and charms, see the Eighth Word below.

14. The original-language text is drawn from Klaeber 1950. On various metrical theories of the Old English poetic line, see Foley 1990: 106–19.

15. The role of South Slavic epic and the comparative method developed by Milman Parry and Albert Lord will be briefly treated in the Fifth Word. For a history of this approach, see Foley 1988; for a bibliography, Foley 1985, available online with updates at <http://www.oraltradition.org>.

16. For a thorough explanation of the misconceived application of a Greco-Roman model to the South Slavic epic decasyllable, see Foley 1990: 85–106.

17. Tedlock 1972: xx.

18. See Hymes 1977 on "measured verse"; further Hymes 1981.

19. See further Abrahams 1962, Labov 1972 (African American); Dundes et al. 1972 (Turkish); Gossen 1974: 97–106 (Mayan) and Parks 1990: esp. 42–88 (ancient Greek and medieval Germanic). More generally, see Ong 1981: 107–12 for citation of other sources.

20. On healing charms in South Slavic, see Foley 1995a: 99–135 and the Eighth Word below; on the poetics of Kuna speechmaking, Sherzer 1998: 118–61; on counting-out rhymes, Rubin 1995: 227–56.

21. See Collins 1998.

22. Much has been accomplished with Native American oral poetry in the last thirty years (see, e.g., Swann and Krupat 1987, Evers and Toelken 2001, and Tedlock 1999 for a glimpse), but so much remains to be accomplished. The only widely available edition of South Slavic women's songs in English translation is Lord and Bartók 1951 (for commentary, see further Coote 1992). Central Asian epic has recently profited from the publication of the *Manas* collected by Wilhelm Radloff (Hatto 1990) and from overviews in Reichl 1992 and 2000.

23. For oral cultures and individuals, see, e.g., Havelock 1963, 1986; on quantitative tests for orality, esp. Lord 1960: 30–67.

24. In the United States we have clear examples of this phenomenon, at both the cultural and individual levels, in both African American (Abrahams 1970) and Native American groups (see note 22 above).

25. The charge and countercharge pattern of discussion that characterized this approach through quantitative analysis was particularly evident in the discussion over the possible orality of *Beowulf* and other Old English poetry. See, in chronological order, Magoun 1953, Benson 1966, and Foley 1990: 207–35; for an overview, O'Keeffe 1997.

26. See, e.g., Coplan 1994 (Basotho); McCarthy 1994 (Jack tales); McDowell 1989 (Sibundoy sayings); McLean and Orbell 1975 (Maori); Rosenberg 1988 and Titon 1988: 253–358 (folk sermons); J. Smith 1991 (Pabuji epic); C. Smith 1964, Seeger 1990, and Zemke 1998 (Spanish ballads).

27. Of course, such genres as jokes and contemporary legends continue to circulate in our print-dominated societies and can provide opportunities for studying oral performance firsthand. Also, the second edition of Lord's *The Singer of Tales* (2000) contains a CD with audio and video samples of South Slavic epic from the Milman Parry Collection that foster secondhand experience of Oral Performance.

28. On Mexican folk-drama, see Bauman and Ritch 1994.

29. See, e.g., de Vet 1996 (Balinese epic); McCarthy 1990, M. Brown 1996, and Niles 1998 (ballads); Warner 1974 (Russian folk-plays). We should also note the initiative associated with the Universität Freiburg working group on orality and literacy, which has applied orality-literacy studies across a wide disciplinary scope in the humanities and social sciences, including literature (as opposed to oral poetry). For a sense of that school's interpretative program as applied to literature, see Erzgräber and Volk 1988 (on medieval English texts), Goetsch 1990 (on modern literature, mostly novels, in English, German, and other languages), and Habermalz 1998 (on James Joyce's *Ulysses*).

30. In addition to Bonair-Agard et al. n.d. and Glazner 2000, see the Poetry Slam International Web site (<http://www.poetryslam.com>) and the Slam News Web site (<http://www.slamnews.com>), two recent videos (Devlin 1998 and Hemstreet et al. 2000), and the units on slam poetry in the Fourth and Seventh Words below.

31. For an excellent contextual study of traditional country blues, see Titon 1994.

32. Milman Parry reports a parallel case involving his field assistant Nikola Vujnović (who was both literate and a *guslar*) in his unpublished field notes, entitled "Ćor Huso," which I discovered in the Parry Collection archive many years after our encounter with Čika Žika. Selections from "Ćor Huso" that bear directly on Homeric epic were published by Adam Parry (Parry 1971: 437–64). For some examples of Voiced Texts from Africa, in which the original texts are memorized rather than written down and read, see the description of Urhobo and Somali oral poetry in Okpewho 1992 (esp. 68) as well as manifold examples in D. Brown 1998. Another example is the North Carolina storyteller Leonard Roberts's oral performance of "Raglif Jaglif Tetartlif Pole," which he recorded from his Aunt Columbia and published in two different collections; see further note 9.

33. For further reading, see Kelber 1997, Horsley and Draper 1999 (New Testament); Niditch 1995, 1996 and Jaffee 1999 (Hebrew Bible); Tedlock 1996 (*Popol Vuh*); Duggan 1973, Vitz 1998, and Taylor 2001 (*Roland*); Webber 1986a (*Cid*); Davies 1992 (*Mabinogion*); and Davidson 1994 (*Shâhnâma*). Voices from the Past are the principal subject of books like Zumthor 1990 and Bradbury 1998a.

34. On the legendary singers described by the Parry-Lord *guslari* and their affinity to ancient descriptions of Homer as well as to modern Mongolian epic singers, see Foley 1999: 49–62.

35. For a digest of available references to Old English oral poets in both the extant poems and the secondary sources, see Opland 1980.

36. On the Coptic hymns, see MacCoull 1999; on the *Shâhnâma,* Davidson 1994: esp. 60–66; on the Latvian *dainas,* Lord 1989 and Vikis-Freibergs 1989b; on rap music as oral poetry, see Wehmeyer-Shaw 1993 and Pihel 1996.

37. See Heissig 1996, Chao Gejin 1997.

38. See further note 35. The idea of *vocality* developed by Zumthor (1987) and Schaefer (1992, 1993), and defined by Schaefer as "a cultural situation that very much depended and relied on the voice for mediation of verbal communication even though writing had already been well established" (1993: 205), describes a phenomenon similar to Voiced Texts.

39. On Old English poetry and comparative analogues, see Niles 1999: 89–119. Three recent hypotheses about the fixation of the Homeric poems are Janko 1990, Jensen 2000, and G. Nagy 1996a: 29–112.

40. See Stock 1983: esp. 3–87 on interactions of oral and written and 88–92 on "textual communities," in which "the text itself . . . was often re-performed orally" (91); also Stock 1990: 1–29.

41. See O'Keeffe 1990: esp. 23–46 and Doane 1994.

42. I explicitly leave out of consideration novels that use oral strategies or refer to oral sources, on the grounds that they are neither poetry nor wholly oral (even in our full sense of "oral poetry"); see, e.g., Obiechina 1992 and Balogun 1995 (African), Rosenberg 1994 (African American). Another genre not treated is the complex hybrid known as the "frame tale" (see Irwin 1995, 1998), which occurs throughout South Asia, the Middle East, and Europe from the ancient world at least until the medieval period and "depicts . . . storytelling events in all their variety and in the process carries many of the keys to oral performance onto the printed page" (1998: 391).

43. For a brief biography of and commentary on Njegoš, see Lord 1986: 29–34 and Mihailovich 1986: vi–vii; on another learned South Slavic poet who wrote oral poetry, see Miletich 1978a, b on Andrija Kačić-Miošić and "imitation oral" style.

44. See esp. DuBois 1995 and Honko 1998: 169–76, 2000b: 8. On the three versions of the *Kalevala* composed and published by Lönnrot between 1835 and 1862, see Honko 1998: 174–75.

45. See the recent collection of essays in the *Journal of American Folklore* on Macpherson's Ossianic poetry: Porter 2001 (on Macpherson's identity and the question of authenticity); McKean 2001 (on the fieldwork legacy); Bold 2001 (on Macpherson's influence on the image of the Celt in America); and J. Nagy 2001 (on connections with Irish medieval literature and modern Irish folklore). See further my response to that cluster (Foley 2002).

Further Reading

Homeric epic: Seventh Word below
Kalevala: Bosley 1989 (English translation); note 44 above

Macpherson/Ossian: Gaskill 1996 (edition); note 45 above
Native American oral traditions: Wiget 1996: 3–132; McDowell 1998; Toelken 1998; Evers
    and Toelken 2001
Old English poetry: Raffel 1963, 1998 (modern English translations); Foley 1990, 1991;
    Niles 1999
Oral-formulaic theory: Foley 1988; Fifth Word below
Slam poetry: Fourth and Seventh Words below
South Slavic oral epic: *SCHS;* Lord 1960; Foley 1990, 1991, 1999
Writing systems: Daniels and Bright 1996

Second Word:
Contexts and Reading

Detachable Speech?

Have your words ever been taken out of context? Imagine you're Hannah Conley, two-term mayor of Olympia, a small town in the midwestern United States. Earlier in the day you were interviewed by a frightfully eager journalist about a burning local political issue. You chose your words with great care and, thinking over the encounter later that evening, you feel comfortable that you expressed yourself clearly and thoughtfully, even though you had to run off to another appointment after three or four minutes. The next morning you read your well-meaning sentences—quoted with verbatim accuracy, to be sure, but now twisted by insertion into a new background. You'd been advocating the preservation of green space along the interstate that skirts the edge of town, believing it was the right thing to do and hoping that all adjacent parts of the community would profit. But suddenly your words don't say that anymore, reframed as they are by the journalist's own agenda. Here's an excerpt from his less than objective column:

> Yesterday voters narrowly rejected the anti-billboard committee's campaign for a moratorium on new sign construction along the interstate. Confronted outside her office, Mayor Conley seemed to dismiss the committee's defeat as inconsequential. "In theory I favored this initiative," she insisted. "Most of our suburbs along the interstate could certainly use a little help, but they're probably well beyond the reach of such propositions, anyway." The mayor then turned on her heel and rejoined a meeting with real estate developers.

What did you wish to say? At least three things: that in general you agreed with the committee's earnest campaign (it was the right thing to do), that the suburbs could always be improved but were already doing quite well (as opposed to other parts of town), and that these same suburbs were physically far enough removed from the corridor in question that they wouldn't be marred by any further sign construction. Such was your thoughtfully crafted "take" on a difficult situation. That's what you said.

Within the new context, however, you find yourself reinterpreted. Now you favor the anti-billboard proposition only in theory (not in practice); now the suburbs can use any help they can get; indeed, now they're in such poor shape that even voter-driven initiatives are powerless to provide much help. Your words, which you intended as caring, engaged, and measured have become uncaring, aloof, and crude. As the sun appears to be setting on your political career, you ponder the discrepancy between what you meant and how you were represented, between your performance *in context* and its reception *out of context.*

What this imaginary scenario dramatizes is the pitfalls inherent in detaching words from their context. Although we embrace the convenient myth of the finiteness and self-sufficiency of speech and text in most of our daily verbal activities, the truth of the matter is much less convenient. All of our utterances, all of our texts are contingent; "total explicitness is impossible," as Walter Ong has often reminded us. How faithfully and with what accommodations does a transfer from one context to another take place? What is the price of assuming a detachability that does not—cannot ever—exist? The mayor may well pay dearly by failing to get reelected after what are (wrongly) perceived as remarks that lack altruism and community concern. What price will we pay if by seeking to "read an oral poem" we dislocate the poet's words into our own context, if we automatically apply our own unexamined assumptions about how poetry works, if we (unconsciously but wrongly) try to force a square peg into a round hole? The potential for "disconnect" looms large enough with a reporter whose assigned task it is to reframe a solicited opinion to suit a newspaper story with its own goals and contingency. It looms enormously larger when we seek to reframe oral poetry as something it isn't.

What Is *an Oral Poem?*

The first of our three remaining questions—"What is *an oral poem?*"—is not at all the same question as "What is *oral poetry?*" In the First Word we were concerned with establishing the lineage and contemporary prevalence of oral poetry, as well as with understanding its scope and diversity across various media. We discovered that oral poetry has an extremely ancient heritage, indeed that written poetry is a relatively recent phenomenon, and we learned that the greater part of the world still composes and uses oral poetry as a staple of social life. We also saw that writing and oral poetry are not necessarily mutually exclusive, that the Great Divide is an invention that doesn't square with reality, and that texts and oral poetry can peacefully coexist and even interact in interesting ways.

But now we pose another question, one that focuses on a singular rather than a collective noun. Now our quarry isn't "oral poetry" as a complex, diverse phenomenon but "an oral poem" as a single item. This shift in perspective brings us face to face with the same issue of detachability that derailed Mayor Conley. The problem lies precisely with the phrase "an oral poem," which seems to name an isolatable object that can stand by itself, complete and independent, like a book on a shelf. Of course, no utterance can ever really answer such a description; not even books themselves can do that. But our automatic assumptions, the unconsciously applied logic for all of our reading, encourage us to accept the illusion of completeness and independence. When we unthinkingly impose a context for interpretation, we are in effect reframing the utterance, refusing it any context other than the one provided by our unexamined assumptions. Until there is reason for us to do otherwise—when we face a poem in another language, for example—we're loath to change anything fundamental in our approach. This kind of "default reading" meshes with our myth of verbal art as a monolith and helps license the construction of a limited canon of works approved for cultural consumption. No matter what we encounter, we make it fit the bill for our purposes. We read it into submission.

So far so good: oral poetry is endemically plural, naturally diverse. However, by using the phrase "an oral poem"—very intentionally in the singular—as part of the title of this book, I mean to force the point yet more insistently. Until recently, the materiality of texts has hypnotized us into pretending that an utterance can be explicit. If we can hold it in our hands, turn its pages, scroll down from one screen of it to the next, it must be finite and determinable. But any oral poem, like any utterance, is profoundly contingent on its context. To assume that it is detachable—that we can comfortably speak of "an oral poem" as a freestanding item—is necessarily to take it out of context. And what is that lost context? It is the performance, the audience, the poet, the music, the specialized way of speaking, the gestures, the costuming, the visual aids, the occasion, the ritual, and myriad other aspects of the given poem's reality. To put the matter as directly as possible, an oral poem's context is nothing more or less than its language, most fundamentally and inclusively construed. And when we pry an oral poem out of one language and insert it into another, things will inevitably change. We'll pay a price.

Consider what happens to the category of oral poetry we've named Oral Performance, for instance. Even if we get to the bottom of how the Tibetan paper-singer is employing that piece of white paper or newsprint, our culturally conditioned reflex will be to textualize him and his song. (To an extent I've committed that very same sin of interpretation by placing his photograph on the cover of this book.) Follow the well-trodden path from event to reframed, fossilized item. We start by videotaping or acoustically recording one of his performances, which then becomes an epitome, an object that we can edit, translate, and publish via the textual network. By reducing event to item we construct "an oral poem" from a performance in context. As a result we increase its audience a thousandfold; now Grags-pa seng-ge's performance reaches far beyond the immediate circle of his friends and relations, his town, even his culture. Or does it?

Here's the paradox. What gets published and circulated is no longer what we experienced. By bringing his song to publication, by refashioning his words to match our system, we've turned a process into a product. Furthermore, we've forever eliminated many of its signals: once his performance gives way to a text, the singer's voice is silenced. Whatever he conveys vocally and gesturally—explicitly or implicitly—is lost, and whatever contribution his audience makes gets deleted as well. In short, whatever is implied by the context in which he performs—let's call it his *poetic tradition*—is sacrificed in the name of textualization. That's the bargain we're called upon to strike: to pretend that the singer's detached words are a reasonable facsimile of his words in context. It's a crippling bargain, because it sells short the singer's art.

How about Voiced Texts? How detachable are they? Although this category of oral poetry starts life as a text, it's always intended primarily for oral performance and reception by a live, present audience. That's its natural context, part of its meaning. The two different ways in which I first experienced one of slam poet Marty McConnell's poems make the point. My initial exposure to her "Treatise on the Abandonment of a Moderately Lucrative Career Track" came as a performance given in AS 229, a café that served as one of the prime venues at the National Poetry Slam in Providence, Rhode Island, in late August, 2000. Picture a small, darkened room with a moderately raised stage at its front, filled beyond capacity with tiers of riveted, cheering audience members who obviously "knew the drill." As harsh red and yellow lights played across the stage, poets lifted their poems off the page and out of memory into crackling, attention-grabbing performance, striving to move, teach, shock, and connect with a highly reactive audience. All this took place in an intensely competitive (though friendly) atmosphere, as slammers also sought to win as many points as possible on the 50 percent content / 50 percent performance scale. Into this electric ambience McConnell injected her words (or her "word" in the South Slavic poets' sense), explaining why she's "for the screamers, the cynics, / & the signmakers":

because my silence was curable
because I own the wrong voice for a rock star
because you can't holler a sculpture
because skywriting dissolves
because metaphor is hard-wired truth
because existence *is* risk.[1]

A few weeks later, in response to my request, McConnell e-mailed me an electronic file containing the text of this poem. It's from that source that I've taken the excerpt above. In quoting it here I'm at a loss to convey the kinetic rhetoric of sound and gesture that drove the original performance in AS 229; I can't help you reexperience what her poem—her Voiced Text—really was. Oh, it's true enough that the "because" clauses line up neatly on the page in visual repetition, but their acoustic force and pulsing rhythm are gone, edited out for the sake of reduction to text. Gone as well are the defiant tone and compelling gestures that so effectively underlined the poem's larger commitment to spoken-word poetry. Very much among the missing is the audience, who so actively participated in the poetic ritual of voicing a text and who became part of the event. It's no exaggeration to say that the performed poem was rooted in their energy as well as the poet's, and that when you and I silently examine this textual shadow we just can't make up the difference, no matter how hard we try. McConnell's poem may have begun as a text, but in its voicing—which in slam poetry is a poem's only reason for being—it transformed into something else. Her "Treatise" was always intended as more than a treatise-text. It wasn't made to languish on the page but to live in the real-time, face-to-face exchange of spoken words. The discrepancy between the electronic text file and the Providence performance couldn't be more categorical: as oral poetry "Treatise" simply isn't detachable from its living context.

The same can be said for the other examples of Voiced Texts that we considered in the First Word. Čika Žika's pamphlet source for his performance of a South Slavic epic proved only the stimulus for an event that had at least as much to do with his individual competence as a traditional singer of tales as with the direct and singular influence of any printed artifact. He could speak the specialized language of epic fluently, and the language mattered more than the artifact. Were we to convert even the acoustic tape of that performance—already a text—into an entry in a printed anthology, we would have detached his poem from much of its meaning. We would have stripped away the context that made it what it was. The case of African American blues, which straddles Oral Performance and Voiced Texts, is similarly transparent. To present an anthology of blues songs culled from performance is, however well-intentioned, to guarantee that they're read out of context. Like our fictional Mayor Conley, we pay a steep price for such radical surgery.

As we move from an audience-centered reception in performance and toward our third and fourth categories of oral poetry, detachability remains an issue. Of course it's harder to assess because our initial and exclusive point of reference is textual. Texts can very effectively mask a poem's history, hiding an act of decontextualization behind a seemingly impenetrable and comfortably familiar facade. For this reason doubts may arise. If all we have is a text— if that's all that survives or ever was—then why can't we proceed without fretting over how it came to exist or how it relates to an oral tradition? In the First Word we saw that even readers of texts must take into account the rules under which the texts they are reading came into existence. We now add the perspective from context: to ignore the poetic tradition from which *an oral poem* (in the misleading singular) emerges is to misread it. Do you want to rationalize Voices from the Past by treating them as literary texts? Then you run the risk of missing cues or misconstruing signals. And why? Because you haven't been careful or patient enough, because you haven't weighed every last letter of every last spatialized verse? No, you run these risks because you're simply using the wrong code, speaking the wrong language, making the wrong assumptions. It's as simple and as far-reaching as that.

Notwithstanding the form in which they survive to us, Voices from the Past preserve signs of their identity as oral poetry. In most cases we can't recover exactly what the poems sounded like or how poets interacted with their audiences or even precisely how these texts are related to an oral poetic tradition. But all is not lost. Perhaps there are descriptions of oral performance within the poems or in contemporary documents. Perhaps there are structural symptoms typical of oral poetry such as formulaic repetition, multiform scenes, pattern numbers, or whatever strategies or units the given tradition uses as its poetic currency. More crucially, and this will bear on our response to the question of "What is *reading?*" below, these structural symptoms will need interpretation. Do we understand Voices from the Past differently because we can recognize such signals? Yes, certainly; even simple sentences in software manuals mean differently if we read all of the words instead of a few. Exactly what do the signals mean? We can answer this tougher question only when we do our best to read such poems within their expressive context, within their poetic traditions. And that kind of reception is the polar opposite of removing them from their natural context to suit our own designs, of separating each one out in order to manufacture *an oral poem,* in order to create something that never was.

With Voices from the Past we're handicapped, to be sure. The reality of mismatched media will intrude in a way that it doesn't with actual performances. The poems-in-documents that have reached us have passed through various stages of transmission, some of them unknown to us. But let's remember that ancient Greece knew Homer as oral poetry, that when our poet says "green fear" (*chlôron deos*) he conventionally means "supernaturally inspired fear," that his feast scenes carry the idiomatic expectation of mediation that is either consistently realized or ironically overturned, and that in telling the *Odyssey* he is shaping a version of an old (probably Indo-European) story that actually places the woman, the Penelope-figure, at its center.[2] Ancient audiences knew the context of his story; they heard it against the background of a poetic tradition. We can learn to listen, too, even if we'll never match their ability. Similar observations can be made for other Voices from the Past, and we'll provide both methods for reading in context (Third through Fifth Words) and a selection of examples (Seventh and Eighth Words) as our exploration continues. But both the methods and the illustrations stem ultimately from a simple caveat: "Don't take Voices from the Past out of context." Don't misread them.

The issue of detachability presents itself in strong relief when we turn to Written Oral Poetry. As noted above, this is a relatively small category, but once again its special position on the spectrum of verbal art offers a telling perspective. We could put things in the form of a question: given his obviously learned status and ready access to texts of all sorts, why did Bishop Njegoš choose to write poetry within the oral idiom of South Slavic epic? The best answer is also the simplest: Njegoš resorted to the "folk style" because it was greatly to his advantage to do so. His poetry is proof positive that not only was he unconstrained by the traditional decasyllabic medium of the *guslari;* he was actually empowered, deriving something positive, even essential, through its unique agency. With the verse-form, the diction, and other telltale structural symptoms came an attached context: an implied background of values, heritage, and myth that he could access merely by dialing to the proper communicative channel. As we saw in the First Word, the same can be said for Elias Lönnrot and the *Kalevala,* for James Macpherson and the Ossian poems, and for scores of Chinese written oral poems. As long as the writers in question "broadcast" on the traditional wavelength and their reading audiences remained "tuned" to the designated setting, their words would work and work inimitably. These poems project a context, a field of meaning from which they cannot be detached without doing violence to their expressive art. Even when printed in a book, each written performance is more than *an oral poem.* Each one is oral poetry.[3]

In addressing the question of "What is *an oral poem?*" let's summarize by boiling our response down to a simple mathematical statement of relationships: "oral poetry is to its context as any utterance is to its language and setting." An example from contemporary colloquial English, a powerful idiom in its own right, may help to illustrate. In order to know whether "Get out of here!" means "Leave!" or "You don't say!"—and further to gauge the degree of seriousness, insult, or playfulness involved—we have to know the speech setting. Who's speaking to whom? With what tone and set of facial cues? Without that context we can't interpret the remark. Just so with oral poetry. To pry words out of performance, even if that performance is a learned author's written composition, is to modify their meaning, perhaps even to destroy the original intent of the words. Just look what happened to Mayor Conley. Staying as much as possible within the specialized language of the oral poetry under examination, striving for as much fluency as we can muster in that idiom, is our best chance to catch all of the signals involved. It's our best chance to hear the whole story.

In answering the question "What is *an oral poem?*" we've essentially glossed a homemade *proverb*—"*Oralpoetry* is a very plural noun"—that we'll be meeting in the Sixth Word. Let's close the discussion by offering a sneak preview of another *proverb* that argues against removing oral poetry from its context and in favor of modifying our own point of view to suit the poetry: "True diversity demands diversity in frame of reference." We'll have occasion to return to both of these bits of pseudo-folk wisdom later on. Now it's time to address our third question.

What Is *Reading?*

Orality isn't simple or monolithic, as the first two questions have taught us. Neither is literacy, and therefore neither is reading. None of these terms identifies a "one size fits all" concept; each of them can mask more than it reveals. Just like oral poetry, literacy and reading represent unified phenomena only in a limited sense: they offer a path into and a perspective on complexity of a very interesting sort. Each term points toward a cache of phenomena that are more or less related, that can be understood collectively in a productive way. Grouping them together can aid us in assembling what physicists call a coarse-grain analysis, a rough approximation.[4]

But this kind of unity has meaning only if we are also willing to credit its innate diversity. Oral poetry comprises many different kinds of verbal art from many different times and places. We have used four categories to provide some organization of its many forms, but of course oral poetry's diversity can't be tidily filed away in four airtight categories. It's much too human for that. Literacy too is finally irreducible to a single set of characteristics: tablet-based cuneiform serves certain social functions and assumes a certain readership, vellum-based uncial letters in medieval manuscripts have a different responsi-bility, and HTML literacy supports a niche activity of a third sort. The struc-tures of logographic scripts, syllabaries, alphabets, and other systems vary wildly. So too does the material technology of literacy—involving an array of surfaces from stone and clay through papyrus, vellum, acid-free paper, and the PC desk-top. Indeed, if literacy names everything from petroglyphs to digital code, how can we ever expect reading to answer any single, uniform definition?

Autonomous versus Ideological Literacy

In thinking about the myriad ways in which people inscribe, manipulate, and interpret textual signs, the contrast drawn by Brian Street (esp. 1984) seems helpful. Street distinguishes between two models, one or the other champi-oned by many investigators. The "autonomous" model "assumes a single di-rection in which literacy development can be traced, and associates it with 'progress,' 'civilisation,' individual liberty and social mobility." Further, he observes, "it isolates literacy as an independent variable and then claims to be able to study its consequences" (2). In other words, this model assumes an archetypal state or phenomenon toward which all societies evolve at varying rates and in idiosyncratic ways. It also licenses theories of cataclysmic media-shifts and binary theories like the Great Divide. Street points out that com-parative views from actual fieldwork reveal stark differences among the ways cultures use literacy (not to mention who is literate and for what reason an individual might resort to written communication). Against this background, the autonomous model "tends implicitly to privilege and to generalise the writer's own conception and practices, as though these were what 'literacy' is" (2).[5] In other words, the danger in this model lies in setting up our own liter-acy as the unquestioned epitome and then using that standard to make one-track measurements of the literacies of other cultures and societies.

Consider a much-discussed instance of incipient literacy. Scholars often speak uncritically about the advent of the Greek alphabet and what they take to be its natural and immediate result: the composing, editing, and regular, general use of a textual *Iliad* and *Odyssey*. From oral tradition we jump directly to reproducible texts available to and usable by some significant number of people—hypothetical (but, we suppose, inevitable) texts that behave suspi-ciously like our twenty-first-century editions of Homer. From this assump-tion it is but a small step to assertions of the greater subtlety and design that literacy makes possible, as well as circular arguments that our *Iliad* and *Odys-sey* are much too well-formed, too complex to be merely oral poetry. One hardly knows where to start in uncoupling this faulty train of reasoning—with the real facts of text-production and reproduction in the ancient world, with the low levels of literacy in ancient Greece, or with the hidden assumptions about the user-friendliness and general availability of the texts, their assumed (but nonexistent) mass readership, and the like. All of these are realities shrouded by the autonomous model, overridden by a culturally egocentric bias that prefers the mirror to the microscope.

But let's limit our analysis to a bare-bones scenario. Suppose we grant the usual date for the entry of the Greek alphabet, about 775 B.C.E. And suppose we assume the quick development of a tablet- or papyrus-based recording technology for translating sounds into scratchings. Just what makes us so confident that over the next few centuries anything like a modern text of Homer's epics could emerge? Or take it a step further. Even if we could import a copy of the modern Oxford standard edition of the text back to ancient Greece, who would or could read it and for what purpose would they choose to do so? And how could such a precious artifact—whether in the contemporary papyrus or the modern clothbound edition—ever be copied in large numbers, even if there were a reading audience to create a demand? Such questions are customarily, even ritually ignored, as we unthinkingly impress the assumptions of modern Western literacy back upon a cultural situation to which they are wholly inapplicable.

And herein lies the problem, which is more our problem than anything else. The autonomous model of literacy—the great leveler of cultural diversity—must view the advent of Greek literacy as an immediate and permanent sea-change. The Alexandrian library is thought to house conveniently usable editions of Homer (when the most that would fit on an unwieldy, twenty-foot scroll is a single book, or one twenty-fourth of one epic). The Alexandrian librarians are not seldom portrayed as modern editors who produced standard editions (when all we have is their kit of editorial markings and no hard evidence of any editions whatsoever). A mass reading audience magically appears to consume Homeric epic texts on the grand scale and the sophisticated level that literacy licenses (when mere literacy rates, never mind social organization, make such an audience patently impossible).[6] Pretending that incipient literacy makes Homer a modern paperback may be a comforting and self-celebratory fiction, but it's no more defensible than conceiving of Derek Walcott's *Omeros* as a bulky collection of two score papyrus rolls instead of the self-contained, mass-market page-turner that it is.

To cope with the natural diversity of literacies, Street proposes an "ideological" model. In place of typologies and extreme contrasts, scholars who advocate this model "concentrate on the specific social practices of reading and writing. They recognise the ideological and therefore culturally embedded nature of such practices" (2–3), instead of culling the operations of reading and writing out of their social embedding and into free-standing abstractions. Once this kind of pluralism replaces the notion of singular, uniform literacy, it's much easier to explain the realities reported from fieldwork: that a given culture may use literacy for some of its verbal transactions and not for others, and that even the very same individual may depend upon oral tradition for certain activities but on texts for others.

Of course, we don't want to overstate the case. Copious evidence of linkages between Western institutions and media development have been brought forward over the last four decades. One thinks of classic works by Marshall McLuhan, Eric Havelock, and Walter Ong, but also of the orality-literacy contrasts persuasively drawn by Jack Goody and David Olson. Elizabeth Eisenstein's magisterial study of the advent of printing demonstrates the enormous social and cultural changes that can be traced to a momentous shift in communications technology. Indeed, the Internet revolution we're experiencing now is perhaps the most immediately persuasive reason to credit radical media-shifts as benchmarks in the history of a given culture's self-management.[7]

But all of that evidence provides us with only a first approximation of literacy and other media-shifts, and then primarily in the West. It provides an overview that chronicles one sequence of events, to which other sequences and situations are silently assimilated. Just as importantly, that overview is painted in very broad strokes, concentrating on outlines and gross anatomy rather than on specificity and the finer details of expressive physiognomy. In the wake of these impressive studies on benchmark cultural shifts, in fact because they have contributed so much, we are left wanting more. We need a larger gallery of portraits, in order to reflect the realistic diversity of different segments of human culture, as well as more precision and awareness of variation in the portraits we already have. To preempt irrelevant assumptions, we should be posing two questions: For just what purposes is literacy used, and who actually uses it?

Observations from various perspectives concur on the reality of the pluralistic, ideological model. From an anthropological point of view, Ruth Finnegan and others have long emphasized that modes of orality and literacy intertwine and affect one another.[8] From a scientific perspective, David Barton and Mary Hamilton have held "that many views of literacy are simplistic in treating it as a single isolable variable; that many views of literacy are ethnocentric in evaluating all developments against our Western alphabetic society; that writing is intimately entwined with other visual symbolic systems; and that writing is simultaneously a psychological phenomenon and a sociological phenomenon" (1996: 813). Indeed, we saw in the First Word that oral poetry contains such phenomena as Voiced Texts and Written Oral Poetry, that literary compositions can be "oralized," and that literacy is no bar to oral composition and performance. It should therefore come as no surprise that literacy and orality, far from being mutually exclusive, support one another in many ways.

So what are the watchwords in thinking about literacy? First, our conception of this complex set of phenomena, grouped together for analytical convenience, should be just as tolerant of diversity as our conception of oral poetry. Second, given that variety, brute measures like percentage literacy or the mere existence of some sort of writing must not lead us down the garden path of assimilating other cultures' literacies to our own. One culture's or group's literacy may not look much like another's. Third and more positively, we should be ready to take what literacy offers in any given situation—according to the specific culture, social stratum, assigned social task, single individual, even the particular "literacy event," as Shirley Brice Heath has suggested. With an open-minded view of literacy commensurate with what really goes on (and has gone on) in the world, we can avoid seeing other communicative ecologies as versions of the particular textual ecosystem we inhabit. And in that way we'll be better prepared to accept an equally diverse concept of something else we tend to take for granted as a single, undifferentiated phenomenon—the act of reading.

The Complexity of Reading: Three Cases

Reading isn't always what you're doing right now. Even within the Western sphere, "ways of taking" from texts are really quite disparate. Manuscripts are one thing: questions arise from the medieval period onward about reading aloud versus reading silently, for instance. Reading without vocalization seems to emerge with the development of word-separation, of inserting spaces between words, as the old *scriptura continua* becomes obsolete (Saenger 1997). And this is to say nothing of earlier curiosities like the back-and-forth *boustrophedon* ("ox-plowing") style of ancient Greek inscription, as economical in its way as the ox that turned and went the other way down the next row. Some of the oldest epigraphic inscriptions in Greek go (from our point of view) backwards, while some writing on statues—most of it in the early medium of Homeric hexameters, incidentally—forms a horseshoe pattern.[9] The standardization of spacing and direction that we expect as a condition of creating texts and a precondition to reading them lies far in the future.

Another relevant and especially interesting phenomenon is the "textual community." As Brian Stock explains, eleventh-century religious orders "read" their important texts by assigning principal interpretation to a single person (1983: 90): "What was essential to a textual community was not a written version of the text, although that was sometimes present, but an individual, who, having mastered it, then utilized it for reforming a group's thought and action." Orality intertwined with this practice in numerous ways, as in discussions, exchanges, and preaching that depended upon group knowledge of the text but which did not reiterate it each time. The lesson is that putting words on vellum or paper didn't automatically make those words textually available to a wider audience; in fact, it often limited or at least filtered their spread. With medieval manuscripts, the primal act of reading initiated a "trickle-down" dynamics.

Or consider the new kinds of reading that printed books rather than painstakingly hand-fashioned manuscripts made possible. Not only did Gutenberg's invention provide a new standardization of materials but it reshaped the entire economy of information. Elizabeth Eisenstein (1968: 7) observes that "to consult different books it was no longer so essential to be a wandering scholar. Successive generations of sedentary scholars were less apt to be engrossed by a single text and to expend their energies in elaborating upon it." With multiple, relatively easily produced copies, texts could be consulted by many more readers concurrently; intellectual exchange could take place across much greater distances and involve more people. Indeed, the three features of what Alvin Kernan calls "print logic"—multiplicity, systematization, and fixity (1987: 54)—profoundly change the rules of the reading game. This is the beginning of the trajectory that brings us to the distributional miracle of the mass paperback and the even wider democratization underway in the new world of the Internet.

Many kinds of reading lie along that primarily Western trajectory, to be sure, although our very modern, very parochial assumptions about what it means to read tend to conceal their tremendous diversity and homogenize their situatedness. But that's only one chapter in the international story of reading, which stretches from the beginning of writing and texts to the present. To open up our sense of what it can and does mean to read, I offer three examples from outside the Western sphere, two of them contemporary and the third ancient.

Foreign Language in an Indonesian Village — We take as a given that the text we aim to read will be written or printed in a language we know. Otherwise, we risk falling victim to the plight of an eminent Armenianist who in 1981 set out to read a public lecture in German to an eager audience in Innsbruck, Austria. He wasn't even a whole page into his performance before all present realized that he didn't know a word of German; indeed, it turned out that his paper had been translated and then converted into phonetic symbols that he vocalized like a laundry list, with nary a pause between sentences or even individual words. His reading consisted of a blur of mechanically generated syllables, meaningless to him and just about meaningless to all present.

But intelligibility comes in different guises, not all of them immediately transparent. Should we insist on ready comprehension as a prerequisite for bona fide reading, we will define out of existence some interesting activities that have important implications in their own settings. Consider an instance reported by James Baker, who conducted fieldwork on the island of Tidore, in the North Moluccas of eastern Indonesia. The people of the village where he worked are devoted Muslims who honor Islamic traditions, including reading the Koran aloud from Arabic script. But here's the catch: they don't understand Arabic. This discrepancy—or so it seems to the outsider—leads Baker to ponder what reading really means (1993: 98):

> We could, of course, consider the activity they are engaged in as one of "reciting," rather than "reading." If at base we think of reading as an activity of interpretation that requires from the start some amount of language competence, then we would have to say that the uncomprehending recitation of written texts is something altogether different. But, if we also think of reading as the socially significant practice of taking up a text and going through the process of actualizing the inscribed words in a temporal sequence, expending real time and personal effort in doing so, then we have something essential to the activity of reading without yet concerning ourselves with comprehension and the interpretations that can follow from it.

He goes on to explain how this pious ritual combines with Tidorese fidelity to their own ancestral traditions, which are oral, in a ritual melding or syncresis.

For us, however, the most telling point is that reading, which we celebrate as at least one analytical step beyond mere base-level comprehension, can proceed in a language unknown to the readers. Reexperiencing and reconfirming faith in a sacred text, the book upon which Islam is founded, is apparently the gist of this practice. Of special significance is the sounding of proper names, "words that live in the practice of speaking and have a persuasive force undeterred by the foreignness of the language spoken" (99). It may seem counterintuitive to us as we pore over our textbooks, manuals, and manuscripts in an attempt to break their code and glean what they have to say, but this kind of reading can serve a purpose—even if the read text is a mix of partially recognizable proper names and largely inscrutable sounds.

Sonorous Texts in Tibet — Reading also fosters scriptural transmission, among many other activities, in Tibet, but it does so in a particular fashion. The following case involves the modern transmission of a text by Tsong-kha-pa, the fourteenth-century C.E. founder of the Geluk order of Tibetan Buddhism and teacher of the first Dalai Lama. Here is Anne Klein's description of what that reading process entails (1994: 293):

> Most textual encounters begin with an oral practice known as *lung*. This term translates the Sanskrit word *âgama,* literally meaning "scripture," and *lung* is in fact the scriptural text itself in oral presentation, read aloud by a teacher to a student in order to create a connection with the entire vocal, scholarly, and ritual lineage of the text. Only after receiving *lung* is one ready to hear oral commentary on the text, to study and debate its meaning and, if one chooses, incorporate it into a meditation practice. It is clear from the importance placed on this practice that, written or oral, a text is not words or meaning alone. Texts also include sound, power, and blessings. Unlike the purely visual text, which is distinctly "out there," causing the reader to shift continuously between the external physical text and his or her own internal responses, the sonorous text occupies inner and outer space simultaneously, but not necessarily conceptual space. During the transmission of *lung* the text is read so rapidly that conceptual grasp of it is minimal; this is a time when the spoken word must be heard, not necessarily understood.

Texts are, in other words, vehicles for creating a holistic acoustic experience, not visual keys to revelatory thought.

It is virtually impossible to recognize this ritually driven, cooperative, oral-and-written activity as what we customarily designate by the verb "to read." Something much different is going on here, something unusual in the contemporary West but hardly unique in the world.[10] Although the chain of transmission begins with the fourteenth-century scripture, the sacred words are immediately embodied by a reader who voices them aloud for a listener. Text becomes experience. In place of the physical artifact we have a "sonorous text" whose most essential form and reality are heard sound. In place of the silent, lonely musing and note-taking to which we're accustomed we have a face-to-face human exchange. And in place of attempts to solve the code and tease out meaning via approved analytical procedures we have a focus on letting the sonorous text resonate through the student. Clearly the teacher's words have power far beyond the mere libretto from which he reads. One can readily understand why Klein observes that "the boundaries taken for granted in reading, writing, and other forms of creativity performed in a Western print-oriented environment seem not to obtain here" (311).

An Ancient Library of Hebrew Scriptures — The more widely we look, the more obvious it becomes that these boundaries don't exist in a great many cultures and situations. Worldwide and throughout history, texts are seldom the replicable objects we buy, sell, and tote around, and readers aren't often the scrutinizing, object-dependent dissectors we assume them to be—on the model of ourselves, of course. For a third case, we journey back in time with Martin Jaffee's re-creation of a library of Hebrew scriptures before 100 C.E. (1998: 321–23):[11]

> Imagine, if you will, a room containing twenty-two books. All of them are composed by anonymous authors, many of whom lived centuries apart. Most of the authors, moreover, are not creative writers. Their creativity consists of compiling into coherent compositions earlier literary traditions—some transmitted in writing and others by word of mouth, some of rather recent vintage and others centuries old. The books are issued on leather scrolls ranging from a few feet to many dozen. . . .
>
> These copies represent a major investment of labor by tanners who produce the writing surface of the scroll and scribes who laboriously copy the text. Sometimes, by error, whole lines are skipped or miscopied. If such scribal mistakes go undetected and uncorrected, later copyists will reproduce the error and transmit it as the genuine text. . . .
>
> Nearly the only people who ever see these books are governmental leaders and officials of the Ministry of Culture. While most people of the country are able to read in at least a rudimentary way, these books in particular are legible only with difficulty. In the first place, they are written in an ancient version of the national language, a version that is spoken, if at all, only by antiquarian scholars. There is also the matter of the copies themselves. The scribal handwriting is a specialized script difficult to decipher. . . . But illegibility is not that serious a problem for most people, since few have looked inside any but the most famous of these scrolls.
>
> . . . what they know of most of the library's contents comes to them from hearing portions of some of the books read aloud by trained declaimers on national holidays, commemorative festivals, and other public occasions.

Perhaps the first thing that strikes us about this strange room is how little it resembles any library in our experience. Only twenty-two books? Well, we have to realize that housing spatial representations of all knowledge in the same place is not a universal goal. Not all libraries are mirror-images of the ancient archetype at Alexandria.[12] Unwieldy leather scrolls of a couple dozen feet? The fact is that manipulable clothbound volumes—sized and mass-produced for marketability, transportability, and easy shelving—are creatures of the "warehouse model" of knowledge storage and retrieval systems. If we wonder how we ever did without such handy, shelvable objects, just think how electronic media are beginning to shrink the warehouse. Errors in copying? Perish the thought; we assume that texts are dependably the same from copy to copy, else how could we really read them? But this too is a modern mania, as is the very idea of "ver-

batim" transmission. And texts that are hard to read and actually read by only
a few people? We should remember that textual democracy—liberty, equality,
and fraternity in reading—has not always been the uniform policy in all societies and periods. Many cultures have only a few specialists to manage, read,
and interpret texts. And even those who do read—whatever they happen to
read—may be doing something quite different from what we expect.

Reading is complex. It names a diverse set of practices across the geographical and chronological expanse of human activity. It cannot be portrayed as
any single practice without disenfranchising dozens of cultures, without defining out of existence a healthy percentage of possible "ways of taking" from
texts. Even the few reading scenarios we have brought forward highlight the
myopia induced by narrow, unexamined assumptions, and hundreds of additional examples await to fill out the picture.

But what would reading look like to someone who didn't do it? How could
it be understood, how could it be framed and contextualized, in oral poetry or
any other medium that depends primarily or exclusively on an alternate technology? What if our parochial concept of reading, so familiar to us that we don't
even think about it, didn't exist? What would an oral poet say about reading?

Reading Bellerophon's Tablet

We had a veiled hint of one oral poet's idea of writing (though not of reading) back in the section on "What the Oral Poets Say." In commenting on the
nature of a *reč* in oral epic poetry, the *guslar* Mujo Kukuruzović distinguished
between a word in writing and a "word" in a song. Although he didn't himself use textual technology at all, Kukuruzović clearly differentiated between
the two media in terms of their building blocks. In writing, a poetic line might
well be four or five or more writing-based words, he observed, but when he
sings epic a "word" is a whole line or more.

For an inside look at how an oral poet conceives of reading texts, we need
go no further than the sixth book of Homer's *Iliad*, to the passage often cited
as the single unambiguous reference to writing in the Homeric epics.[13] The
episode involves Proitos's wife Anteia's ruthless revenge on virtuous Bellerophon, whose only crime was to resist her extramarital advances. Miffed by his
denial, Anteia turns the tables: she reports to her husband that it was Bellerophon who nefariously pursued her and asks for his murder. Proitos, seeking
to delegate the nasty job, saddles the unsuspecting Bellerophon with a "folding tablet" to deliver to Anteia's father, the king of Lykia. The message inscribed
on the tablet? Apparently, "Kill the bearer." Here's how Homer tells the tale
of a most deadly memo in a world where memos didn't exist (lines 166–80,
with a few words intentionally left untranslated):[14]

So [Anteia] spoke, and anger took hold of the king [Proitos] at her story.
He shrank from killing [Bellerophon], since his heart was awed by such
    action,
but sent him away to Lykia, and handed him murderous *sêmata,*
which he inscribed in a folding tablet, enough to destroy life,
and told him to show it to his wife's father, so that he might perish.
Bellerophon went to Lykia in the blameless convoy
of the gods; when he came to the running stream of Xanthos, and Lykia,
the lord of wide Lykia tendered him full-hearted honor.
Nine days he entertained him with sacrifice of nine oxen,
but afterwards when the rose fingers of the tenth dawn showed, then
he began to question him, and asked to be shown the *sêma,*
whatever he might be carrying from his son-in-law, Proitos.
Then after he had been given his son-in-law's wicked *sêma,*
first he sent him away with orders to kill the Chimaira.

For those unfamiliar with the story, the encrypted death-sentence is never successfully imposed. Not that the Lykian king doesn't try. When Bellerophon disposes of the monstrous Chimaira, he's sent against the Solymoi, the Amazons, and some local champions—all with the same result. His apparent invulnerability prompts Anteia's father to reevaluate the situation, and the one-time executioner ends up offering Bellerophon his unmarried daughter and half of all he owns. The reversal is complete and the death-warrant is less than a memory.

So much for Bellerophon's problems; we have a few of our own to wrestle with. For one thing, what exactly was written on that folding tablet? Critics have haggled endlessly over the likely code of the inscription. Some lobby for ideographic symbols, some for alphabetic letters, others for something more pictorial or abstract. Second, how did the Lykian king actually get the message? Presumably, he had to read it or have someone read it to him. The Greek original offers us no help here—literally, he asks to "see" (*idesthai*) the "sign" at line 176, after which he "received" (*paredexato*) his son-in-law's message. Neither verb helps us to understand what—if anything—Homer knew about the reading process.[15]

However we choose to answer these two questions, another quickly follows. Is the tablet evidence that literacy and reading were part of Homer's own world, perhaps even influential in his composition of the *Iliad?* Or do we owe the story of the tablet to an imported folktale that happened to mention a communicative medium not in general use in the archaic Greece of Homer's time and certainly not employed by oral poets? Again, opinions differ, but the preponderance of scholars shy away from viewing a (mythological and poetic) artifact as (ethnographic) evidence for contemporary literacy and reading. Still, the tablet and whatever is written on it do raise some challenges, and not only for the bearer. No wonder the scholars are stumped.

Homer's own view, on the other hand, is much more straightforward. Unencumbered by worrisome hypotheses about what might have been, he explains the scratchings in his own terms—as what he calls *sêmata*. Usually translated simply as "signs" (and then subject to reinterpretation as letters or some other graphic unit), *sêmata* are emphatically not letters in Homeric Greek. Even the ancient commentators warn against understanding them as written letters.[16] Over the course of the *Iliad*, the *Odyssey*, and the Hymns, we encounter fifty-eight instances of the noun *sêma* or its plural *sêmata*. No matter what their particular function in this or that situation, they share a basic and primary meaning as "tangible symbols that point toward larger concerns or ideas that would otherwise remain hidden or secret, windows that open onto emergent realities knowable in no other way" (Foley 1999: 3). Homeric *sêmata* include such pregnant signs as Zeus's omens, funerary markers for heroes, the telltale scar on Odysseus's thigh, and the olive-tree bed that stands as the key to Odysseus's and Penelope's reunion at the climax of the *Odyssey*.

Now let's factor this core meaning back into the reading of Bellerophon's tablet, focusing on how Homer portrays its contents and power. In doing so we need to think in the poet's terms, not ours. For Homer it's not even remotely a question of ideographs, alphabetic letters, or any other system of inscription. Nor does the visual and cognitive gymnastics of what we mean by reading ever come into play; that's not the point either. Least of all do *sêmata* constitute evidence of writing and reading technology at the root of the making and earliest transmission of the poems. Instead, these symbols stand as evidence of another technology of representation, a technology in which simple cues lead to complex wholes, in which tangible markers bloom into intangible implications. Omens have life-or-death consequences; funeral markers betoken heroic achievement and imperishable fame; the scar and the bed play essential roles in the end-game of the *Odyssey*. Modest in themselves, these *sêmata* are of crucial importance for what they project, and therein lies their power. Just so with the scratchings on Bellerophon's folding tablet: these signs also expand to an insistent and powerful meaning, prescribing nothing less than the murder of the man who presents them.

At their core, Homer's *sêmata* have absolutely nothing to do with writing or reading texts. Like a keyword in a book index or a URL on the Internet, they furnish a pathway—quick and immediate—to information that is otherwise difficult or impossible to come by. Writing and text, Homer is saying by three times calling Proitos's message *sêma(ta)*, are a species of this special sign-language, not the other way around.[17] By explaining the unfamiliar technology in terms of a technology he does use, Homer focuses not so much on the sign as on its signification, not so much on what the tablet-*sêmata* are but on what they do. And what they do is to deliver a message in code. In order to complete the transaction, the Lykian king must *read* that message—and here I broaden the definition of "read" to match the definition intended in this book's title, *How to Read an Oral Poem.* To read, from this point onward in our deliberations, is to decode. In the most fundamental sense, then, the tablet's message isn't written at all—no more than the messages encoded in Zeus's omens, the olive-tree bed, or any of the other *sêmata* throughout Homeric oral poetry are written. Homeric signs index important and mysterious phenomena; they cue crucial matters such as identity, the future course of events, even the ultimate reality of life and death. All they await is a reading that will break their code. To that kind of reading—of both *sêmata* in particular and of oral poetry in general—we now turn.

Notes

1. Quoted with the permission of M. McConnell.

2. For discussion of these and many other idiomatic expansions, see Foley 1999.

3. See Sale 1999 for a fascinating reading of Virgil's *Aeneid* as a text whose (written) formulaic diction rhetorically projects the "myth" of a Roman oral epic tradition that of course never existed, but whose facsimile existence lends a powerful (because pseudo-Homeric) authority to Virgil's poem.

4. I feel it necessary to affirm, in the strongest terms, that literacy and reading are sprawling, complex fields in their own right, with extensive histories of scholarship and lively debate. They enter the discussion here as ancillary topics because our main emphasis must remain on ways of understanding oral poems. Nonetheless, I have tried to offer additional avenues in the "Further Reading" section.

5. Chief among those whom Street cites as advocating the autonomous model is Jack Goody (e.g., 1987). See esp. Goody 2000: 1–25 for responses to various critiques of his prior work.

6. See esp. Harris 1989: 3–115.

7. See esp. Olson 1994, Olson and Torrance 1991; Eisenstein 1979; Hobart and Schiffman 1998; O'Donnell 1998.

8. See Finnegan 1988 and 1977, rpt. 1992. For the various uses to which literacy was put in ancient Greece, as well as the interactions between oral tradition and written media, see esp. Thomas 1989 and Harris 1989: 1–146. Olson observes that "the history of literacy . . . is the struggle to recover what was lost in simple transcription" (1994: 111). Given the cornucopia of oral poetries eligible to undergo transcription, all with different expressive features and strategies, how could we expect anything other than *histories*—plural—of literacy?

9. On the history of ancient Greek inscriptions, see Powell 1991: esp. 119–86.

10. Cf. Digges and Rappaport 1993 on the intertwining of literacy, orality, and ritual practice among indigenous peoples in highland Colombia.

11. Daniel Boyarin (1993: 11) notes that "'reading' in ancient Jewish culture signifies an act which is oral, social, and collective, while in modern (and early-modern) Europe it signifies an act that belongs to a private or semiprivate social space." For a full explanation of the ancient Hebrew situation, see Niditch 1996.

12. See esp. Canfora 1990, Foley 1998b.

13. For a fuller discussion of Bellerophon's tablet, with references to the interpretive background and the implications of the tablet-signs for Homeric poetics in general, see Foley 1999: 1–5, 277–78.

14. After Lattimore 1951.

15. On Greek verbs for reading, which imply voicing and hearing along with visual and cognitive activity, see Svenbro 1999: esp. 38–46; also Chantraine 1950.

16. See esp. the scholion to *Iliad* 6.168 (a) that identifies them as *eidôla* ("images, phantoms"), a term that Homer uses to name dream-images and shades of the dead; further reference at Foley 1999: 278, n. 6.

17. It's also a species of what Homer and his audience do as they transact the *Iliad* as oral poetry. See further Foley 1999.

Further Reading

Diverse literacies: Clanchy 1979 (medieval England); Harris 1989 (ancient Greece and Rome); Hladczuk et al. 1989 (bibliography); Hudson 1994 (European Renaissance to Romantic period); McKitterick 1990 (early medieval Europe); O'Keeffe 1990 (Anglo-Saxon England); Small 1997 (ancient Greece and Rome); Street 1995: 55–73 (Iran) and 1993 (cross-cultural methodology); Swiderski 1988 (south India); Thomas 1989 (ancient Greece)

History of literacy (primarily in the West): Graff 1987

History of reading (primarily in the West): Cavallo and Chartier 1999; Manguel 1996; H. Martin 1994

Models of literacy: Finnegan 1988 (literacy and orality); Goody 1987, 2000 (autonomous model); Hobart and Schiffman 1998 (information storage and thinking); Kintgen et al. 1988 (theoretical, historical, educational, and community perspectives on literacy); Olson 1994, Olson and Torrance 1991 (writing and its effects); Ong 1982 (orality and literacy); Street 1984, 1993, 1995 (ideological model)

Oral poems and texts: Haslam 1997 (Homeric epic); Sargent 1994 (Chinese lyric)

Silent reading: Saenger 1997; Svenbro 1999

Traditional signs: Foley 1999

Varieties of reading: J. Boyarin 1993

Third Word:
Being There: *Performance Theory*

Much of our discussion so far has focused on the first two questions underlying this book and its title: (1) "What is oral poetry?" and (2) "What is an oral poem?" In the First Word we discovered that oral poetry isn't any one thing. It names forms of verbal art as various as oral performance, voiced texts, voices from the past, and written oral poetry. In the Second Word we found that oral poetry isn't a *thing,* or *things,* at all. Even the apparently innocent phrase "an oral poem"—with its connotations of singularity and detachability—is a dangerous misnomer. Instead of identifying an utterance in context, "an oral poem" points toward a freestanding item. In fact, we learned that the poet's words can't be pried out of their natural, nourishing base in the poetic tradition without fundamentally changing their meaning.

We could say it even more simply: *diversity* and *context.* The First Word established the inherent diversity of our subject: the Tibetan paper-singer, the slam poet, Homer, and Bishop Njegoš all compose oral poetry. We understand their oral and written performances best when we understand a double-sided truth—that theirs is a shared enterprise also enriched by inevitable differences. The Second Word concentrated largely on context. As we saw, each of the four categories of oral poetry depends in some important way on the poetic tradition from which it derives and the living situations in which it is composed and received. Oral Performances are rife with signals that fall victim to the always-reductive process of textualization. Voiced Texts move in the opposite direction, assuming their intended form only in performance and drawing their meaning from certain expectable "givens" on the part of poet and audience. Voices from the Past are texts but more than texts, revealing telltale features and structures with idiomatic meanings. Even Written Oral Poetry depends upon the oral poet's specialized language and its traditional implications. Across a diverse spectrum, context matters.

In the Second Word we also began to wrestle with the third of our four questions, "What is *reading?*" by sampling the international variety of activities too often artificially compressed into a single concept: the act of reading. By itself, the history of reading in the West—stretching from tablet and manuscript to Internet—puts the lie to our unexamined assumptions about what it means to engage the technology of the written word. Reading just isn't as uniform a phenomenon as paperbacks or even home pages can make it seem. Broadening the perspective to include ancient and non-Western cultures, we saw evidence of a yet greater variety of reading acts. Our small collection of examples from widely different places and eras included a foreign but nonetheless intelligible language in Indonesia, sonorous texts in Tibet, and a curious-looking library of ancient Hebrew scriptures. In the final scenario from the *Iliad* we saw how Homer portrays writing and reading—explaining a technology he doesn't use in terms of one that he does. As the Lykian king reads Bellerophon's folding tablet, he's decoding "signs," to be sure, but at the most fundamental level these signs have nothing whatsoever to do with writing.

What Do We Mean by *How?*

Diversity, context, and different kinds of reading; these will be the watchwords as we move toward methods for reading oral poetry. "What is *reading?*" now gives way to the fourth in the series of questions posed above: "What do we mean by *how?*" In order to answer it, we now embark on a three-Word survey of popular, proven approaches that will eventually lead to real-world applications in the Seventh and Eighth Words. But first let's take a moment to remember the reason we need such a menu of approaches and to sharpen the focus of our final question.

Ways of Reading

To read is to decode, to generate meaning from signs. We don't need an alphabet or even a text to do that. As stipulated toward the end of the Second Word, what we need is a method that will break the code of the communication. With oral poetry, as with Bellerophon's tablet, the usual assumptions about textual logic prove either irrelevant or insufficient to the task. Something more is necessary—something that may well prove complementary to our usual assortment of interpretive tools, though not already a part of it. To be precise, what's required of us is flexibility and adaptability of a particular sort. We must be ready to suit our thinking and frame of reference to oral poetry, rather than demanding that oral poetry suit our tried-and-true (but very parochial) ways of transacting the business of verbal art. Verbal art must come first, its readers second. If we don't turn off the default switch, if we are unwilling to expand and diversify our notion of reading to fit the bill, then we will have reduced oral poetry to a text. Instead of opening up its unique and challenging expressive resources, we will have read it into submission.

To take realistic account of the diversity of oral poetry and the crucial importance of context, the "how" must involve a variety of perspectives, not one but many nontextual approaches. Let's be clear about exactly why this is important. First, because oral poetry is itself heterogeneous, we need a full menu of methods, a collection of perspectives that will allow us to understand the whole range of Oral Performances, Voiced Texts, Voices from the Past, and Written Oral Poetry. What is more, as mentioned above, these four categories are themselves only convenient, generalized clusters imposed upon a virtually infinite array of possibilities. Each of the four "types" sponsors enormous variety within itself, as attested by both the eons-long heritage of surviving oral poetry and its vast international scope today.

But the need for pluralism in approach goes beyond even this remarkable diversity of forms. As an article of interpretive faith I steadfastly maintain that no one method, no matter how promising or finely honed, will ever pass muster as the single "best" perspective, even if we confine ourselves to just one performance or work of oral poetry. No one approach can ever be as enlightening or fulfilling as a combination of approaches, any more than a single photograph can offer as full a visual representation as can multiple shots from different angles. To match the demonstrated variety of oral poetry's "ways of speaking" we need a correspondingly diverse menu of "ways of reading."

For this reason I seek to provide a critical repertoire whose strategies can be deployed as the need arises and the occasion suits. The Third through the Fifth Words will thus concentrate on developing a reader's kit of options, both because each option has something unique and useful to contribute and because all of them taken together can help us become a better audience for oral poetry. One of our *proverbs* in the Sixth Word puts it this way: "True diversity demands diversity in frame of reference."

Three Perspectives

Over the next three units I will be describing three different methods for reading oral poetry: Performance Theory (the Third Word), Ethnopoetics (the Fourth Word), and Immanent Art (the Fifth Word). Each method has proved useful to scholars and students of folklore, anthropology, and literature, and each has substantially advanced our understanding of oral poetry.[1] Although the three approaches have distinctly different histories and evolutions, they also share some fundamental principles. Among their common concerns are a sensitivity to the role of context, a commitment to understanding and portraying verbal art on its own terms, and an awareness of expressive signals beyond the usual repertoire of textual cues. In a nutshell, these various approaches all champion what I have elsewhere called *word-power*, the special, idiomatic way in which oral poetry accesses meaning.[2] Whatever the particular approach, then, each one strives to decode and represent the more-than-textual implications of the given Oral Performance, Voiced Text, Voice from the Past, or Written Oral Poem.

Why focus on these particular methods and which of them is the most useful? Such questions are almost rhetorical, but that doesn't mean we shouldn't squarely face them. I've chosen these three approaches because over the past fifteen years or more they have proven extremely effective for the study of oral poetry worldwide. That's most certainly not to deny the contributions of other methods. On principle we should welcome the inclusion of any and all perspectives, since more arrows in the quiver can only aid investigation.[3] But for our present purposes it has seemed appropriate to limit the number of approaches in order to strike a sensible balance, that is, to avoid narrowness on the one hand and the telephone-directory mentality on the other. Taken together, these three ways to read an oral poem provide both a repertoire of reading strategies and a unified theoretical focus.

As to which of the three is the most useful, that will depend entirely on the oral poetry under consideration and the aims of the investigator. In fact, the most honest response is to refuse the question, to deny the very notion of unconditional preference or absolute usefulness. As indicated above, only via multiple perspectives can we come to a fair and suitably nuanced appreciation of how oral poetry works, what it does, how its audience responds, and so on. Choosing any single perspective—by itself, every time, no matter what the conditions—will severely constrain our viewpoint and limit our understanding. Like all verbal art, oral poetry deserves more than that: it deserves a diversity in approach to match its endemic diversity of content. To the extent that each of these three methods helps us (in its own way) toward fluency in the language of oral poetry, it will have done its job. Each tool can certainly serve a useful function, but the overall kit offers us the best chance at successfully reading oral poetry.

How Performance Theory Works

> Q: What difference does performance make?
> A: Performance is part of the meaning.

In 1973 I had my first opportunity to watch and hear a South Slavic *guslar* perform an *epska pjesma*, an epic song, live. The occasion was the annual observance of the birthday of Vuk Stefanović Karadžić, the famous and beloved nineteenth-century linguist, ethnographer, and collector of oral poetry. The place was his native village of Tršić, Serbia. So institutionalized an event was this that a permanent stage had been erected in a nearby field to serve as a natural amphitheater for the thousands of people from all over Europe who each year come to observe what amounts to an international celebration.

But the professionally constructed stage and the massive crowds weren't the venue for this oral poet's performance. He plied his trade under a spreading elm tree adjacent to Karadžić's ancestral home, a modest three-room white-washed building up a hill about a half-mile from the official goings-on. Sitting on a rough-hewn picnic table and surrounded by about two dozen listeners, he sang the story of an early twentieth-century battle in which Serbs had distinguished themselves. As we approached, we first heard the characteristic whining melody of the single-stringed *gusle* used for instrumental accompaniment, and then, as we edged toward the periphery of the gathered audience, the equally typical rhythm and melody of the poet's ten-syllable lines, one verse after the next in a regular series of vocal and instrumental pulses. A few steps closer and we could make out some of those verses: heroic formulas for famous heroes and places, grand descriptions of horses and armaments, and other sound-bytes drawn from the shared traditional wordhoard. In fact, it would have been difficult not to hear these "words," since they were delivered in a full-throated voice that was almost a shout. I knew immediately why the traditional term for singing epic—the way the *guslari* themselves describe what they do—is *turati*, "to drive out or impel." Performing epic in the South Slavic tradition is hard, physical work.

It's also highly participatory, or at least it can be. While we stood on the rim of the small group assembled around the *guslar*, various things happened. A few people wandered in and out, apparently unmoved by what was going on, but most of the audience paid rapt attention. However, even the most deeply engaged of them behaved little like the exquisitely silent, dependably polite coteries that grace poetry readings at colleges, universities, and other public forums in the United States. The most involved of the singer's audience responded by calling out alternate or additional lines, or by loudly offering observations about the action of the saga unfolding before them. One old man seated near the singer's feet thrust aside his lapel just as the song reached a heroic climax, proudly exhibiting a collection of medals that he'd won for bravery in battle. This kind and level of audience involvement—I'd call it audience participation—reminded me of ethnographic reports published by Matija Murko, who observed performances of oral epic all over the South Slavic lands in the early twentieth century. Murko merrily told the story of a bard who received perhaps the ultimate critical review: during one of his rest-breaks the audience greased the string of his *gusle,* rendering it unplayable and terminating that night's performance without discussion or appeal.[4]

I tell this small tale of the Tršić *guslar* for a reason. That initial performance of South Slavic oral epic—experienced after much study of texts and some acquaintance with the acoustic recordings made by Parry and Lord—was not even remotely what I expected. It was more vivid, more arresting, more demanding, more contingent. The audience played a much larger and more determinative role in the moment-to-moment reality of the evolving song than I had suspected, and the singer depended a great deal more on encoded, implied meanings than I had understood from an inventory of texts. Some years later, after tuning in to a Belgrade television program that promised an oral epic performance but delivered only four solemn academics in baccalaureate robes droning ostentatiously from hymnal-shaped prompt-books, I realized from another perspective what it means to detach oral poetry from its traditional performance context. That first day in Tršić was not simply an eye-opener; it was an ear- and mind-opener as well.

What made this small glimpse so special, so utterly different from poring over a text? As the question-and-answer sequence that begins this section suggests, the difference lay in the fact that performance was part of the meaning. Consider Richard Bauman's classic account, specifically his observation that

> performance represents a transformation of the basic referential . . . uses of language. In other words, in an artistic performance of this kind, there is something going on in the communicative interchange which says to the auditor, "interpret what I say in some special sense; do not take it to mean what the words alone, taken literally, would convey." This may lead to the further suggestion that performance sets up, or represents, an interpretive frame within which the messages being communicated are to be understood, and that this frame contrasts with at least one other frame, the literal (1977: 9).

The mere fact—and of course it is more than a mere fact—that the Tršić poet was actually singing his epic song live made the experience palpably different from turning pages in a detached textual artifact. In Bauman's terms the performance engaged another field of reference, another frame, another context. It called upon those present to decode another set of signals that came into play precisely because the song was happening then and there, in a live exchange between oral poet and oral audience.

What is more, the game was being played according to certain rules. All of the participants were transacting their business according to an unspoken agreement, under a communicative contract that governed music, specialized language, audience response, and other aspects of the ongoing situation. That the contract was implicit rather than explicit hardly diminished its force or effectiveness. If anything, its status as an understood, behind-the-scenes agreement only increased its word-power. Its rules had become part of the grammar of the performance, as invisible and yet as powerful as the grammatical rules you and I are using to negotiate this sentence.

Because I had studied some texts and a few available recordings at that stage, I had an elementary fluency in the language of South Slavic epic performance. But my ability to "read" the *guslar*'s more-than-textual song was quite limited, and I certainly couldn't emulate the much greater fluency of native speakers with a history, in some cases a lifetime, of participation in the poetic tradition. Still, a performed play differs radically from a closet drama, even for theatergoers on their very first visit. Just so, the Tršić performance opened my eyes and ears to a new dynamic of presence, audience, and exchange. And it's precisely this dynamic at which performance theory aims. It seeks to break the code of what happens in all dimensions of the event, from the verbal component through the nonverbal dimensions of music, physical gesture, costume, and other constitutive aspects of what's transpiring. It seeks to read the signs, whatever the signs may be.

Keys to Performance

In Bauman's terms what cues the event—what shifts the gears of communication—is one or more *keys to performance.* By invoking these signals the performer communicates via a recognizable shorthand, alerting the audience to the kind of experience in which they will be collectively engaged. Bauman enumerates the following as examples of such keys: (1) special codes, (2) figurative language, (3) parallelism, (4) special formulas, (5) appeals to tradition, and (6) disclaimers of performance. Very few performances will feature all of these cues, and most will also depend upon signals beyond these six. Since no two expressive acts can ever be identical, diversity mandates that keys naturally vary from one tradition, genre, individual, and instance to another. Furthermore, as Bauman himself stipulates (1977: 22), any list of features is by definition culture-specific. The responsible reader must learn the particular oral-poetic language in order to know which features serve as keys to performance, and exactly what shape they take within a particular tradition or genre. That's what fluency means. Nonetheless, his short list of six characteristics gives us something to work with as we try to understand how performance induces its own frame of reference. Let's look at some examples.

The *guslar* at Vuk Karadžić's homestead was employing a number of *special codes,* to cite Bauman's first key. One of them was his singer's dialect, a peculiar version of the South Slavic language that little resembles the "street talk" of Belgrade, which lies perhaps an hour to the north by car, or of any other specific locale. Up-to-date urbanites describe it as archaic and filled with curious words and forms from other regions, not to mention highly stylized. Fellow villagers would find it curiously old-fashioned and filled with Turkish words they didn't ever use (or sometimes even know), if indeed they stopped to think about such things. The *guslar's* chosen dress, especially the white shirt with flowing sleeves, knee-length black pants, and shoes with turned-up toes (*opanke*), amounted to another code, marking him as a member of the Orthodox peasantry who had donned his "Sunday best" for the occasion. Our research team saw the same costume donned for the same purpose some years later during our fieldwork in the village of Orašac. The vocal and instrumental melodies the singer used to summon the traditional context of oral poetry were a third signal, serving initially as an instrumental overture and throughout the performance as a continuing nonverbal reminder of the historical and cultural "wavelength" for the event. Each of these signs was a key, a way into the experience—at least for the initiated. It's well to remember that any language, no matter how powerful or subtle it may seem, requires fluent hearers as well as fluent speakers.

Special codes aren't restricted to the category of Oral Performance. Consider the many codes that key the Voiced Texts of slam poetry: the close atmosphere of the club where the event takes place, the stage lights, the performance style, the judging ritual, even the high-energy introductions for each team and individual.[5] All of these aspects index the poets' performances, situating this one night's activities in this particular spot against a larger backdrop of associations and linking the specifics of the here-and-now with a generic context based on other places and times. Voices from the Past provide us only a text to deal with, but to a degree special poetic dialects survive the media-transition. The infamous Homeric language—many-layered both historically and geographically—attests to that. What Homer speaks is a variety of ancient Greek never spoken by anyone except for composing hexameter poetry, so its use evokes a frame of reference. Likewise, although Written Oral Poetry has no access to meaning-bearing features like tone, gesture, and costume, it can and does depend heavily on the stylized poetic language to set the stage for an imagined or rhetorical performance. Neither Bishop Njegoš nor Elias Lönnrot sang before a live audience, but they were performing nevertheless. When they wrote—whether in South Slavic decasyllables or Finnish octosyllables—they were in effect keying performance via the special code of the epic language. They were effectively saying "interpret what I say in some special sense; do not take it to mean what the words alone, taken literally, would convey."

The characteristic of *figurative language* is of course not limited to live performance in particular or to oral poetry in general. Indeed, we can find some version of every one of Bauman's keys in text-based literature and in everyday speech, so we shouldn't think of any single feature as an infallible litmus test for genuine oral poetry, of whatever sort. What matters is the particular kind and regularity of figurative language (or special codes or any other key). The question to be asked is not whether we can locate this or that feature in a given poetry, but whether the feature is truly constitutive of the poetry. Is it a signal, a telltale detail, an encoded message meant for hearers or readers?

Consider the force of a heroic simile, which normally does little or nothing to advance the storyline but includes important directions on the reading process. If the *guslar* at Tršić had described two horses charging across a plain in the following way, for example, he would have been invoking performance and creating a traditional frame of reference:

> The foam fell on their rounded rumps
> and from the rumps it fell to the plain;
> one would say that lambs were being born.
> From their nostrils flames emerged
> and set fire to the mesh on their forelocks.
> Clouds of smoke billowed before them
> as if Venetian rifles were being fired
> whose smoke was poisoned.
> Like hares they crossed the level plain;
> like wolves they took to the mountains.
> Like two fiery dragons on phantom steeds,
> all day long until nightfall they crossed the ranges.

These are Avdo Medjedović's words—or should I say his "word"?—from a 1934 performance of *The Wedding of Smailagić Meho*.[6] Via this extended byte of figurative language he was doing much more than simply marking time or decorating his narrative. He was prescribing how to read his epic story, how to decode his song, by reinforcing its character and most basic identity as a performance networked in a poetic tradition. He was implying at least as much as he was saying, telling his audience not just what happened but how they should interpret what happened. He was saying "hear this against the background of our epic tradition."

This same key also finds its way into other categories of oral poetry, such as Voiced Texts. Poets of all stripes use figurative language, as we noted, but slam poets often turn to highly charged political and ethnic imagery that over the course of performances by numerous poets becomes recognizably idiomatic. In her "releasing the stone to fly," Lynne Procope observes that

the engravings on our surface are an anticipation of our
survival
and our substance is hope
our matter is more than divine
we are what god intended with free will
so i choose to love this black man
rewrite struggle in the hard lines on his back
    i choose to love him black
but never in the hope that he will love me back.[7]

In delivery such images, running against the mainstream current of a privileged society personally unacquainted with the struggle against poverty and prejudice, take on an urgency that can't be conveyed on the page. And this is not to mention the sound-rhetoric of gestures, tonalities, emphases, and the like that can themselves become figurative and engage the audience in the insistent present of the spoken-word event.[8] That's why slam poets perform and that's what voiced texts do; they demand attention and inspire participation.

As for Voices from the Past, again the keys translate to the medium of oral-connected texts, at least to an extent. Consider the highly formal, multi-line similes so typical of Homer's poetic language, a good many of which gloss the clash of armies in the *Iliad* by ironically juxtaposing deadly warfare to the untroubled innocence of natural, domestic scenes. Listen to how Homer portrays the thousands of Greek warriors at Troy as they mill anxiously about, their blood up, eager to have at one another (Book 2, lines 469–73):

As the myriad hordes of murmurous flies
that swarm through a farmer's stables and pens
in springtime, when milk overflows the pails,
so many Achaeans faced those Trojans
raging to devastate the enemy.

I've italicized the pivot-words *As* and *so* in order to emphasize two of the features that identify this Homeric key to performance. Once again, figurative language does much more than prettily embellish the basics; it alerts the audience to the nature of what is transpiring and tells them how to take it. With Written Oral Poetry, traditional figures of speech can and do survive from living oral poetry into authored texts never meant for live consumption. Such is the power and resiliency of the traditional language that it can key performance even in text-bound forms of oral poetry, provided the readership can "hear" the signals. Actual voicing, hearing, and live participation may not be a part of the equation in Lönnrot's *Kalevala* or Macpherson's Ossian poems, but performance imposes an interpretive frame nonetheless.

Like figurative language, *parallelism* is a feature of most poetries, whatever their origin, nature, or audience. But once again the distinction lies in the particular kind and regularity of the characteristic in question. Is it a dependable characteristic, a constitutive feature of performance in the tradition in question and does it therefore cue the audience? Is it one of the signals in the expressive repertoire of the performer, used idiomatically to help create a framework for reception? For the Tršić *guslar,* the answer was most certainly yes. He was participating in a tradition that fosters and draws meaning from certain sorts of parallelism. One basic and far-reaching symptom of the widespread parallelism in South Slavic epic is the additive, pulsating nature of his and his fellow poets' verse-making. With rare exceptions, each ten-syllable line is syntactically, rhythmically, and musically complete in itself, an independent entity related to neighboring decasyllables only as one proximate member of a usually temporary alliance. Each verse is a freestanding unit with a poetic life of its own.

The opening of Halil Bajgorić's performance of *The Wedding of Mustajbey's Son Bećirbey* (lines 1–7) illustrates this additive, granular organization:

Oj! Djerdelez Alija arose early,
Ej! Alija, the tsar's hero,
Near Visoko above Sarajevo,
Before dawn and the white day—
Even two full hours before dawn,
When day breaks and the sun rises
And the morning star shows its face.[9]

One line-unit follows the next, one name or time designation parallel to another, with each verse structurally independent from those that flank it. The lines work together in this passage, of course, but each one can and does exist in combination with other decasyllables elsewhere in the poetic tradition. Like beads on a string, as Aristotle says about the elements in a periodic style, the increments that make up the whole are parallel, but themselves discrete.[10] This phenomenon should come as no surprise. In "What the Oral Poets Say" the *guslari* as much as told us the same thing when they insisted on the integrity of whole lines as "words," explaining that our concept of a word just didn't square with theirs.

Do we find parallelism in other oral poetries, particularly those involving texts? Yes, indeed, as long as we don't insist on defining this cue too narrowly.[11] The Voiced Texts performed by slam poets feature parallel lines, images, and larger structures, with the relationships between paired or grouped elements driven home in a visceral acoustic way in the heat of live performance.[12] Voices from the Past, like *Beowulf* or the Old French *Song of Roland,* are well known for the additive, byte-like texture of their narratives both line to line and scene to scene, and Written Oral Poetry behaves similarly. To the extent that we're fluent in the language of the given oral poetry, to the extent that we know what to listen for, we can read such signs. And what exactly do they stand for? For the moment, let's be content with understanding their word-power as an invocation of performance, an invitation for all present to communicate according to the implied rules of the game.

Special formulas ramify throughout many oral poetries, prominently enough that they encouraged the development of Oral-Formulaic Theory, which is in turn linked to Immanent Art, one of our three "ways of reading."[13] But we're getting ahead of the story. These special phrases, like the *guslar*'s (and Bishop Njegoš's) "well-wrought tower" or "shaggy brown horse" or Homer's "wine-dark sea" or the Old English poets' "foamy-necked ship," turn up again and again. When they recur they serve a structural function, to be sure, but they also act as prompts, invoking the context in which the audience is to construe the poet's words. Those fluent in the language of oral poetry have heard these formulas before; there's nothing new or original or iconoclastic about them. Nor should there be, since their effectiveness depends on their idiomatic quality. For the audience who can read them, such signs aren't dead-letter clichés but more-than-literal cues on how to proceed. Precisely how we should decode them is a subject for Immanent Art, which deals with the word-power of formulas. For now, the important point is that such formulas key performance, whether live or in a text.

At the same time, we should recognize that special formulas, like any other poetic feature, won't be of equal importance in all oral poetries. A vast scholarship exists that proves such variability beyond a doubt: while formulas are the stock-in-trade of oral poets in some traditions, they're relatively rare phenomena in other traditions. For another thing, Voiced Texts seem not to depend as heavily on recurrent bytes or "words." In slam poetry, for instance, recurrent phrases are not common, primarily because poets compose in a much more wide-open species of language. Rather than dipping into shared reservoirs of poetic diction like those available to Homer, the *guslari*, and many other performers, slam poets mold their texts more individually. Theirs is thus a more personal, idiosyncratic craft at the level of nuts-and-bolts phrasing; they use words much more often than "words." If there is a formulary aspect to slam poetry, it lies chiefly in the recurrent style of delivery, in the tonal, gesticular, and other kinesic aspects of performative expression.[14]

Variability in the density of special verbal formulas reinforces at least two lessons. First, there truly is thoroughgoing diversity in oral poetry; a feature that qualifies as a key in one poetry may well be rare in another. Second, and complementarily, no single feature can ever qualify as a litmus test for performance across a spectrum of oral poetries. Just like different languages, oral poetries have their own sets of operating rules. We reduce them to a single simplistic model at our peril.

Among the six features cited, the closest we come to a universal signal is probably the *appeal to tradition*. Either explicitly or implicitly oral poets are constantly establishing and reestablishing the authority of their words and "words" by reaffirming their ties to an ongoing way of speaking, to an expressive mode larger than any one individual. We might think of this key as the nontextual equivalent of a footnote or a subheading or some other cueing device. It creates a frame of reference within which the poet will operate and identifies for the audience what well-marked path to follow. The Tršić *guslar* began his performance with just such a nontextual device, a prologue or *pripjev* to his song, similar in form and function to the *pripjev* with which Halil Bajgorić began a performance of *Halil Rescues Bojičić Alija* (lines 1–9):

> Oh my gusle, maplewood gusle,
> Speak now and ever,
> Speak softly, loudly—
> The gusle is mine but it's played for all of you.
> I will sing a song of truth,
> Which I heard from my father
> In one thousand nine hundred
> And twelve by count,
> A song about a certain hero.

Applicable not just to a single story but to any song about any "certain hero," this coded appeal to tradition uses a number of strategies to fulfill its keying function. The singer speaks to his accompanying instrument or *gusle*, the symbol of epic performance in the South Slavic tradition, claiming it as his own but stipulating that the poem is performed for the audience (as are, by extension, all songs that make up this oral poetry, whenever and wherever and by whomever they are sung). He pronounces it a song of truth, and backs up that assertion by citing his avowed source and the supposed date he learned it. Fieldwork teaches us that such sources and dates are rhetorical rather than actual, a distinction without a difference for the *guslar* and his audience. As always, it's not the literal but the idiomatic, performative meaning that really counts.

Performers use this same key in other kinds of oral poetry as well. The prologues to the Old English *Beowulf* and to the ancient Greek *Iliad* and *Odyssey*, all Voices from the Past, are familiar analogues to the *guslar*'s *pripjev*.[15] In invoking the muse, for example, Homer addresses the source of oral epic poetry in his tradition, and from that direct, unambiguous linkage flows the story. We would have difficulty finding a clearer appeal to tradition than the first ten lines of the *Odyssey:*

> Sing man in me, O muse, the many-turning one who very many times
> Was driven back, after he had sacked the sacred citadel of Troy.
> He saw the cities of many men and came to know their minds,
> and on the sea he suffered many woes in his spirit,
> striving to win his soul and the homecoming of his comrades.
> But he could not save his comrades, though he tried;
> they perished on account of their own reckless crimes,
> the fools, who devoured the cattle of Hyperion's son Helios.
> For this reason their day of homecoming was lost to them.
> From somewhere, O goddess, daughter of Zeus, speak of such things to
>   us as well.

More than providing an outline of the ensuing action, this prologue seeks to tap the wellspring of myth and oral poetry, to frame the story in a known and dependable context. What follows will be delivered in performance and on the authority of that source. The appeal to tradition acts as a kind of oral *imprimatur.*

Written Oral Poetry works in a cognate fashion, though of course it's limited to a textual incarnation of performance. Voiced Texts may refer to tradition via methods that are more oblique. Consider, for instance, slam poetry's ritual of the "sacrifice poet," the slammer who begins the event with a separately scored, noncompetitive performance to warm up the audience and help calibrate what follows for the judges.[16] This too is an "appeal to tradition" that links the present proceedings to the historically recent but widespread movement of spoken-word poetry in North America. But appeals to tradition are hardly restricted to prologues or warm-ups. Like the other keys, they take shape within the dedicated, specialized language of the particular oral poetry. Each "wordhoard," as the Old English poets called their tradition, requires a differently notched set of keys to unlock it.

The final entry in Bauman's short list of six features, *disclaimer of performance,* turns out not to play any major role in the South Slavic epic tradition exemplified by the Tršić singer. If anything, the *guslari* are only too eager to affirm their individual mastery of epic performance. But demurral by a performer—essentially the "Unaccustomed as I am to public speaking" gambit that breaks the ice for a speech before a large audience—is not uncommon among oral poetries. Bauman mentions both Cree storytellers' denial of expertise and "the plateau Malagasy, for whom the elaborate assertion of verbal incompetence is a diagnostic feature of *kabary* performance" (1977: 22). Notice what's going on: saying you can't means asserting that you can and you will. This is another good lesson in the expressive nature of all of the keys; every one of them is nominal in form but institutionalized in meaning. What functions as a resonant signal in one oral poetic language may well have no special force in another. It may not even exist in that other tradition. Each oral poetry maps its reality onto a different set of signs. As for keying performance, those signs—like Homer's *sêmata*—are fundamentally nontextual.

From keying performance we'll move in the Fourth Word to examine another "way of reading": the approach called ethnopoetics. Although our perspective will shift, many of the same concerns will be surfacing. Once again, we'll be inquiring about the more-than-textual aspects of oral poetry; we'll be asking how to understand its special character and, in the case of ethnopoetics, how best to transmit that understanding to readers of editions and translations. In short, our focus will remain both on word-power (in the ordinary sense of words) and on the power of "words."

Notes

1. See also Foley 1995a, which explains and illustrates each approach at length and identifies the theoretical basis that they share.

2. See "Dovetailing: Word-Power," in the Fifth Word below; also Foley 1995a: esp. 56–59, 102–8.

3. One of the most prominent and interdisciplinary approaches has been developed by a consortium of departments at the Universität Freiburg, which looks at living oral traditions, texts from the ancient world to the modern novel, and historical and philosophical works. Most of this school's writings are in German, many of them published in the ScriptOralia series issued by Gunter Narr Verlag; for an overview of some of its main ideas in English, see Oesterreicher 1997. Also worthy of mention as another useful method is Paul Zumthor's work on medieval (oral-connected) traditions (e.g., 1990).

4. Murko 1990: 122.

5. See further the description of an actual slam event in the Seventh Word, as well as the ethnopoetic transcription of a slam performance in the Fourth Word.

6. *SCHS* 3: 108, with lineation introduced.

7. Bonair-Agard et al. n.d.: 26.

8. See further the application of the approach called ethnopoetics to Procope's "elemental woman" in the Fourth Word below.

9. Quotations from Halil Bajgorić's performances are taken from my own editions of *The Wedding of Mustajbey's Son Bećirbey* (Foley 2003) and *Halil Rescues Bojičić Alija*. These performances were recorded by Milman Parry and Albert Lord in June, 1935 (for details, see Kay 1995: PN 6699, 6703).

10. *Rhetoric*, III.9. Aristotle relates this style to poetry and memorability.

11. As a general caveat, we should be careful to allow for *tradition-dependent, genre-dependent,* and even individualized versions of any poetic feature. See further Foley 1990: 5–19.

12. See note 5 above.

13. See further the Fifth Word below.

14. See note 8 above.

15. For an ethnopoetic analysis of the prologue to *Beowulf,* see the Fourth Word.

16. See further the description in the Seventh Word.

Further Reading

Performance theory: Bauman 1977, 1986; Bauman and Briggs 1990

Applications to ancient Greek epic: G. Nagy 1996b; to Old English narrative poetry: Foley 1995a: 201–6; to Hispanic verbal art in New Mexico: Briggs 1988; to Mexican *corridos* and Scottish storytelling: Bauman and Braid 1998; to Mexican folk drama: Bauman and Ritch 1994

Application to text-making: Fine 1994; Foley 1995b

Related scholarship: discourse-centered approaches: Sherzer 1998, Urban 1991; ethnography of speaking: Bauman and Sherzer 1989; folklore and cultural performances: Bauman 1992

Fourth Word:
Verbal Art on Its Own Terms:
Ethnopoetics

Q: Does oral poetry need to be read differently?
A: Diverse oral poetries need to be read diversely.

Our second way of reading also focuses on the nontextual, but it enlists textual representation as part of its overall program. As the name etymologically indicates, ethnopoetics—the poetics of each *ethnos* (of each group, nation, or tribe)—starts by stipulating that poetries are plural. Each has its own shape, identity, and rules. Given the tyranny of Western poetic models, such advocacy of pluralism marks an enormous step forward. By keeping this simple, common-sense precept in mind, we can avoid egregious errors like classifying Native American verbal art as prose because it lacks a syllabic line, or denying the presence of epic in Africa because extended narratives from that continent little resemble the "classic" Homeric epics.[1] And what emerges after we discard crippling preconceptions and stop trying to force round (non-Western) pegs into square (Western) holes? At the very least, we open up the liberating possibility of suiting our way of reading to the way in which the oral poetry actually works.

Reading, Representing, and Reperforming

As an approach, ethnopoetics follows a three-part agenda. First, it seeks to *read* or understand oral poetry on its own terms, within the indigenous cultural matrix. For Dennis Tedlock, one of the originators of this method, that impulse has meant learning to hear and interpret the performative aspects of oral poetry—everything that gets lost as we transfer the story-event to a story-item. Voice quality, volume control, intonation, and especially silence are taken as constitutive dimensions that deserve decoding because they're part of the performance.

For Dell Hymes, the other early architect of ethnopoetics, the shortfall between our presumptions and the reality of oral poetry is chiefly structural. By failing to recognize units like lines, verses, stanzas, scenes, and acts—all of them defined by rules different from those we're accustomed to—we've unjustly denied the title of "poetry" to a great deal of Native American verbal art. For both scholars, the fault lies in unexamined assumptions that have masked the true nature of oral poetries. We have assumed that we know what we're looking for, and that it's always the same thing, no matter what the cultural background. By ignoring the individual poetry's reality, we've deleted crucial aspects of the poet's and tradition's art. It's as though we removed every second or third word or paragraph from a novel and then tried to make sense of it; oral poetry read from the wrong perspective becomes a shadow, an unintelligible echo of itself.

To correct this misapprehension and to restore as fully as possible the experience of each poem, ethnopoetics proposes the latter two actions on its agenda: to *represent* oral poetry on its own terms and by doing so to foster the reader's more faithful *reperformance.* This commitment has led to new insights as well as to some radical experiments that test the limits of page-bound representation. Hymes's structural scoring of Northwest Coast tales, most of them originally transcribed in run-on prose in the early twentieth century, reveals balances, relationships, divisions, and correspondences of detail that the hypothesis of prose had submerged. Not only the texture of the story but its characterization, its dénouement, and even its most basic plot come into clearer focus as ethnopoetics dissolves the parallax induced by employing the wrong rules for reading. Tedlock uses variations in typography to stimulate the reader's re-creation of the performance by portraying loudness, rising and falling intonations, pauses, and the like, and thereby to restore part of Zuni oral poetry's heard reality. Capital letters, lines rising and falling in waves, various fonts, verse boundaries—all of these visual cues are made to serve an acoustic purpose. In both cases the arena of the page also becomes an arena for reading, representing, and reperforming oral poetry.

Scoring Oral Poetry

All types of oral poetry can profit, to varying degrees and in different ways, by approaching them through ethnopoetics, by asking what particular features a culture understands as constituting poetry. The most obvious application is to Oral Performances, which depend so directly on the very signals that ethnopoetics seeks to recover and to encourage the reader to take into account as part of the reading and reperforming process. In relation to the Tršić *guslar* described in the Third Word, a number of performance-based cues would have to be added. Beyond the usual strategy of separating out poetic lines and the like, a performance-text could also include coding for vocal and instrumental music, for phrases that serve proverbial purposes, for couplets and other small groupings that amount to whole "words," and for larger narrative segments. Why? Because each of these dimensions is more than inessential or ancillary; each of them is part of the song's meaning. Our usual method of text-making, based on written Western poetry, has accustomed us to think of rhetorical strategies as confined to the black-and-white medium of spatialized words—what we take as the "core" of poetic expression. But the fact is that what we privilege as the single truly important channel for communication is only one of many channels. By reducing a South Slavic oral epic performance—or any oral performance—to a staid, sanitized procession of uniform, one-dimensional lines tidily arranged on the page, by effectively stripping the life from it, we fall victim to a reading so partial that it must be called a misreading. Ethnopoetics aims at rebuilding the living organism of oral poetry instead of rummaging through its calcified bones. In that sense it amounts to a forensics of oral poetry.[2]

Meanwhile, in the interest of briefly illustrating the range of ethnopoetic applications, let's focus on Voiced Texts and Voices from the Past. I choose these two categories because, as we should expect given the endemic diversity of oral poetry, each demands a different perspective in order to achieve optimal results. Looking at the two of them opposite one another will give us some idea of the range of this approach. For Voiced Texts, whose origin is textual but whose medium is live performance, the methods espoused by Tedlock are more useful and appropriate. By attending to the *performative* dimensions of slam poetry—to vocal qualities of all kinds including the rhetorical force of pausing and silence—we can lift the poet's creation off the page and embody it in our own reperformance. For Voices from the Past, on the other hand, whose oral-connectedness remains in play but whose performed reality is forever masked by fragmentary textual remains, the strategies used by Hymes are more penetrating. Here it is the *structural* dimensions of poems like *Beowulf* that call for attention because of the expressive responsibility they bear. Experiencing a work of verbal art according to the units and patterns in which it was made amounts to playing by the rules—to reading, representing, and reperforming it on its own terms.

Voiced Texts: Slam Poetry

To show how ethnopoetics can open up dimensions of oral poetry that conventional printed media institutionally ignore or obscure, I offer a comparison of two versions of Lynne Procope's "elemental woman." What is provided immediately below is the beginning and the end of the poem, with the two parts separated by a row of asterisks. The left-hand column presents the text as formally published in the collection entitled *Burning Down the House* (Bonair-Agard et al. n.d.), frozen outside of its natural life in performance. The right-hand column is my transcription of Procope's live performance of the same poem—or is it the same?—as recorded on the videotape *nycSLAMS* (Hemstreet et al. 2000).[3] To make sense of the transcription, you as reader and reperformer must do two things: first, consult the digest of symbols that precedes it to learn your cues; and second, perform it aloud yourself. This exercise, like ethnopoetics itself, is participatory. It will work only if you directly and personally experience the difference between visually perusing the minimally coded published text and reperforming the living poem according to the textual prompts.[4]

line = breath-group bounded by pauses

\# = short pause (less than one second)

\#\# = long pause (one second or longer)

rising ^{letters} = rising intonation

falling $_{\text{letters}}$ = falling intonation

CAPITALS = loudness

italics = words spoken rapidly and together

undividedwords = phrase spoken as a single word

<u>underlining</u> = hand gestures (as observable)

[] = a continuous poetic line

(**occasional stage directions**) bold & parentheses

Published Text

I want to be some kind of elemental woman

the original born before my time
   i have lived this life before;
     on the banks of the orinoco,
       the ganges,
         the nile . . .

Live Performance

I know I need to be someKINDof

\#\# ele^{men}$_{\text{tal}}$ woman

you <u>know</u> # the o<u>rig</u>inal

SORTof

born before my time

because we have

lived this life before
on the banks of
the Ori<u>no</u>co # the <u>Ganges</u> # and the <u>Nile</u>

disbelieving the line,
because i have struggled
down freedom's road and
marched blood red streets in
new york city

SORTof
DISbelieving the LINE
because # I have
[STRUGgled down^{FREE}dom's ROAD
and
marched BLOOD red STREETS in New
York City]

un-repressed by religion
even though i have burned in salem
and been stoned in Jerusalem
yet still i am faithful, elemental
woman

TYPEof
UNrePRESSED by religion
because I have # BURNED in Salem
and been STONED # in # Jerusalem
yet # STILL # FAITHful
ele^{men}tal woman

i need to be an elemental woman
not for this moment but for my life

I think I need to be someKINDof
ele^{men}tal woman
not for THIS MOment
but for my LIFE

*   *   *   *   *   *   *   *   *

i want to be an elemental caribbean
woman

I need to be someKINDof
ele^{men}tal Ca^{rib}bean woman

(smile)

and i will sing a love song—
i will be that love song.
resonating so i can hear it sung in my
next life!
a millennium from now to wonder;

who that woman really was!?!

And I # I think I need to sing a love song
oh, maybe no,
I need to <u>BE</u> that love song

[resoNATing so # I can hear it sung in
my NEXT life
a milLENnium from now and wonder]
WHO # THAT # WOMAN # really WAS

that hint of melodic memory in the
   minds of
men who passed my pride in the street
and wondered when i learned respect
   was spelt—self

I need to BE that love song
[a hint of a melodic memory in the
   minds of
men who PASS my PRIDE in the
   STREET and
wonder when I learned respect]
was spelt SELF

that song—of my sisters who stood beside me
before the mirror, to help me wash off
another layer of paint and fade cream
sisters who stand with me now as i speak
   my reality

I need to BE that love song

[of my sisters who STAND beside me
before the mirror and watch me wash off
another layer of # paint and fade cream]
sisters who SING with me
as I # SPEAK # MY # REALITY

(more softly and ethereally)

that i am the womb
before the creation of space

[that I am the womb
before the <u>creation of space</u>]

that i have recreated my self
in my own image

[I have # *recreated my self*
in my # <u>*OWN image*</u>]

to find the spirit of the living goddess is
   in me
that she is me and always will be
—elemental woman

so that *the <u>secret</u> of the living goddess* is <u>IN</u>
   me
<u>sister</u> # she <u>IS</u> me
<u>and</u> she <u>always</u> <u>WILL be</u>
<u>ele</u><u>men</u>tal <u>wo</u>man

    Even more than keeping track of visual discrepancies between the two col-
umns, actually performing the transcription illustrates how ethnopoetics
works and what enacted features it foregrounds. If performance is the embodiment of a Voiced Text like "elemental woman," then an ethnopoetic transcription amounts to a "how-to manual" for that embodiment. Of course, there
are disclaimers to consider. No version of such a manual, no matter how carefully or exhaustively planned and executed, can ever capture the whole reality
of the oral poem. In the final analysis, the experience and its representation

are never the same thing; they are neither superimposable nor interchangeable. One person's "take" may emphasize certain features while another person's script may concentrate on other sets of cues. And the danger always looms of so burdening the prompt-text that the reader may find it difficult or impossible to follow all of the directions concurrently; there can be too many balls to juggle all at once. But an ethnopoetic transcription does offer a way to partially recover what the conventional printed page deletes: the living, present dimensions that constitute a performance. It invites readers to take an active and participatory role, to join the oral poet's oral audience.

Let's do precisely that, keeping an eye on the published version and an ear on the transcription. We can start very generally by noticing that the performance diverges from the fixed text in a number of ways, demonstrating the trademark suppleness, or variation within limits, that is a hallmark of most forms of oral poetry. More specifically, those departures take the form of a preference for breath-group units and oral-style, delivery-friendly rephrasing. Instead of the declarative free verse of the book-poem version, the performance organizes itself in bytes of utterance, usually marked at both ends by short or long pauses. Silence, not white space, provides the line its bookends. And just as pauses punctuate the flow of the performance, defining its "words," so small expletives like "SORTof" and "TYPEof" announce and introduce its parts, weaving them together in an aural fabric. These features have little if any meaning for the writing poet or her text-bound readership, but without their expressive contribution the performed poem loses a great deal.

Procope uses many other performative strategies to (re)make her poem in living form, strategies that are not employed—can't be employed—in the fixed medium of the unvoiced text. Pauses lead to syncopation and emphasis within breath-groups, and stanzaic structures appear as not only logical but also performance-based units. Additionally, recurrent lines resonate along the acoustic length of the poem. The title phrase "elemental woman" is one of these echoes, always in the sound-shape

ele^{men}tal woman,

indicating a rising and then falling intonation preceded by a short pause. As the performance proceeds, this phrase acoustically knits the presentation together, lyrically amplifying its unity. The performed poem does more than sit impassively on the page: by keeping the multidimensional vocal reality of the idea front and center, it plays on our ears rather than our eyes. Likewise with the refrain-like "I need to BE that love song," which occurs only once in the published version but three times in the performance. The latter two instances are hardly "added" or "extra," however. By serving as an acoustic division and an interface between significant, integral ideas, this echo reinforces the stanzaic logic of the latter part of the poem. And again it does so aurally, not visually. Each of these sets of recurrences is in effect a key to performance, an invitation to the audience to respond on a designated channel.

Depending on how much of a burden we feel comfortable in placing on the reader (and reperformer), we can also include nonverbal signals such as gestures and facial expressions in such prompt-texts. I've inserted a few such signals in the transcription. Underlining, for instance, indicates that Procope accompanied her speaking with rhythmic hand movements, and the stage direction (**smile**) describes her facial rhetoric just before she begins the last section of the performance.[5] Coding such features encourages the audience-participant to understand the performance as an embodied, visceral experience, as not only a sounded but also a felt reality. Of course, no symbols or markings, no matter how specific, can ever convey the precise ways in which the poet used staccato jabs to drive home her vocal emphases as opposed to the encompassing, spherical motions with which she manually illustrated her statement

> [that I am the womb
> before the creation of space].

But the mere notation and realization that her physical body is an expressive instrument awakens us to what performance is and how we must approach its urgent reality. If such transcriptions of performative features succeed in helping readers voice and literally em-*body* texts, they accomplish their purpose.

Now that you've reperformed Procope's "elemental woman," visit the *HROP* home page and join her audience. The selection presented there is the video from which I made the performance-text given above. You might even want to try scoring her performance yourself.

Voices from the Past: *Beowulf*

Most people encounter the Anglo-Saxon epic *Beowulf* in one of a number of modern English translations. Not unexpectedly, these translations strive after "good poetry" in the modern idiom, so that the work will stand on its own. If the only contact between poem and reader is through a translation, so goes the argument, then the translation cannot afford to look backward; it has to be its own poem, no matter how "unfaithful" to the original. The problem is that even such a praiseworthy aim as this masks a deeper problem: under such conditions, we simply aren't reading *Beowulf* on its own terms. To be more precise, only to the extent that Old English and modern English poetics over-lap are we reading this oral poem on its own terms. Even spending the time and effort required to learn the Old Germanic tongue of Old English won't entirely solve the problem, of course. We'll still be left with the nagging mat-ter of textual representation. How do we score the poem in order to foster playing by the rules? How do we put the voice back into *Beowulf?*

Let's start with a word about method. With Voices from the Past, which survive only in manuscript and are typically accompanied by little or no de-scriptive information, we can't identify the kind of living performative cues typical of voiced texts or oral performances. The truth is that we won't even be able to pronounce finally and definitively on the relationship between our unique manuscript of *Beowulf,* enshrined in run-on lines across a series of sheepskins, and its active performance in Anglo-Saxon England. Such is the inevitable price imposed by time and circumstance. Still, we can't afford to ignore the expressive dimensions of what is—notwithstanding the mute me-morial—an oral poem. How then should we proceed?

Instead of relinquishing our responsibility to read *Beowulf* on its own terms, we can profitably turn to another, equally useful brand of ethnopoetics, one that has been effectively employed to enhance both live performances and long-silent texts: the structural focus championed by Dell Hymes. His strate-gy is to foreground the oral poem's most basic organization, and to do so on its rather than on our terms. Thus he seeks to reinstitute those features that survive the journey to written records: fundamental units and divisions, from the level of the line through large narrative increments, units that conventional text-making obscures or overrides. In the process, texts are reinvigorated with something of their lost idiomatic force. Indeed, it should be stressed that Hymes developed this method specifically to breathe life back into Native American texts whose recording left only faint, run-on prose traces of com-plex and poetically sophisticated works. Instead of settling for the misreading of prose, he urges us to conceive of a different kind of poetry, one in which the texture of verses, stanzas, scenes, and acts is partner to the story line. By portraying Native American texts according to their own rules rather than defaulting to our unexamined assumptions, he restores the poetry in them. He makes "words" from words.[6]

We can do something similar with other Voices from the Past, provided that we are willing to think within the target language. As an experiment to illus-trate what sorts of representation are possible and useful, I include immedi-ately below two versions of the opening lines of *Beowulf.* On the left is a liter-al, word-for-word translation of what the manuscript contains; on the right is an ethnopoetic, "word"-for-"word" translation. Of course, any edition or translation of the poem already moves significantly away from the crude, bulky block of print on the left and toward what we have learned to expect of poetry—lines, word order, punctuation and capitalization, and so forth. But here's the catch. These conventional editions and translations aren't moving toward *Beowulf* and Anglo-Saxon poetics, but rather toward a "party-line" or consensus concept of what poetry ought to be—how it ought to look and how it ought to work. Since Anglo-Saxon poetics overlaps with this modern concept to some degree, since its terms converge in some ways with our terms, any such presentation can claim ethnopoetic progress. But along with that illusory progress comes the distortion inherent in converting a poem to something it isn't, in reading it into submission. The right-hand column reinstitutes some of the major units and patterns found in the original Old English as a guide to becoming a more fluent audience for the poem.[7]

Literal translation from the manuscript	*Ethnopoetic translation*
	Prologue
Lo of the spear-danes in year-days of the chieftain-kings the glory we have heard how these noblemen valor performed often scyld scefing from troops of injurers from many tribes mead-benches withheld terrified princes after first became the destitute one found he of this a remedy experienced grew up under clouds with honors prospered until to him each of the neigh-bors over the whale-road obey had to tribute to yield that was a brave king	Lo! We've heard in year-days of the Spear-Danes' glory, the chieftain-kings', how these noblemen performed valor.
	Inset story
	Often Scyld Scefing withheld mead-benches from troops of injurers, from many tribes; 5 he terrified princes after the destitute one was first found; he experienced comfort for this, grew up under the clouds, prospered with honors until each one of the neighbors over the whale-road had to obey him, 10 to yield tribute to him. That was a brave king!

[The story of Scyld, the first hero, continues; lines 12–19]

Proverb

| So must a young man good things accomplish with brave | So must a young man   accomplish good things   20 with brave gifts   in his father's household, |

gifts in his father's household
so that by him in old age afterwards may stand chosen
companions when war may
come the people may serve
by praiseworthy deeds must
among of nations each a person prosper.

so that chosen companions   may stand by him
afterwards in old age,   his people may serve him,
when war may come;   by praiseworthy deeds
must a man prosper   among each of nations.   25
Sea voyage / Ship-burial scene (26–52)
Danish royal genealogy (53–67a)
Building of Heorot (67b–85)

In making the ethnopoetic transcription in the right-hand column, I have tried to transfer as many of the oral poetic features of Anglo-Saxon verse as possible.[8] Thus the passage illustrates the typical metrical structure of *Beowulf* and other Old English poems in both whole lines and half-lines (the latter marked by mid-line spaces). That is, the poetry is inherently duplex: the increments in which it is made are not just lines or half-lines but both. Although this two-tiered organization usually goes unrepresented in translations, it contributes a crucial expressive dimension. For one thing, the characteristic pulsing rhythm— not of syllables or textual words but rather of larger "words" organized by stress patterns—identifies the channel for communication, setting the reader on the poet's and tradition's track. It helps to designate the special language in which the communication will take place and thereby to activate the idiomatic associations that a poet and fluent audience bring to the transaction. It makes a connection and opens the dialogue between poet and reader.

This two-level rhythm also supports the additive, paratactic style that further determines *how* as well as *what* the poem means. By presenting the information in small, relatively self-contained, byte-size nuggets, this style requires readers to participate in making poetry; it asks them to merge the segments into an integral whole, to weave the individual threads into a single handsome fabric. Thus the "Spear-Danes" of line 2a and the "chieftain-kings" of line 2b identify the same people, elsewhere called the Scyldings after their eponymous ancestor Scyld Scefing; each name is another facet of the same jewel. In line 5 the Danes' enemies are collectively identified as both "troops of injurers" and "many tribes." Within the poet's way of speaking, this doesn't constitute tiresome repetition but rather a pair of alternate pathways to the same reality. If we linked this excerpt to a larger sample of Old English poetry, we would see that many lines and half-lines also recur in other poems, that they are themselves traditional and bear idiomatic meaning. Even within this limited selection, however, we can appreciate the general poetic strategy. And we can see the pressing need to rescue both lines and half-lines, as well as the trademark rhetorical style they support, from misrepresentation and consequent misreading. Neither the run-on prose of the manuscript nor the customary left-justified increments so dear to Western poetries will suffice: what we need is a representation of the kind of poetry that *Beowulf* really is. We need an ethnopoetically defensible poem-script.

Toward that end I have added some segmentation and labels to cue the reader's reperformance of the poem's early stages. The first "word," the **prologue** (lines 1–3), has numerous parallels throughout Old English poetry. Its typical components—in particular, the exclamatory "Lo!" together with an idiomatic phrase summoning the mythic past ("in year-days") and a verb of hearing that includes the audience as part of its collective subject "we"—combine to produce a clear, recognizable signal that marks a heroic beginning and forecasts a traditional tale.[9] From this ritualized start the poet proceeds to the first of many **inset stories** in *Beowulf*.[10] Although such loops in the narrative have lives of their own, they always maintain a reliable connection to the main story; for example, they commonly rehearse the history of an important ancestor or heroic exploit that has some direct linkage to matters at hand. But they also entail switching gears, or perhaps switching "words," a practice that the *Beowulf* poet describes as finding "another word bound in truth" and as "exchanging words" (870b–71a, 874a). By labeling the story of Scyld Scefing as one of these tales-within-a-tale, we identify the traditional poetic strategy behind it and help the reader to understand the story on its own terms.

Another strategy frequently employed by the poet is the **proverb.** This common gambit embeds the specifics of a particular situation in the overarching traditional network that informs all individual moments. It builds a bridge between the particular and the generic, the momentary and the traditional. How better to round off the description of Scyld Scefing's model heroism and kingship (4–19) than to link his brief biography to approved cultural practice via a proverb (20–25)? Inserted proverbs are a common strategy in oral poetry, especially epic,[11] and it's not too broad a generalization to say that much of the language of oral poetry is in some way proverbial. Proverb, idiom, and traditional expression are closely related.

The next byte of narrative, ethnopoetically labeled **Sea voyage / Ship-burial scene** (26–52) highlights the double focus of *Beowulf* and so many other Voices from the Past in their portrayal of a unique event via a traditional pattern. Although the apparent subject of this passage is the ship-burial of Scyld Scefing, it is also and equally a sea voyage. That is, the poet, called the *scop* in Old English, describes the funeral by deploying a five-part sequence of actions that he elsewhere uses to narrate an actual journey over water; the same sequence structures Beowulf's trips to and from Denmark later in the poem.[12] In all three cases he's unfolding the same map of traditional expectation: (1) the men accompany the hero to the ship; (2) the vessel waits, moored; (3) the men board, carrying treasure; (4) the ship departs; and (5) the passengers reach the destination and encounter a coast-guard. But what the *scop* does at the poem's outset is intriguingly different—and remarkable. He uses that same traditional structure, presumably a familiar pattern for both poet and audience, for a nontraditional purpose: to point up the uncertainty of what lies at the end of Scyld Scefing's voyage. Everything proceeds as expected except that no destination is cited; "men don't know," says the poet, "who received that burden" (50b–52). The funeral is a voyage whose destination remains unspecified, while nothing is known about the coast-guard who may or may not await Scyld's arrival. The shortfall is striking. In this hybrid poetics, the words indicate a ship-burial while the "word" suggests a journey by sea, a journey that lacks the customary completion. The "word" causes another shift of gears and an arresting effect.

Beyond this point the narrative of *Beowulf* moves toward a history of the Danish regency, in preparation for the introduction of the current king Hrothgar, and eventually to the building of the great hall Heorot, the symbol of political might, social order, and cosmic balance that is compromised every night by the monster Grendel's attacks. A faithful ethnopoetic description will chart these and other structural increments as the expressive bytes they are.

At all levels, then, from the half-line and whole line through the largest units and patterns, the structural brand of ethnopoetics can help make us aware of the impact of these "chunks" on the poetry they constitute. By scoring *Beowulf* and other voices from the past, by encouraging reperformance not on our imposed terms but on their inherent terms, we can learn to read and reperform such oral poems better. By insisting on the "words" as well as the words, we can in some ways join an audience from whom we're separated by centuries or even millennia.

From the performative and structural brands of ethnopoetics we now turn our attention to a third "way of reading," the approach called Immanent Art. This method concentrates on the trajectory from structure to meaning, and asks not just what the expressive units are but, as precisely as possible, *how they mean*. Our itinerary for the Fifth Word will include tracing the genesis of Immanent Art from what is widely known as the Oral-Formulaic Theory, as well as constructing a model for its application to various categories of oral poetry.

Notes

1. Johnson 1980, entitled "Yes, Virginia, There Is an Epic in Africa."

2. On editing projects aimed at this goal, see the Post-Script at the end of this volume.

3. Let me acknowledge my debt to Anne-Marie Foley for her invaluable assistance in transcribing this performance.

4. In one respect this transcription utterly fails to represent the reality of the performance situation: it doesn't take account of the audience reaction and participation. I have not tried to include that dimension here (a) because I wanted to avoid overloading the page with instructions and (b) because in reperforming this oral poem you're not interacting with *that audience*.

5. Note that the alternation between medium shots and close-ups on the videotape makes it impossible to see, and therefore to chart, all of Procope's hand gestures. What I include here is meant only as an illustrative sample.

6. This method has now been extended to more than thirty Northwest Coast Native American traditions.

7. One word of caution: reading ethnopoetic transcriptions, as you may already have discovered with the scored prompt-text of "elemental woman" above, is harder work than plowing more familiar fields. Reacting to and processing poetry that is configured in a radically different way is something like confronting culture shock: it requires patience and an appetite for diversity.

8. Let me stipulate that one substantial casualty of the transferral to modern English has been the required alliteration between half-lines that governs Anglo-Saxon verse. Modern English, so distant in some ways from its Germanic roots, does not offer the resources to effectively mirror this feature.

9. For details on this signal, see Foley 1991: 214–23.

10. On the role of such inset stories, often called "episodes and digressions," in *Beowulf*, see Bjork 1997.

11. See further Foley 1994.

12. See lines 205–303a and 1880b–1919. For a fuller discussion of these passages, see Foley 1990: 336–44.

Further Reading

Ethnopoetics (overview): DuBois 1998; Foley 1995a: esp. 17–27
Performative ethnopoetics: Tedlock 1983, 1990, 1999 (Zuni, Quiché Maya)
Structural ethnopoetics: Hymes 1981, 1989, 1994 (Northwest Coast Native American)
Application of ethnopoetics to text-making: Fine 1994; Foley 1995b; Hanks 1989

Fifth Word:
Traditional Implications:
Immanent Art

Q: What difference does repetition make?
A: "Words" aren't repeated by rote; they recur because they're
   idiomatic.

The approach through Immanent Art certainly owes something to both
performance theory and ethnopoetics, but it is particularly indebted to what has
come to be called Oral-Formulaic Theory, also known as the Parry-Lord Theory because of its genesis in the writings of Milman Parry and Albert Lord. To
distinguish the approaches plainly, Oral-Formulaic Theory elucidates the structure of oral poetry, while Immanent Art asks how that structure means. Notice
that I didn't say *what*, but rather *how* it means. On the one hand, Parry-Lord
Theory identifies quanta or bytes of language—"words" as the South Slavic epic
singers refer to them—as the building blocks of oral traditional narrative. Its
major thrust is to identify and describe the inventory of flexible construction
materials available to the poet, to discover and explain how phrases and scenes
and larger patterns vary within limits from one performance to another, from
one singer to another, and so forth. Immanent Art, on the other hand, seeks to
understand the idiomatic implications of these multiform "words." It concentrates on the recurrent phrases and scenes and story-patterns not as ends in
themselves but as indexes of more-than-literal meaning, as special signs that
point toward encoded traditional meanings. It aims beyond a nuts-and-bolts
grammar and toward a working fluency in the language of oral poetry.

The Great Experiment

To grasp the methods and goals of Immanent Art as a way of reading, we need
to understand its origins in one of the most far-reaching research programs in

the humanities over the last century.[1] The story begins with a young classicist, Milman Parry, who in the 1920s confronted the stubborn impasse of the celebrated Homeric Question—simply put, "Who was Homer?" Two contemporary orthodoxies offered competing solutions: the Analysts envisioned the *Iliad* and *Odyssey* as the work of one or more master editors who assembled and molded parts composed by others, while the Unitarians championed a single genius author for both poems in their entirety. To his everlasting credit Parry accepted neither position, choosing instead to interpret Homer's poems as *traditional* creations, as the collective bequest of generations of poets who handed them down over centuries. In his earliest writings, the M.A. thesis of 1923 and doctoral theses of 1928, he demonstrated the existence of the *formula*, a traditional byte of diction, which he defined as "an expression regularly used, under the same metrical conditions, to express an essential idea" (1971: 13). He also charted the systematic deployment of such familiar phrases as "swift-footed Achilles" and "ox-eyed Hera" as they combined and recombined with various verb phrases to constitute whole hexameter lines. Even at this early stage he was glimpsing how oral poetry worked in word-groups, that is, in "words."

But Parry wouldn't actually put the "oral" in oral poetry until he took two further steps, both of them comparative and both based on living oral traditions. First, under the influence of contemporary fieldwork in central Asia and the Balkans, he began to see that the structural characteristics he had discovered in the Homeric texts were also typical of living oral poetries. A bridge between the silence of ancient texts and the immediacy of modern-day experience was built, and his hypothesis of composition during performance, supported by the poet's command over a ready-made way of speaking, soon followed. Traditional poetry, Parry theorized, had also to be oral poetry.

The second step turned out to be the crucial one because it required him to leave the library and its texts behind and to join the oral bard's audience. In 1933–35 he and his student Albert Lord undertook a field expedition to then-Yugoslavia designed to test Parry's textually derived hypotheses in the living laboratory of South Slavic oral epic tradition. Concentrating on the region we today call Bosnia, and with the able assistance of their interpreter and interviewer Nikola Vujnović, himself a *guslar*, they recorded what Lord often called a "half-ton of epic" on aluminum discs and via dictation. These hundreds of epic songs became the basis of the Milman Parry Collection of Oral Literature at Harvard University. They have been selectively published in the series *Serbo-Croatian Heroic Songs*.[2]

This enormous sample of indisputably oral narrative made possible a comparative analysis of South Slavic oral epic, sung chiefly by preliterate *guslari*, and Homeric epic, which Parry had theorized must have been both oral and traditional. The results were dramatic: both poetries were highly formulaic, for example, as the two tables below illustrate:[3]

Formulaic Diction in Homer

τὸν *him*		πολύτλας δῖος Ὀδυσσεύς (8) *much-suffering divine Odysseus*
τὴν *her*		θεὰ γλαυκῶπις Ἀθήνη (1) *the goddess gray-eyed Athena*
τοὺς *them (masc.)*	δ' αὖτε προσέειπε *but addressed in reply*	μέγας κορυθαίολος Ἕκτωρ (3) *great flashing-helmed Hektor*
		ἄναξ ἀνδρῶν Ἀγαμέμνων (5) *the king of men Agamemnon*
τὰς *them (fem.)*		Γερήνιος ἱππότα Νέστωρ (1) *the Gerenian horseman Nestor*

Formulaic Diction in South Slavic Oral Epic

		nahod Simeune *the foundling Simeon*
Veli *Said*	njemu *to him*	Todore vezire *Todor the high counselor*
	njojzi *to her*	Miloš čobanine *Milosh the shepherd*
	njima *to them*	srpski car Stjepane *the Serbian emperor Stephen*
		Kraljević Marko *the king's son Marko*

Moreover, each epic tradition depended on a repertoire of typical scenes that varied within limits, portraying the same actions from instance to instance but shape-shifting to suit the particular environment of the individual situation. These larger "words" described such recurrent events as the arming of a hero, or assembly, or caparisoning a horse, or traveling to a destination; they too were ready-made bytes of traditional language. Each instance was systemically similar to other instances, but adjusted to harmonize with its immediate surroundings.

Both types of "words"—formulas and typical scenes—lay at the compositional basis of the poetry of Homer and of the *guslari*. Later research added a third level of recurrence: the story-pattern or tale-type, like the return pattern that underlies the *Odyssey* and myriad South Slavic songs. The conclusion seemed inescapable. Since the symptoms matched, Parry and Lord were to claim, then the underlying cause must be the same. These precious shards of ancient Greek poetry must be all that survives from a long-standing and widely distributed poetic tradition like the one they found in the former Yugoslavia. Textual analysis was buttressed by analogy; book-work was borne out by fieldwork.

Once the genie was out of the bottle, the Oral-Formulaic Theory spread quickly and widely. With the publication of Lord's seminal book, *The Singer of Tales,* in 1960, Old English, Old French, and Byzantine Greek poetry were brought into the comparative fold. Proceeding by analogy from the epics of the *guslari,* Lord claimed famous poems from these three medieval, text-based traditions for the expanding realm of oral poetry. Suddenly, *Beowulf* could be understood as a performance, the *Song of Roland* could be explained as the work of an oral bard, and *Digenis Akritas* revealed roots in oral tradition. And this significant broadening of the theory proved only the beginning of the process. The next four decades saw rapid comparative applications to more than one hundred different traditions, among them Chinese, Japanese, Russian, Albanian, Basque, Bulgarian, Sanskrit, Indonesian, Tamil, Australian Aboriginal, and Hawaiian, as well as the Hebrew Bible, the New Testament, myriad traditions from Africa and Native America, and Hispanic traditions from both the New World and the Old World. Scholars discovered formulas (recurrent phrases), themes (recurrent scenes), and story-patterns both in living oral traditions and in ancient and medieval poems that we know only from manuscripts. Suddenly a whole new universe of poetry announced itself as oral or at least oral-connected. The *guslar*'s influence had reached far afield indeed.

But the Parry-Lord explanation also caused some scholars to object. Oral-Formulaic Theory was too mechanical, they argued; it abandoned basic concerns about meaning and art to structural determinism. This situation presented a double bind. On the one hand, the objection was reasonable and called for a thoughtful response. Indeed, Parry's own focus on usefulness as the primary motivation for oral traditional structures—for instance, his contention that the celebrated "rosy-fingered dawn" line meant merely "when day broke" or that "much-suffering divine Odysseus" reduced simply to "Odysseus" (1971: 13–14)—permeates the long history of this approach and raises legitimate questions. On the other hand, adherents of the new approach felt that they could not responsibly ignore the real evidence of the building blocks of oral poetic language. Oral-Formulaic Theory had provided an important perspective on the dynamics of many oral poetries around the world, and denying telltale structures would amount to throwing out the baby with the bathwater.

So there sat the problem, intransigent and divisive, forcing scholars to make an impossible choice between structure and aesthetics. Whereas the Parry-Lord theory brilliantly explains the apparent miracle of textless composition, it does leave us largely without an explanation of the *guslar's*—or Homer's or the *Beowulf* poet's—poetic artistry. Because it leans so heavily on the idea of usefulness for singers composing in performance, the Oral-Formulaic approach cannot say enough about the depth and quality of their craftsmanship.

From Structure to Meaning

For this precise reason Immanent Art insists on treating oral poetry as first and foremost a species of *language,* with all of the systematic pliability and expressive power we recognize in language. More than that, it seeks to restore what grammars and dictionaries are ill-equipped to provide: the dimension of idiomatic force. Instead of concentrating solely on the structure and morphology of formulas, typical scenes, and story-patterns, Immanent Art asks about the traditional implications of these "words," about how they mean. When a *guslar* begins a performance, striking up a familiar tune on the *gusle* and speaking in decasyllables, what frame of reference does he summon? When singers express themselves via formulaic phrases or typical scenes or familiar story-patterns, what ideas do they stimulate in an audience or readership fluent in this specialized language? Immanent Art assumes that such a language—no matter how useful it may prove in a practical, get-the-job-done sense—is also a finely honed instrument for articulate and economical communication. Structures and patterns exist not merely as mechanically useful items but as vehicles for meaning and artistry.

Let's apply this point of view to "much-suffering divine Odysseus," for example, a phrase that names the hero no fewer than thirty-seven times in the *Odyssey*.[4] Is this often-used "word" merely a filler, a convenient and dependable way to identify Penelope's husband in a metrically acceptable byte of verse, or is something else going on? Immanent Art contends that this and other noun-epithet formulas are keys or switches—not unlike links on a Web page—that summon a larger context via a specialized code. They bring the named persons or objects or places to center stage by idiomatically accessing their traditional identity, in much the same way as parents and other storytellers evoke a well-known personality with the label "Little Red Riding Hood" or the nightly news tells the latest tale of the economy by citing the "tech-heavy NASDAQ." Such names harmonize not with unique situations or events, since they weren't made for any unique situation or event, but within a traditional network. Like any idiom, they have a larger-than-literal responsibility.

That's why we can't afford to read such formulaic phrases—or any "word"—too shallowly. Odysseus won't always be suffering every time he's called "much-suffering," any more than Achilles will always be running whenever Homer refers to him as "swift-footed" or the sea will be compellingly "wine-dark" during any particular nautical expedition. What matters isn't literal faithfulness to the specific moment at hand, but traditional fidelity to an idiomatic way of speaking. Indeed, how else can we explain the poet of the *Homeric Hymn to Hermes* identifying the messenger-god as the "mighty slayer of Argos" only a few minutes after he's born? Argos-slaying lies in Hermes' future, to be sure, but even such a prodigious and mischievous talent as he is can't (and doesn't) manage the feat as an infant. Once again, the special name—the "word"—refers to his traditional history, to his fuller identity outside this or any other moment. How does the phrase mean? It means timelessly, nonsituationally, and *traditionally:* not just "Hermes," but "Hermes [in his larger mythic presence]." The modest, concrete part stands for the complex, implied whole.

The Model

To address this kind of idiomatic, indexical meaning, Immanent Art employs three interlocking concepts: register, performance arena, and communicative economy. The first of these, *register,* names the special language used both by oral poets to make their poems and by audiences and readers to hear and read them. The term derives from the field of anthropological linguistics and was brought into the study of oral narrative by Dell Hymes, who defines registers as "major speech styles associated with recurrent types of situations" (1989: 440). Thus, for example, the *guslar*'s way of speaking amounts to the lingua franca uniquely suited to the purpose of composing and receiving South Slavic epic.

We can grasp the concept of register via a brief exercise. Choose any newsworthy event that took place sometime in recent history and consider how you would describe it to three different people: your closest friend, a parent, and the dean of the local college or university. Imagine that you are trying to convey, as nearly as possible, precisely the same information about what occurred—who, what, where, when, and why. Now imagine further that a fieldworker has videotaped your three presentations just as they happened. When the tapes are replayed, you discover, much to your surprise, that they differ quite graphically. You selected a different level of formality for each person, you assumed different attitudes and knowledge on the part of each audience, and in general you carefully tailored your word-choice, rhetoric, gestures, intonation patterns, and the like as you suited each communication to the individual. Without thinking much about it, you used a repertoire of registers.

Within a shared, traditional medium like oral poetry, registers are expressive vehicles shared by many speakers and hearers. Thus the Tršić *guslar* described in the Third Word was performing within the South Slavic epic register as he entertained local listeners outside Vuk Karadžić's house in 1973; Avdo Medjedović, Halil Bajgorić, and dozens of other singers were employing very much the same way of speaking when Parry and Lord recorded them in 1934–35; Old Man Milija, Tešan Podrugović, and hundreds of other bards tapped into a version of that special language when Karadžić and his colleagues wrote down their South Slavic epic songs from dictation in the first half of the nineteenth century; and even the anonymous *guslar* who sang the oral song(s) that Petar Hektorović published in 1568 as *Fishing and Fishermen's Conversation*—the earliest full transcription that survives from this tradition of oral poetry—made his narrative in a closely related register. Indeed, it's this same way of speaking, fragmentary bits of which date from as far back as the eighth century c.e., that the nineteenth-century Montenegrin intellectual Bishop Njegoš commanded so fluently that he could compose his own oral poems while "writing in performance."

Why did this curious register—and other such specialized languages throughout history and around the world—survive so long? What advantages allow them to be so resilient, to persist even into written composition? One might think that the more arcane and less mainstream the species of language, the more fragile its makeup and the more tenuous its continued existence. But the fact is that archaic words and alternate dialect forms live on in many oral poetic registers even as the "everyday language" evolves and streamlines itself more rapidly and more thoroughly. The *guslari*, for example, depend on Turkicisms that one hears nowhere else except in their epic singing; they even use a type of past tense that has completely fallen out of the everyday language. Their poetic register is a mysterious mix of old and new, of alternate forms, of everything one doesn't expect in a language. How and why does such an unusual way of speaking persist?

Immanent Art provides a two-part answer: dynamic structure and idiomatic meaning. First the dimension of structure. These systematic ways of speaking support composition; once poets learn to speak them fluently, they can make oral poetry in performance. Although they may do so with greater or lesser success, depending of course on their individual abilities, fluency opens the door. And once established as a dedicated medium, a focused register will persist because it's governed by stricter rules for variation than are broad-spectrum everyday languages. We need to be careful here: oral poetic registers will bend but not break; they will foster rule-governed variability but resist radical change or wholesale replacement. Variation within limits is the register's lifeblood, but as with any language there are limits. "Much-suffering divine Odysseus," for example, doesn't vary at all, but it can combine with many different partners to produce a large inventory of sentences. We could put it this way: composite "words" are bigger and more systematically useful than their constituent words. Registers evolve, of course, they don't stand still; but systematic structure does exert a selective inertia on their evolution. Structure is one aspect of their traditional identity.

But the second half of the answer is the crucial part—a register offers unique access to the implications inherent in a poetic tradition. It's the key that unlocks the wordhoard, the license to communicate with unmatched economy, the switch that brings into play an unspoken frame of reference. It's the reason, as a *proverb* borrowed from the Sixth Word puts it, that "Oral poetry works like language, only more so." Because registers are more highly coded than everyday language, because their "words" resonate with traditional implications beyond the scope of multipurpose street language, they convey enormously more than grammars and dictionaries (based as they are on the everyday language) can record. For this reason—because they offer ready access to meaning that otherwise lies out of reach—registers can and do persist beyond live performance and into texts. Registers don't just get the composing job done; they connect oral poems to their oral traditions.

So much for the specialized language in which many oral poets create their poetry; just where do they go to ply their trade, to meet their audiences? At one level, the answer couldn't be simpler or more obvious. Every performance occurs in its own time and at its own place: we've long realized that even the "same" poem varies, sometimes radically, from one poet to another, from one venue to another, from one day to the next. In that sense oral poems are made and remade over a wide variety of geographical and chronological contexts. We can learn a great deal about individual performances and overall variability by paying close attention to such individual contexts.

In another and more vital sense, however, all poems and performances in a given tradition take place in the same *performance arena*. By this term Immanent Art identifies not the actual physical spot or chronological moment but rather the virtual space and time in which the poet and audience—more accurately, poets and audiences—transact their traditional business. From this perspective it's the enactment or ritual of oral poetry that creates the place, rather than vice versa. With the onset of performance, however it's signaled, something changes: applicable rules for composition and reception lock into place and participants begin using the designated register. They code-switch because of a change in social situation, a shift in virtual venue. While every experience of a given story or charm or epic will vary within limits, all experiences take place in the same performance arena.

Indeed, because fluent participants have learned just "where to go" and "what to say" when they get there, the exchange that is oral poetry can occur with maximum *communicative economy*. Instead of having to cast about for a common language, they know which one to use. What is more, the register to which they turn isn't just any language. Employed for the single purpose of making and hearing or reading oral poetry (and having forsaken all of the more general functions that everyday language has to serve), the oral poet's "way of speaking" is a sensitive but durable instrument that promotes highly efficient expression. Sing one particular note, and everyone in a Romanian village knows the ceremony is about to begin; strike two smooth stones on the table, and the Chinese storytelling audience awaits the tale's beginning; say "Once upon a time" and every child knows that a fairytale's on the way; cry "Hwæt!" ("Lo!") and the audience for Old English oral poetry readied themselves for the onset of the narrative. Such cues create a performance arena, prescribe a register or channel, and set up a situation in which the implications of "words"—however "words" are defined in the given tradition—become an active part of the experience. Immanent Art shows how oral poets converse in coded structures with traditional implications, how they use the leverage of idiom to help shoulder the expressive burden. Under such conditions, a few "words" can mean a lot, and vivid, many-layered communication can proceed very economically indeed.

From Model to Application

The way of reading called Immanent Art thus seeks to open up traditional referentiality, to understand how the single instance resonates with implicit meaning. As a method it applies in different ways to all types of oral poetry. Oral Performances like those given by South Slavic bards offer an immediate example of what this approach can add to our listening or reading. When a *guslar* evokes the performance arena with musical and verbal signals, the fluent audience code-switches from everyday language to the language of epic, from mere words to recurrent, idiomatic "words."

Suppose the singer begins with the line "Pocmilijo Ograšćić Alija." A quick glance at any standard dictionary will result in a translation on the order of "Ograšćić Alija was grieving," and we move on to the next line in search of elaboration. Outside the performance arena that's an acceptable procedure, but within the arena it assumes the wrong register and leads to misreading. For one thing, the noun-epithet formula for this hero should call to mind a network of other adventures in which he finds himself enmeshed, events that remain unrehearsed in the present song but may well have important bearing on the hero's motivation for actions that do actually occur in the present story. Unlike characters in a novel, figures in many oral poetries live beyond the edge of any page and outside the covers of any book. Code-names like the six-syllable formulaic phrase "Ograšćić Alija" not only get the hero identified in a systematic fashion; they also cue that individual's larger biography, (re)creating a presence beyond the orbit of any single performance or song.

And what is this larger-than-textual-life hero actually doing? Why, for instance, is he grieving? In a novel we'd need to wait until the next paragraph or even chapter for a flashback explanation or some other indication of how the drama will play itself out from this point onward. But within the idiomatic register of South Slavic epic poetry this single decasyllabic "word"—"X was grieving"—implies nothing less than the following: a Turkish hero, long imprisoned in a Christian ban's jail, is crying out in misery; his strident complaints are keeping the ban's infant son from nursing, thus threatening the boy's life and the continuing royal lineage; soon the banica, wife to the captor, will petition her husband for the prisoner's release. If the ban refuses to intercede or throws up his hands in resigned defeat, she will conduct the negotiations with the enemy herself. This generic map will take on greater detail as the actual story proceeds. We'll learn the names of the principal characters, hear the ban and banica argue over issues of power and responsibility, meet the prisoner in his rags, and so on. We can't predict the exact details, of course, but we know the general sequence of events well in advance. Indeed, the entire rest of the story, which mirrors the *Odyssey* in its portrayal of the long-absent, returning hero, is also contained in that one-line cue. What this single decasyllable *implies* idiomatically dwarfs what it seems to say explicitly. This is one way in which "Oral poetry works like language, only more so."

Numerous other examples can be summoned to illustrate how "words" work as powerful signals in Oral Performances; clearly, they're much more than structural prostheses that assist the poet in composing under the pressure of live performance. Let's be content with examining two additional bytes, one a phrase and the other a typical scene. When a *guslar* calls a woman a *kukavica crna* ("black cuckoo"), for instance, he's idiomatically affirming that she is already or soon will be widowed. Moreover, this coded name and its attached status have real and threatening consequences. In the highly patriarchal society of the South Slavic epic, the phrase speaks not only to a woman's bereavement but to her consequent loss of identity. Without her husband's kin network to support her, she will effectively cease to exist. Dire straits are institutionally implied, not literally but through the special resources of the register.

At the level of the theme or typical scene, consider the celebrated "word" that describes the arming of the hero in the epic songs of the *guslari*. Oral-Formulaic Theory long interpreted this multiform, traditional sequence of actions—dressing and equipping the hero with familiar items one at a time in a regular order—as a useful compositional ploy. But it's much more than that. Such protagonists don expectable clothes and armor as well as strap on equally expectable weapons, all right, but what happens next will surprise anyone who remains outside the performance arena. Instead of immediately entering battle, heroes conventionally depart on a journey to a far-off locale, where they eventually undertake a dangerous and usually covert mission, during which, to make matters worse, they'll have to deal with a duplicitous character whose allegiances are always in doubt. Exactly how that generic skeleton is fleshed out depends on certain aspects of the particular story—the gender of the hero, the particular subgenre of epic (return, wedding, siege of city, and so forth), and other details. But the overall traditional pattern holds, as the "word" creates a map or frame of reference that contextualizes the individual arc of the given story or performance. It's maps like these that guide the audience or reader through the story's topography.

Of course, not all Oral Performances depend to the same degree or in exactly the same fashion on the units of formulaic phraseology, typical scenes, and story-patterns. As discussed in the Second Word, any method—whether it be Performance Theory, Ethnopoetics, or Immanent Art—can offer only one possible perspective on oral poetry. In some instances one approach may bear more fruit than another, and in any case we certainly shouldn't assume that any "way of reading" is the final or the only way. It's also well to keep firmly in mind that each of these "words" takes different shapes in different oral poetries: phrases depend upon their metrical dimensions, which in turn depend upon the idiosyncrasies of the given language and the historical evolution of verse-forms. Since languages differ, the registers they support must differ. As always with oral poetry, the watchword is variety.

With Voiced Texts we encounter another form of oral poetry that responds to the approach through Immanent Art, but with a twist. Since these poems are composed in writing, usually in a much less formulaic language, their verbal structure can be quite open-ended. In terms of their individual diction, or rather its ghost as silently represented on the page, they do not necessarily share a great deal with other text-based poems. Nonetheless, as we saw in Lynne Procope's "elemental woman" examined above in the section on ethnopoetics, recurrent lines and patterns do occur within Voiced Texts, and they accrue meaning to themselves as the performance progresses.

In fact, that's the key point here. The register in which slam poetry is delivered, while not a systematically structured idiom like that of South Slavic oral epic, does take on a number of performance values. Social criticism, intonation patterns, strategically placed pauses, hand gestures that mark emphases and rhythms, a competitive attitude—all these and more are essential, constitutive dimensions of the register used in the performance arena of slam poetry. Precisely because poets communicate via such idiomatic signals, they communicate with unique economy and power, with far more implicit meaning than an unvoiced text can manage. Even if some of the signals are personal, more a feature of the poet's own idiolect or unique performance than of a shared register, they work in a similar way. Immanent Art shows that Voiced Texts, like Oral Performances, depend on idiomatic cues; the crucial difference is that many of these cues are performative rather than verbal and can be transmitted to textual representation only with difficulty and only approximately. What Immanent Art reveals is how these poems mean in performance, which is of course the very arena where Voiced Texts live.

Voices from the Past, or at least some closely related ancestor of what survives to us, once lived in a similar performance arena. We can have no direct experience of the earliest stages of their existence except through hypothetical reconstruction, but Immanent Art can still open a door or two. By concentrating on the implied meaning of their "words," we can avoid some of the pitfalls inherent in a merely textual reading and at least partially understand their registers on their own terms. Although access to purely performance-based signals is forever barred by the accidents of time, place, and the medium in which they survive, we can to an extent enter the arena and speak the language. To some degree we too can join the audience.

Just how do we accomplish that feat of reading, now that poems like the *Odyssey* live only as fixed manuscripts, forever divorced from actual performance? The first step is the analysis that Oral-Formulaic Theory brought to bear on ancient and modern texts: the distinction of "words" from words. Can we identify the formulaic phrases, typical scenes, and story-patterns that recur in whatever samples we have at our disposal? In short, can we establish a grammar for the poem's register? Can we figure out how the specialized language works? In doing so we'll need to respect the idiosyncrasies of the particular register involved, keeping the diversity of oral poetry securely in mind.

But such a grammar can never be the end of the process; true fluency demands more than a mechanical grasp of a language. The crucial next step is to inquire into the idiomatic implications of the "words" we've managed to find. In order to gauge the traditional referentiality of a unit, we'll need to gather together a number of recurrences from different situations or environments and ask what more-than-literal meaning (if any) they all convey. Just like the non-native speaker of English who has to hear "Y'all come back" or "mother of all battles" in a number of different contexts to glean a sense of its meaning, so the non-native reader of Voices from the Past has to encounter idiomatic signals across a spectrum of usages to understand their role within the register. Now it may be that there simply aren't enough recurrences to provide a clear sense of that kind of immanent meaning; the reality is that manuscript poetries usually boast only quite limited resources. In such circumstances we'll have to be satisfied with a partial victory: while the implications of one phrase or scene may be effectively unearthed, those of another may elude our best efforts. Still, although we're likely to remain at the mercy of fragmentary or selective records in dealing with Voices from the Past, a partial victory is better than simply admitting defeat.

As a practical illustration of this method and policy, let's examine a formulaic phrase and a typical scene from the Homeric poems.[5] Both units or "words" recur regularly enough to support inquiries into their idiomatic implications. The phrase is *chlôron deos,* which literally means "green fear" and recurs ten times in various narrative contexts in the Homeric epics and hymns. Translators have struggled with how to render this small nugget of diction, customarily settling for metaphorical equivalents like "pale fear," "sallow fear," or "blanching terror." But while such solutions adequately serve the target language, they just don't get at what the phrase signals. An examination of all ten occurrences in their different contexts shows that *chlôron deos* amounts to code for "supernaturally induced fear." There is nothing in either Greek word to prompt such a conclusion, but the composite "word" is another matter. Whatever the situation—from Zeus's ominous thundering in *Iliad* 7 to the macabre gathering of the shades in the underworld in *Odyssey* 11 and on to Metaneira's terrifying glimpse of divinity in the *Hymn to Demeter*—"green fear" cues not a color or a metaphor but an idiomatically recognizable state of mind. If we're fluent in Homer's register, we know precisely what he's talking about. We've heard it all before.

Similarly, the typical scene of Lament for a fallen warrior, another traditional "word" in the Homeric register, recurs six times in the *Iliad.* As a group, these instances collectively chart the sort of variation within limits that we expect of such multiform units. The mourners change (Briseis, Andromache, Hekabe, and Helen), as do the heroes mourned (Hektor, Patroklos), but a three-part pattern frames each instance within a recognizable generic structure. No matter who's the speaker or the object of the Lament, the map calls for (1) an address to the slain warrior, (2) a narrative of personal history and future consequences for the mourner, her kin, and the rest of her people, and (3) a readdress of the departed hero for a final intimacy. Along with this structure comes the idiomatic force of the typical scene: the woman's loss of identity and the impending destruction of her family and potentially her nation—not unlike the implications of the South Slavic epic phrase "black cuckoo."

But from the perspective of Immanent Art the story doesn't end there, since there is in fact a seventh lament that idiomatically forecasts what the others can only certify after the fact.[6] I speak of Andromache's plea to Hektor at lines 405–39 of *Iliad* 6, as she attempts to persuade her husband to do (what is for him) the unthinkable, that is, to stay inside the walls of Troy with her and their infant son Astyanax instead of returning to battle. Her words are that much more poignant because they also take the form of the Lament "word": because she pleads with him in this resonant way, her very speech-act pronounces him already a dead man. Hektor stands there alive in front of her, but Andromache is already singing his death-dirge.

Immanent Art looks at Written Oral Poetry from a similar perspective, with the sole major difference being that in this case there never were any nonverbal signals to perish during a reduction from live performance to textual transcription. For an example of the persistence of the South Slavic epic register as a structural and meaning-bearing vehicle, I reach beyond Bishop Njegoš's early poetry, so rife with traditional phraseology and narrative patterns, to his *Gorski vijenac* (*The Mountain Wreath*), published in 1847. Generally considered his magnum opus for its celebration of historical events in Montenegro and its concern with issues of long-lasting political and social import, this poem nonetheless draws its most fundamental poetics from South Slavic epic. And it is an undeniably oral poetics. As Vasa Mihailovich observes, *The Mountain Wreath* "is written in the pure language of folk poetry, a language that never ceases to astound the reader and listener" (1986: xi). Of course, the reason why it moves a reader or listener is that it means a great deal more than it literally portrays, that it embeds this high-minded drama of the Montenegrin struggle for honor, justice, and freedom in a traditional context. The idiomatic register creates a performance arena for both the writing oral poet Njegoš and those who "hear" him "singing." How better to stoke the nationalist home fires than by implicit appeal to the authority of tradition?[7]

Dovetailing: Word-Power

In the Fifth Word we have concentrated on explaining the approach called Immanent Art. The three-part model of register, performance arena, and communicative economy speaks to oral poetry's idiomatic power, to the implications that are inherent in the paired acts of composing and reading oral poems. Most fundamentally, it tries to make explicit what Oral Performances, Voiced Texts, Voices from the Past, and Written Oral Poetry imply. By learning to negotiate the specialized language fluently, at least as fluently as circumstances allow, we can seize an opportunity to join the oral poet's audience.

Immanent Art shares a great deal with our two other ways of reading, Performance Theory (Third Word) and Ethnopoetics (Fourth Word). Each one of them seeks to illuminate the special dynamics of oral poetry—not just the fact of performance but how that fact influences our understanding of what's going on; not just the performative or structural dimensions but how those dimensions affect the reader's reperformance; not just the formulas, typical scenes, and story-patterns but the traditional implications of those "words." To summarize, the three perspectives are linked by a common attention to what I have elsewhere called *word-power,* a term that describes how words of all kinds engage contexts and mediate communication.[8] To draw a *proverb* from the Sixth Word, we could say that all three ways of reading recognize that "Performance is the enabling event, and tradition is the context for that event." From the act of performance—whether live or rhetorical—and the fact of tradition—the context for any utterance—emerges a poem's word-power.

In the Sixth Word we will be leaving this rumination on ways of reading to enter on a different kind of exposition, one that's in a sense the most traditional unit in this book and in another sense an admittedly bogus enterprise. Let me explain. In order to take advantage of its unsurpassed word-power, I will be introducing the (pseudo-) traditional *proverb* as a medium for explanation and discussion. "A Poor Reader's Almanac," far less genuine a collection than Ben Franklin's, will aim at recalling core concepts about oral poetry through a series of carefully constructed, homemade maxims. This new strategy marks a shift in the overall presentation. We began with four snapshot scenarios of oral poetries and then gave the poets the floor before spending four chapters—or "words"—on the volume's title, *How to Read an Oral Poem.* Now we shift gears again, with the intention of providing the reader yet another perspective on the fundamentals of oral poetry. Even though the *proverbs* to come are the furthest thing from genuine, it's my hope that they will do one of the things that real proverbs are meant to do: embody complex ideas in simple, memorable form.

Notes

1. For a history of the origins and development of Oral-Formulaic Theory, see Foley 1988. An annotated bibliography is available in Foley 1985, with updates in *Oral Tradition;* the entire bibliography can be consulted and searched online on the *HROP* home page. See also the recent survey by McCarthy (2001), as well as an application to film studies (Eades and Létoublon 1999).

2. See *SCHS* as well as the Parry Collection Web site at <http://www.fas.harvard.edu/mpc>.

3. This set of examples is excerpted from Parry 1971: 379.

4. The table above indicates that the first noun-epithet formula combines eight times with a verb phrase meaning "in reply addressed him/her/them," and so on. The remaining twenty-nine occurrences of "much-suffering divine Odysseus" are partnered with a variety of other verb phrases ("and then indeed pondered," "and then answered him," "and then rejoiced," etc.), illustrating further dimensions of the systematic pliability of Homer's and his tradition's formulaic diction.

5. For more examples of the method and its results, see Foley 1999: 201–37 (traditional phraseology) and 169–99 (typical scenes).

6. This analysis assumes that the Lament "word" had a traditional currency, that is, that it was not simply a phenomenon of the *Iliad* alone. Any occurrence would thus resonate not simply (or even primarily) with the others in this poem, but against the audience's larger experience of traditional epic. For a full discussion and reference to analogues in modern Greek lament, see Alexiou 1974 and Foley 1999: 188–98.

7. In our own time the Milošević regime used traditional musical and poetic forms to boost their "national revival" platform and identity among the ranks of the Serbian people. See Gordy 1999: 103–64.

8. For more on this term and its application, see Foley 1992 and 1995a: esp. 53–59, 95–97, 102–8. I have elsewhere defined "word-power" as "that particular mode of meaning [made] possible only by virtue of the enabling event of performance and the enabling referent of tradition" (1995a: xiv) and as identifying "how words engage contexts and mediate communication in verbal art from oral tradition" (1995a: 1).

Further Reading

Immanent Art: Foley 1991, 1995a: esp. 29–59, 1999: esp. chaps. 4–8; Bradbury 1998b (ballad); Horsley and Draper 1999 (New Testament)

Oral-Formulaic Theory: Parry 1971; Lord 1960, 1991, 1995; Foley 1985, 1988; McCarthy 2001; Zumwalt 1998: 82–83, 92

Sixth Word:
A Poor Reader's Almanac

Why *Proverbs*?

The Sixth Word has a double focus. It will summarize many of the central theoretical points raised in the First and Second Words by rephrasing them as a series of ten homemade *proverbs*. Why *proverbs*? Whatever else they may be, true proverbs (without the asterisks) are the instructional medium par excellence of oral tradition. By encoding wisdom in a quickly digestible and widely applicable form, they reveal the underlying unity of superficially diverse actions or situations. One could think of proverbs as axes or linchpins—only in this case their role is to line up disparate human experiences instead of separate wheels, gears, or other moving parts.

As explained above in the Prologue, the term *proverb* denotes a nongenuine, absolutely made-up maxim that I've created to serve as a quick mnemonic for core ideas about reading oral poetry. Such maxims naturally lack some crucial features of true proverbs: they have no traditional heritage, no cultural background, and (in some cases) no controlling metaphor. Indeed, it's impossible to emulate a real proverb simply by coining a phrase, no matter how "catchy," nor is it my aim to add to the traditional cultural storehouse of wisdom-sayings. My only goal is the very practical one of offering another perspective on our book-long subject—reading oral poetry.

Of course, we already know how to use true proverbs. For example, you see a half-dozen computer enthusiasts huddled around the latest marvel of desktop hardware, happily oblivious to everything else going on around them; or you see the same eight or ten players arriving for their regular pickup basketball game every Saturday morning all summer long, no matter what else their weekends may hold. "Birds of a feather flock together," your friend comments, and you smile in instant recognition. By citing that "old saw" she's neatly indexed both situations, linking them via a sound-byte of traditional wisdom about human behavior in general. And another thing. Notice how economically your friend has managed to convey something quite complex, the gist of which might be paraphrased as follows: "Let me observe that both of these situations involve the predictable natural gathering of an otherwise heterogeneous group of individuals ostensibly committed to a singular and consuming interest or activity." Thankfully, she didn't resort to anything quite so cumbersome. By citing the birds and their feathers, she avoided that kind of clumsiness and took advantage of the idiomatic power of proverbs.

It is just that brand of idiomatic power that I hope to engage here and to reengage in the case studies that make up the Seventh Word and the South Slavic ecology of oral poetry that is the subject of the Eighth Word. Formulated for rapid digestion and ready memorability, our ten made-up *proverbs* speak to the special challenges of reading oral poetry. If the experiment works, they will speak very economically, reconstruing core concepts from the First through Fifth Words even as they provide a unifying context for the diverse collection of oral poetries we'll meet later on. As an alternative to abstractions and theoretical models, which of course have their own validity, we can use these "new saws" as a kind of shorthand to instantly remind us of full-length explanations. That is, we can use them as cues to invoke a frame of reference indexically. (And frame of reference, as we have seen already, is the name of the game.) As ungenuine as the *proverbs* admittedly are, they aim at imitating the function of true proverbs by automatically calling to mind basic ideas that might otherwise require paragraph after paragraph to rehearse exhaustively. If they work correctly, the maxims will point to key concepts as quickly, dependably, and unambiguously as a URL fetches a home page: via the equivalent of <http://www.oraltradition.org>, if you like. As modern as clickable links on the Internet, this strategy is also as ancient and universal as oral tradition. Cite the "sound-byte"—the "bigger word" or *reč,* as the South Slavic poets would say—and the whole idea blooms.

Immediately below, then, you'll find "A Poor Reader's Almanac," a series of ten homemade *proverbs* intended to evoke fundamental ideas about reading oral poetry. Each *proverb* is followed by a few sentences of explanation and then a brief "exposition" that draws out its meaning and presents an example or two to illustrate its operation in practical terms. As generally applicable as I hope these facsimile maxims prove, I also trust that the real-life "data" of the attached examples will provide some ballast, showing how the *proverbs* work and emphasizing the fact that no set of generalizations can ever completely circumscribe the inherent variety of oral poetry. In other words, general principles and specific applications, the warp and the woof of any responsible study of oral poetry, will continue to share our attention in the present section as throughout the book. As for organization and sequence, the first four *proverbs* focus on crucial issues in oral poetry, performance, and tradition; numbers five through seven treat applications and analogies; and numbers eight through ten return to the core challenges of "reading," audience, and unity within diversity. The initial *proverb* is the most seminal of the ten, while the last is meant as the capstone for the entire group.

An Almanac of *Proverbs*

1. Oral Poetry Works Like Language, Only More So

Oral poetry is not a "thing" but a process, not a set of discrete items but an interactive way of speaking. It uses a special language to support highly focused and economical communication, taking advantage of implications unique to that language.

Exposition — We begin from the obvious but sometimes overlooked point that oral poetry *is* a language. As a language, it depends on conventions but is ever-fluid; it follows rules for structure and syntax, but those rules enrich rather than diminish its power to communicate. As for vocabulary, linguists tell us that the relationship between a word and its meaning is arbitrary: we may say "horse" in English, but French speakers say "cheval" and South Slavic speakers "konj." None of these is any more accurate than the others; none can lay claim to being *the word* for the four-legged beasts of burden we know as Arabians, palominos, and other breeds. The more crucial point, however, is that each word has also become culturally institutionalized as a sign that points—unerringly because idiomatically—in the desired direction. However arbitrary the collection of sounds in "horse," "cheval," or "konj" may seem, speakers who employ these terms are observing a social contract that effectively reads "Let X = Y," where X is the sign and Y its signification. Intelligibility depends on the sturdiness of that equation as words move from one speaker to another through time.

Oral poetry works the same way, only more so. Along with the words and definitions we can locate in dictionaries and that solve the mysteries of many kinds of language, oral poetry uses a much broader array of expressive strategies. One of the more widespread of these strategies is the "bigger words" described earlier by the South Slavic bards in "What the Oral Poets Say." We recall the more-than-literal sense of "black cuckoo," for instance, which denotes a woman who has lost or stands to lose her husband. There's nothing in the separate integers "black" or "cuckoo" that offers any hint of what their poetic sum might be, but without doing the math we can't read that phrase as anything other than an attractive metaphor. Or consider Homer's *chlôron deos,* "green fear," long a headache for translators seeking to plumb its metaphorical depths. As we've seen, if we collect all of the instances of the phrase in the *Iliad* and *Odyssey,* what precipitates out is not "pale" or "wan" or "unripe" terror but rather a supernaturally induced fear. Although no lexicon will lead us toward that conclusion, "green fear" demonstrably amounts to code for an emotion that stems from a divine source. That's its "more so." The lesson is simple enough: to read this or any of the other "bigger words" of oral poetry, we must be able to speak the right language.

And there are many other aspects of "more so" as well, many other ways in which oral poetry goes beyond the conventions of everyday language and its expressive repertoire. For example, most such poetries depend on dimensions of speech in performance such as silence, variation in loudness, pitch, tone, and so forth. These are properties of all spoken language, to be sure, but in oral poetry they often become institutionalized cues that help to channel audience reaction. Some cues, like shouting, may already have a broad, base-level implication: people who raise their voices are usually understood to be emphasizing a point, whether out of excitement, anger, surprise, or whatever. But oral poetries characteristically narrow the possible range of such features, streamlining their implications, so that an audience "in the know" will automatically interpret increased volume as a signal with only one possible implication. Raising one's voice may therefore cue a familiar situation. From plural possibilities the idiomatic language selects a singular meaning, creating a particular frame of reference. Any signal can be mapped in such a fashion, just as you might map a macro to a certain key-combination on your computer keyboard.

In this and many other ways, oral poetry is usually more densely coded than everyday language, in order to promote economical exchange. Signals from numerous other levels of performance can also cue the audience: for instance, the visual language of gesture and costume or the melodic and rhythmic language of voice or accompanying instruments. Looking at things from another direction, we must concede that oral poetry forfeits a great deal of its "more so" when it's silenced, immobilized, and spatialized on a page, when it's reduced to the form and dynamics that we text-consumers find most familiar and convenient. Our first *proverb* warns that we must reach beyond the familiar and convenient; we can't afford to settle for something oral poetry isn't, or something less than oral poetry is.

2. Oralpoetry *Is a Very Plural Noun*

The radical otherness of much oral poetry has tempted many people to imagine a single, uniform category, something we might call "oralpoetry" (not a misprint!). But this is much too tidy a concept for such a tremendously broad and varied body of verbal art. A single category of oral poetry will pass muster only if we are willing to understand and engage the diversity within it.

Exposition — Research from the field and from the study agree: oral poetry is a highly diverse category of verbal art, much larger and more varied than written poetry. Of course, written poetry itself hardly ranks as an orderly collection of cookie-cutter items. If we recall, for example, the marked differences between the written works of Geoffrey Chaucer and Charles Baudelaire, or of John Keats and Langston Hughes, or of Euripides and Robert Browning, the blanket term "poetry" fairly bursts at the seams. What do the *Canterbury Tales* and *Les Fleurs du mal* have in common? What links "Ode to a Nightingale" to "The Negro Speaks of Rivers" or *The Bacchae* to "Soliloquy of the Spanish Cloister"? The dimensions of language, literary tradition, genre, prosody, and numerous other features preclude a too-unified idea of poetry, even within verbal art limited solely to the page. We dare call such a cornucopia of diverse forms by the common name of "poetry" only with a double handful of qualifications firmly in mind.

If written poetry presents such a formidable challenge to categorization, imagine how daunting oral poetry must prove. Once we factor in all the additional dimensions that oral performance entails—voice, audience, gesture, music, and the rest—the compound possibilities threaten the viability of any classification, no matter how flexible. It simply becomes hard to conceive of any single genus that could contain so many variant species. The spectrum outlined in Four Scenarios above, ranging as it does from the epics of the Tibetan paper-singer to North American slam poetry and on to South African praise-poetry and Homer's *Iliad* and *Odyssey,* should by itself raise serious doubts. When we go on to extend the list to Native American coyote stories, Serbian magical charms, Tulu work-songs, and many dozens more oral poetries across the world from ancient times to the present day, formal description fails entirely. We are left to wonder, with many anthropologists and folklorists, whether "oral poetry" really has any clear, sustainable, and useful meaning as a type or category of verbal art.

The way out of this dilemma is to shift our perspective from what oral poems are to what oral poetry does. Instead of worrying over products so diverse that they make *oralpoetry* a very plural noun, we'd do better to concentrate instead on expressive processes. What demands does performance make on us as listeners and readers? What sorts of special languages are we asked to speak? What role do traditional context and audience expectation play? Questions like these, posed and discussed above in the First and Second Words, led to the formulation of a four-part system for oral poetry: Oral Performances, Voiced Texts, Voices from the Past, and Written Oral Poetry. To match this variety of contents we then suggested a varied menu of approaches or ways of reading: Performance Theory, Ethnopoetics, and Immanent Art.

We'll be revisiting these ideas telegraphically in our *Poor Reader's Almanac* of *proverbs*, seeking to understand "how *oralpoetry* means" from another angle. Of course, we shouldn't harbor any illusions about the focus on dynamics rather than objects; it won't solve all of our problems. In the final analysis, "oral poetry" is a concept applied externally, from outside the experience of any oral poet or audience. As such, it exists primarily as an analytical convenience to help contrast the enormous variety of oral and oral-derived forms to written poetry (which of course boasts its own very substantial inventory of individual forms). Still, insisting on process rather than product will bring us a little closer to our double goal of understanding unity through diversity. To help maintain this perspective on dynamics and process, we could coin an auxiliary *proverb*: "Don't ask what it is; ask how it works."

3. Performance Is the Enabling Event, Tradition Is the Context for That Event

The very act of performance keys response by designating a particular channel for communication, by cautioning the audience to "take what follows in a certain way—not literally, but according to the expressive contract in force." Tradition comprises the body of implications summoned by performance and shared between performer and audience. Because tradition characteristically varies within limits and is always subject to revision by individual poets and audiences, it is the furthest thing from a monolith. Both performance and tradition enjoy an afterlife in oral-derived texts, where they persist rhetorically, continuing to foster the exchange between poets and readers.

Exposition — Performances encourage audience reactions merely by being performances. Readers of texts can find a quiet corner, pause periodically to take a break or get some refreshment, and proceed at their own pace. Their engagement is incremental and self-determined, measured by bookmarks and bookends. But participants in performances are enmeshed in experiences larger than themselves (even if no other audience members are present); the burden is on them to adapt to idiomatic ways of speaking and hearing, and to do so on demand. The event of performance—and it is an event rather than a thing—requires all present to open the chosen channel for communication, a channel with a history and a currency far beyond any single message it carries. When we enter the performance arena, a virtual space defined by the activity it fosters rather than by actual geography, we are called upon to subscribe to a set of rules that shape the event. Performer and audience communicate through the language best suited to the undertaking, via the idiom that will accomplish the purpose most economically. We use the tool most appropriate to the job at hand.

Consider the recurring event of slam poetry. The dimly lit café, the unadorned microphone, prior competitions, and not least the audience's raucous cheering prepare us for the language of social criticism. Even those of us new to the medium come to learn what we're in for. After some experience we won't expect polite pondering, opaque musing, or metaphors drenched in literary allusion. We'll come to expect "an orator accountable to the audience," as slammer Roger Bonair-Agard puts it.[1] To make sense of the proceedings, we'll need to co-create the performance arena along with the poet, tuning our sensibilities to his or her wavelength, interpreting the special language on its own terms.

The Serbian funeral lament or *tužbalica,* a dirge for a recently departed loved one that is individually crafted by the closest female relative according to the rules for this genre, is another such event. The performative meaning of laments draws from their setting in the village cemetery, from the grave-goods spread out in front of the singer, from her reperformance of the poem at regular intervals over the weeks, months, and years following the death, as well as from structural conventions like the characteristic eight-syllable line. For their part, audiences—and they are genuinely welcome as co-participants in this most public of rituals—are presented with a problem in reception. They must grasp the cues that the performance makes available; they can enter the arena only by understanding the dedicated language spoken there. Disparate as they are in their specific cultural roles, slam poetry and funeral laments share at least one fundamental quality: the enabling event of performance itself conveys meaning in both oral poetries.

Likewise with the framing context of tradition. The first-time audience member at a poetry slam may well be mystified by what's going on. The competitive spin (complete with judges, a rating system, number cards, and team as well as individual contests), the particular delivery styles favored by this or that person or group, the menu of most frequent topics or perspectives—all these dimensions may initially appear strange and unfamiliar. And why shouldn't they seem puzzling? The inexperienced listener may simply be unable to "read" them, unable to place them in context due to a lack of "cultural literacy." But with some knowledge of the slam tradition these cues begin to make sense; they start to signify something. True, performance of the same poem by the same poet characteristically shifts from one night to the next, and audience reaction is notoriously unstable—not least because every audience is made up of different individuals. But the tradition that contextualizes that variation, the background that frames each unique performance, remains as stable as any language ever can. Does that mean "fossilized" or "verbatim," like photocopies or identical printings of a textbook? No; to expect that kind of stability is to misunderstand tradition. It is to reduce process to product, language to text, the dynamic experience of oral poetry to a static collection of things.

Strange as it seems to us text-consumers, it's only in rule-governed flexibility—the mutable language of performance—that tradition lives and persists. Only in systematic variation will we find consistency and stability in oral poetry. The tradition of Serbian funeral lament is no different in this regard: it can't ever be reduced solely to any one of its instances, even though each instance stands for the tradition *pars pro toto,* the part for the whole. The identity of the lamenter will change from one performance to another, as will the person mourned; the circumstances of the death will vary, as will the locale, family members left behind, and so forth. But certain cues remain. The mourner will speak in octosyllables, she will make use of a specific vocabulary of "bigger words," she will pull a black kerchief around her head, she will set out a generous spread of food and drink to nourish the community of those who visit the gravesite to share her grief, and she will return to this performance arena regularly, as custom demands. Her chant frames the stark reality of her loss in a ritualized context, using familiar signs and their cultural implications to weave the uniqueness of any single event into the broader tapestry of life-passages in her village. Whatever the specifics of any one lament, it depends for its meaning on the event of performance and the context provided by tradition. Without performance and tradition oral poetry loses its defining features.

Nor does the advent of texts necessarily mean leaving event and context behind. Performance and tradition remain crucial to reading oral-derived (oral-connected) poetry, whether we're dealing with textualized Oral Performances, Voices from the Past, or Written Oral Poems. In any case reading oral-derived poetry from texts makes real demands on us as latter-day audiences. Performance can be induced rhetorically, as when Homer invokes the muse or the *Beowulf* poet shouts "Lo!" (*Hwæt*! in Old English) to grab our attention. In such cases we're called upon to cooperate in the fiction of a performance event, tune to the designated wavelength, and join an imagined audience ready to "hear" the poem from a certain perspective. The bottom line is that we aren't excused from communicating via the traditional idiom if oral poetry exists only as a text. Poems composed in a particular traditional register must be received in the same register, to the extent that such fidelity is possible over gaps of space, time, and culture. Our knowledge of the living oral poetry in question may in some cases be fragmentary or even nonexistent, as with Voices from the Past, like manuscripts from the ancient and medieval worlds or, closer to our time, the Native American tales that were written down from actual performance in the early twentieth century before the general availability of acoustic recording devices and before their oral traditions perished. In such cases the full experience of spoken and heard realities will remain forever beyond our reach. But vestigial voices can still be heard—even if faintly—and we do these poems an injustice if we don't listen just as carefully as we can.

4. *The Art of Oral Poetry Emerges* through *Rather Than* in spite of *Its Special Language*

The oral poet is no slave to convention. On the contrary, it's by virtue of conventions that oral poets and their audiences gain access to a wealth of "additional" implications that can be transmitted in no other way. Oral poetry operates according to the social contract of a shared and focused poetic language.

Exposition — No doubt the most talked-about phrase in Homer's *Iliad* is "swift-footed Achilles," which appears more than two dozen times even though the hero it names is offstage for much of the epic. But mere frequency isn't the heart of the problem. More troublesome is the frequently heard objection that the designation of "swift-footed Achilles" often seems awkwardly out of place, as when he huddles in earnest discussion with the embassy sent by Agamemnon to try to talk him into rejoining the battle for Helen and Troy (Book 9.307, 606, 643). True, Achilles is aggressively stubborn and the deliberations are animated, to say the least, but his speeches to Odysseus, Phoenix, and Ajax entail no fleetness, no running, no physical action of any sort. Situations like these present us with tough questions: Why is Achilles repeatedly and illogically referred to by this same formulaic phrase? Doesn't Homer have other, more suitable ways to describe him depending on the particular scene or activity?

In response to potentially embarrassing questions like these, critics have developed two theories. The early version of Oral-Formulaic Theory holds that "swift-footed Achilles" is simply a metrical filler or stop-gap, a way of identifying the hero that fits snugly into Homer's hexameter line and combines easily and systematically with other phrases. This theory understands poetic composition as something akin to a jigsaw puzzle, with the performer assembling prefabricated pieces into metrically acceptable units. The counter-opinion holds that the great poet can rise above mere reflex to choose the most appropriate formulaic phrase, and often does just that. Much ink has been spilled on the nature of such "appropriateness." Of course, the mechanical model has severe shortcomings: any approach to Homer's poetry must do more than offer a mechanical solution or it isn't worth our while. The "master-poet" model also leaves much to be desired, since it pits the genius poet against his own poetic tradition, the captive bard heroically struggling against the fetters of the hexameter.

But the major drawback shared by both models is the failure to understand that "swift-footed Achilles," like any other feature of oral or oral-derived poetry, "works like language, only more so." Suppose, for a moment, that we moved beyond counting recurrences of the phrase and beyond figuring out how it interlocked with other "bigger words" to complete the jigsaw puzzle. Suppose that we credited each item with being the product of a process, and further with being a signal that stands for something specific in the context of the poetic tradition. Instead of a tired old cliché forced on Homer by the relentless pressure of composition in performance, let's imagine an idiomatic sign, an economical cue that ushers Achilles onstage—not running, mind you, but with his heroic character and mythic history encoded in and activated by this telltale detail. From such a perspective it isn't his remarkable foot-speed that counts, but what the tradition means by this evocative "bigger word." Then the sound-byte "swift-footed Achilles"—as well as all of the other formulaic names that Homer uses again and again—takes on fresh meaning. They become signs rather than ends in themselves, indexes rather than static data. They "work like language, only more so."

As an analogy not so far removed from oral poetry, consider what happens in performed drama. In addition to the director's blocking, the designer's sets, and the playwright's speeches, characters' identities can be cued by their costumes, gestures, gaits, dialects, or other idiosyncrasies. A detail associated with one person and one person only—whatever that detail might be—can speak volumes by indexing a complex human personality on the head of a pin. Phrases like "swift-footed Achilles" do something similar, if we are prepared to read the code, to appreciate the "more so" of this special way of naming, to treat it as an idiom rather than a cliché. For the poet and audience (and the latter-day readership) aware of the implied network of the poetic tradition, such names— "ox-eyed Hera," "much-suffering Odysseus," "blameless Aigisthos," and dozens more—are always more than mechanical fillers or cherished opportunities for rising above the anvil chorus of lockstep repetition. They are highly echoic sound-bytes that resonate with traditional meaning.

5. The Best Companion for Reading Oral Poetry Is an Unpublished Dictionary

Because oral poetry depends on traditional resonance, our standard lexical resources may prove inadequate to the task of reading. Consulting the "*un-published dictionary*" means tapping into idiomatic implications that lie beyond literal, textual meaning. By employing this new and more functional kind of resource, we can begin to sense how "the art of oral poetry emerges *through* rather than *in spite of* its special language."

Exposition — We've seen above how "black cuckoo," "green fear," and names like "swift-footed Achilles" can't be read only literally. Now consider an even bigger word: a whole scene that recurs time and again, varying within limits. Such scenes abound, especially in narrative poetry, and have often suffered the same critical reception given to recurrent phrases. For some analysts, typical scenes are problem-solvers; they rescue the poet from performance anxiety, providing a tried-and-true vehicle to move the story forward. For others, poetic expertise means reaching beyond traditional structures, with praise reserved for the artist who succeeds memorably despite the heavy millstone of prefabricated patterns.

The oral-derived poem *Beowulf,* a text-bound refugee from early medieval England, depends on a number of such typical scenes. We considered one of them, the "sea voyage," in the Fourth Word, and raise it again here because it illustrates how false the dichotomy of mechanism versus art really is. How does the Old English oral poet get the hero from his Swedish homeland to the Danish court and back again? The answer is via a five-part sequence culminating in arrival, mooring of the ship, and a reception by the coast-guard on the other side. Both the outgoing and the incoming voyages in *Beowulf* follow this scheme, varying within limits to allow for the particular details of each trip. If these were the only two sea voyages in the poem, we might be tempted to side with those who favor the mechanistic explanation: after all, the storytelling job gets done, and done expeditiously. Or we might prefer the "master-poet" argument, downplaying the scene's consistency and celebrating its variability over these two instances. But the third instance, which is the traditional vehicle for Scyld Scefing's ship-burial, tweaks the pattern memorably. Instead of the goal prescribed by audience expectation—completing the journey and meeting a guardian figure—the poet pleads agnosticism. Scyld's funeral is portrayed as a sea-voyage, but with a telling difference: his destination lies beyond the orbit of human knowledge. Such a famous person's departure would be striking enough, to be sure, but the word-power of the sea-voyage scene gives it an added idiomatic depth. Most to the point for our *proverb*, it's a depth of implication beyond the scope of even the most exhaustive dictionaries and lexicons.

This example from *Beowulf* makes a crucial point and raises a serious question. First the point: even oral-connected poetries, which survive only in textual form, may depend on strategies we associate with actual performance.

Voices from the Past aren't necessarily a dead end. Although rediscovering the "more so" of such works will always be more difficult and more partial than experiencing a living oral tradition, it can be accomplished, at least to an extent. And here's where the question comes in: just how do we go about reading or even compiling an "unpublished dictionary"? How do we learn the language if all we have to work from are a few samples?

As discussed above in the Fifth Word, we can gain some fluency—non-native though it will always be—simply by setting all available instances of a signal side by side, then comparing the instances and asking how the signal works and what it means idiomatically. Phrases and scenes may well bear more than literal meanings, as with "swift-footed Achilles" or the sea-voyage pattern in *Beowulf*. But we can't know until we conduct the background work and give ourselves a tutorial in the poet's language and its implications. On one level this kind of language-learning has been going on for centuries; it's called criticism. On another level, recent research has begun to focus on what amount to entries in the "unpublished dictionary" advocated by this *proverb*; we are starting to create materials for a new kind of Companion for Reading Oral Poetry. The analysis can be painstaking (since it involves working in a new language), but the gain in understanding—in *fluency*—is well worth the effort.[2]

6. The Play's the Thing (and Not the Script)

Reading a dramatic script silently and alone is categorically different from experiencing a staged play as a member of the audience in a theater. A similar distinction must be drawn between understanding oral poetry as just another written text and reading it on its own terms. Even if we're able to experience oral poetry only through a written or printed transcription, we still can't afford to treat it as "closet drama."

Exposition — "The play's the thing / Wherein I'll catch the conscience of the King," says Hamlet at the end of the second act. He plans to stage a facsimile of his father's murder for presentation before his uncle Claudius; then, by watching the usurping king's reaction he'll ferret out whether Claudius was, as he suspects, the perpetrator of the deed. Note that Hamlet will conduct no question-and-answer interview, nor will he give his uncle a letter or manuscript to peruse at his leisure. Only the immediacy and firsthand involvement of a play—where actors fashion a special reality and audiences react to it spontaneously—will suit his purpose.

Hamlet's instinct is unerring. Performances are, as the third *proverb* urges, enabling events. Much of their ability to convey meaning resides in their direct and continuing engagement of the audience according to agreed-upon rules. By their very nature, performances make demands and channel response.

Dramatic productions, whether *Hamlet* as a whole or its "play within a play" or an ever-evolving folk drama from Mexico or South Africa, rely on just such channeling to stimulate a more-than-literal response. Reducing the living experience of a play to the silence of a script entails all sorts of compromises: among the casualties of this radical shift of medium are voice(s), gesture, blocking, and a wealth of visual aspects (set design, costuming, and so forth). Closet drama and living enactment aren't the same thing at all.

Just so with oral poetry, which stands to lose a great deal of its word-power when converted from performance event to the kind of textual item so highly prized by contemporary Western culture. As discussed in the Fourth Word, the very problem of representing oral poetry faithfully in a text lies at the heart of the approach called ethnopoetics. Clearly, our responsibility doesn't end with actual oral events. Even when oral poetry survives only in manuscript, the imperative remains: we must project the "play" from the "script" as best we can, converting the object (back) into an event as far as possible.

7. Repetition Is the Symptom, Not the Disease

Recurrent phrases, scenes, and other features mark oral poetry to varying degrees. But they don't really "repeat"; one instance doesn't relate primarily to another, any more than similar sentences spoken days apart in different locales are "repetitions" of one another. Recurrent features represent the inevitable products of a consistent, rule-governed process rather than recycled items from a limited inventory.

Exposition — One of the most prominent features of many oral poetries is what appears to be repetition. When a phrase like "black cuckoo" recurs, or we run across another instance of an assembly scene or a sea-voyage, we assume we're dealing with something repeated, something used and then reused a second, third, fourth, or however many times. As logical as it might seem, however, this knee-jerk judgment can cripple the way we read oral poetry. It has done so in the past.

Let's start by remembering that oral poetry has rules for composition and reception, whatever they happen to be in any particular poetic tradition or genre. These rules focus and sharpen a poet's way of speaking and an audience's "way of hearing" by prescribing a channel for communication. So what's the upshot? In many cases this dynamic will lead inevitably to what appears to be rote repetition of phrases, scenes, intonation, musical accompaniment, hand gestures, and the like. And we know how the modern sensibility deplores repetition. But the root cause of consistency in this case is simply not mere iteration; consistency happens because the speaker follows the rules. We don't merely *repeat* "To your health!" or "A votre santé!" but rather use such phrases because the social situation warrants it, and only when the situation warrants it. No other "bigger word" will do as well. Just so, oral poets don't repeat themselves or find themselves locked into an expressive straightjacket; rather they use the specialized language fluently and idiomatically. This is a crucial distinction: seeing far enough into the process to diagnose the true "disease" of patterned language versus settling for the superficial "symptom" of recurrent features. Such a diagnosis allows us to see how oral poets are in full and idiomatic control of their traditional language, no matter how "repetitive" it may seem to an outsider. They are no more slaves to their way of speaking than any of us is enslaved by speaking French, English, Swahili, or whatever.

Of course, this distinction between external symptom and underlying disease, between recurrent features and the systematic language that is their origin, also bears on the art of oral poetry. Art stems from the dextrous and idiomatic control of a process, and not from manipulation of its discrete products as "repeated" items. One example is Homer's deployment of the modest-sized but powerful phrase "But come . . ." (*all' age[te]*), which occurs no fewer than 154 times over the epics and hymns. At first sight no bit of speech could appear more workaday and repetitive. Plugged into the beginning of a Homeric line, it seems merely to get things started, to help a character reply to someone else. But within the code it signals much more. Structurally, "But come . . ." is open-ended but focused: it leads regularly to a verb of commanding, either an imperative or a subjunctive. Idiomatically, this "bigger word" dependably initiates a call to action, marking a dramatic change in the status quo every one of the 154 times it turns up. Achilles uses the phrase with cogency on a number of occasions, for instance. In the first book of the *Iliad*, he summons its rhetorical punch to encourage Agamemnon to consult a seer who can explain Apollo's anger at the Greeks, while in Book 24 he deploys it to try to convince Priam to break his fast and share a meal of reconciliation with his son's killer. In these and the scores of other Homeric instances, it's not repetition but idiom that matters. Even as simple a sound-byte as this small phrase "works like language, only more so."

8. Composition and Reception Are Two Sides of the Same Coin

Poet and audience are partners in the same process: making and receiving are inextricably linked. Fluency is a two-way street in any language-based transaction.

Exposition — Oral poets compose in a specialized register, a rule-governed and resonant language, under the assumption that the original and primary audience will understand the poem on its own terms. They do not expect their performances to be translated into other registers. They do not expect audiences to "misread" their poems by imposing false criteria. That much said, there is of course no such thing as absolute fidelity, nor would such an ideal even be desirable. As with any communicative event—from an elaborate political speech to a simple "Hello"—response will vary within limits, just like oral poetry itself. Because each person brings variant experiences, attitudes, and abilities to a given performance, everyone "reads" it somewhat differently. Nonetheless, the event of performance and the context of tradition provide a significant and empowering frame of reference. In the end, the best analogy remains language itself: the oral poet implicitly asks his audience to "read" idiomatically, to receive the message on the same wavelength used to send it. Within that arena there is room for individual as well as traditional meaning. Just as with language itself, both are vital.

The link between composition and reception—let's call it intelligibility— also has important consequences for readers of Voices from the Past. If we persist in transferring the *Odyssey* or *Beowulf* or the *Song of Roland* into a literary frame of reference, deleting the implications of their special registers, we should expect some dissonance. Not complete cacophony, since the registers of oral poetry naturally overlap a good deal with other ways of speaking that make up the menus or expressive repertoires within various languages. But there will be times when we can't "read" the "bigger words" or other idiomatic features, no matter how many (published) dictionaries we pull off the shelf. We'll wonder why Beowulf isn't called something other than "Ecgtheow's son"; we'll be deaf to a telltale shift of loudness or intonation in a Zuni story; we'll miss the full richness of some of Homer's most moving scenes. Without receiving on the appropriate wavelength, we won't be aware that Andromache's plea for Hektor to forsake battle in Book 6 of the *Iliad* takes the form of a traditional lament for a fallen hero, and that she is essentially speaking to a dead man. We'll overlook the narrative pattern that drives Achilles' and Priam's ritualistic bread-breaking in Book 24, and the larger and deeper context it provides for closure of the great epic.[3] Even when an oral poem reaches us only in manuscript, we need to see both sides of the coin, to understand what consequences the poet's composition has for our reception. Intelligibility and art depend upon it.

9. Read Both behind and between the Signs

Oral poetry's signs, whether "bigger words," performance arenas, or other signals, point toward coded implications. They ask audiences and readers to recognize them as idiomatic—to read behind the signs. But we can't afford to forget what lies between such signs. Appreciating local differences and variations at every level of an oral poem or performance will complement our grasp of their recurring, traditional background.

Exposition — Variation in oral poetry is not an inconvenience or a symptom of imperfect composition or transmission, nor is it something to be avoided whenever possible. It is the necessary condition of oral poetry, the very heart of the matter. As we look at or listen to various performances, even of the "same" poem, each one will seem both familiar and unfamiliar; each one will lead us through unmapped territory as well as well-trodden ground. And not only is there plenty of room for uncharted areas on our reading itinerary; the truth of the matter is we can't do without them. Just like language, only more so, oral poetry thrives on its ability to vary within limits. Every instance of a "classic" situation or incident is somehow different from all others; every context is unprecedented as well as generic; each poet and poem and performance is in some fashion unique. If we fail to take realistic account of these aspects of uniqueness, we falsify the hybrid nature of oral poetry as both traditional and particular. We lose half of every poem's expressive force. Put more positively, it's precisely at the intersection of traditional and particular, of idiomatic and literal—of what lies behind the signs and what lies between them—that the art of oral poetry lives.

The example of Serbian magical charms or *bajanje* offers an opportunity to weigh both sides of our responsibility. First, the performance itself is a kind of proverb or sign, aligning the present act of curing with other cures undertaken by this and other practitioners and their patients. The performance creates an arena for the event; as a sign it announces what's taking place. And yet every instance, every curing act, is also unique. Each of them involves one particular patient, one particular healer, and one particular outbreak of whatever malady needs treatment. Second, the practioner will dependably intone some familiar phrases, always whispered sotto voce, but in the process she will unfailingly vary the order of the charm's parts, adjust its structure and phraseology to the specific disease to be removed, and address her patient by name. She will tailor the event to the situation at hand. Can so personalized a procedure truly be a traditional remedy? Yes, of course: it uses a series of signs with powerfully idiomatic implications. As we shall see in the Eighth Word, these implications are highly coded, and reading behind them takes some doing. But the healer and the ill person must also read between the signs, allowing for the changeable specifics that the signs can't address. Administering *bajanje*—as an act of both oral poetry and healing—involves both sides of this double dynamic.

By practical necessity, this book concentrates primarily on what lies behind the signs. Let me openly admit that the presentation is skewed in this way, but quickly add that I've done so for what I consider a defensible reason. For it's "behind the signs"—in the density of coded implications that a performing poet asks an audience and readership to recognize—that oral poetry differs from the kind of poetry that we are most accustomed to reading and thinking about. For text-consumers nurtured on page-bound poetry, it's this dimension that much more urgently needs our attention here. With *proverb* 9, however, we've set such practicalities aside for a moment. In real-life engagement with oral poetry, it is neither desirable nor even possible to ignore what lies between the signs. If it were, "bigger words" would soon degenerate into tired clichés; poets would be indistinguishable from one another; and one performance would be just as good, bad, or indifferent as any other. In short, oral poetry would become a boring cache of replicas. Or put it this way— would we be content to restrict the repertoire of everyday conversation to a couple of dozen stock sentences and gestures, with no opportunity for variation? Of course not: everyday conversation—not to mention oral poetry—is much more interesting than that. Because this book aims at repairing an imbalance that has held sway for a long time, I'll continue to stress the signs and their implications in the Seventh and Eighth Words. But let's agree that an evenhanded, balanced approach—one that pays due attention to what lies both behind and between the signs—is ultimately the only responsible way to read oral poetry.

10. *True Diversity Demands Diversity in Frame of Reference*

Understanding the vast variety of world literature requires patient pluralism as we seek to discover what it means. The past twenty-five years or so have taught us that canons, however they're formulated, are unsustainable impositions. Within the sphere of oral poetry, an even broader spectrum of forms, we encounter an added challenge: we must pay special attention not just to *what* but more fundamentally to *how* a poem means. To the extent we can, we must situate performances and oral-derived texts within their expressive contexts and "read" them on their own terms.

Exposition — Oral poetry is in a unique position to foster diversity in the study of verbal art. It offers the chance to reach well beyond any customary canon of world literature to a wide variety of forms, ethnic groups, and viewpoints that have long gone underrepresented or even unrepresented. Think of the possibilities. No longer do we need to settle only for what's been enshrined in often-reprinted editions and anthologies or, for that matter, in texts of any kind. No longer must we limit the sample by geographical area or chronological era; since oral poetry is a virtual universal at some point in every culture's history, we're limited only by what survives and can be collected and made available. As a matter of both definition and principle, works from all peoples and all ages are invited, indeed encouraged, in order to truly democratize verbal art. No more "rounding up the usual suspects," no more deferral to imposed norms, no more blind loyalty to unexamined assumptions.

What's more, we need not and cannot shrink the enormous and varied universe of oral poetry to forms that happen to have made their way into written literature, such as epic, lyric, drama, ballad, elegy, folktale, and the like. The palette of verbal art in human culture is not nearly as limited as that. Oral poetry can acquaint us with an exciting variety of additional genres, such as, among myriad others, riddles, laments, charms, love songs, work songs, dueling games, genealogies, recipes, prayers, verbal maps, folk histories, and even proverbs. Some of these nondocumentary forms are picked up as momentary features of written literature, but most have been silenced by their failure to gain a secure foothold in the world of texts. They haven't qualified for admission to the textual canon. Even within medieval European literature, where oral and written poetry coexist and a few such genres survive, these additional genres suffer the ignominy of being termed "minor," a coded label that distinguishes them from the "major" genres that have gone on to spawn significant numbers of literary progeny. Likewise, the segregation of expressive forms into literature for literary scholars and folklore for folklorists, along with the false charges of elitism or irrelevance from both sides, simply dissolve if we refuse the canon-based presumptions that underlie them. Oral poetry offers us an uncompromised opportunity to study the roots and present reality of human culture at large, not solely or primarily the story of Western culture as refracted through texts.

But diversity is more than contents. To match its enormously wider spectrum of forms, oral poetry requires an analogous diversity of perspectives. It won't be enough—not nearly enough—to collect more and more treasures for the Museum of Verbal Art if we insist on mounting the same sorts of exhibits, effectively predetermining how visitors to the collection will react. To do oral poetry justice, we must learn to present these newly discovered forms on their own terms, so that museum-goers can understand how they work.

What does this mean in practical terms? For one thing, it means that we can't treat oral poems as something they aren't. Performances don't happen in a vacuum but in contexts, with audiences, and with certain rules in place for composition and reception. Performances demand particular reactions beyond the realm of texts; we've got to play the game according to the applicable rules, as best we can. Diversity demands that we take account of such crucially important dimensions because they help to make oral poetry what it is. Nor can we afford to treat Voices from the Past or Written Oral Poems as we would any other work that reaches us as a text. Scholars and readers have been comfortable in doing so for centuries, of course—celebrating the Homeric epics as the first in a long line of "great books," for example—but we can't any longer defend that misapprehension. What we've learned about the *Iliad* and *Odyssey,* as well as *Beowulf* and many other oral-derived monuments, invalidates the strategy of reducing them to texts. They're much more than texts, and diversity demands that we enlarge and pluralize our perspective to accommodate their complex and fascinating identities.

In the Post-Script we'll examine some new strategies for presenting oral poetry, including electronic media and the Internet. For now, however, I offer a few brief examples of how and why frame of reference matters, with the goal of illustrating why diversifying our frame of reference is a necessary step in learning how to read oral poetry.

Consider first the variety of perspectives we need in order to "read" performances from the former Yugoslavia. Epic will provide us a well-known example—something everyone recognizes wherever it occurs, right? But for quite a few years specialists couldn't agree over whether there was any epic at all anywhere on the continent of Africa. It turned out they were looking for European epic, so no wonder they had trouble finding it. Well, then, let's limit the area covered to Europe; based on what seems to be a familiar and relatively stable form, reading epic poems from that region should present no problem. Given the prevalence of epic in Western traditions—think of Homer, Spenser, Milton, Tasso, and so on—we feel confident about the frame of reference in which to place these sometimes massive stories. But what if each performance of oral epic were "a" version rather than "the" version? Scholarship has established beyond doubt that there isn't any such thing as an archetype or master-version. And what if these epics existed not as freestanding stories but as networked cycles, with each tale "complete" only by reference to the implied poetic tradition? Again, research shows that every oral epic performance implies but does not necessarily rehearse all of the complexities of character, situation, event, and the like. What then? How do we proceed? Where's our frame of reference?

Or try narrowing the focus within South Slavic epic. Take Tale of Orašac, the unlikeliest hero you'll ever meet.[4] Various performances dramatize parts of his eccentric behavior but none provides what we'd call a standard biography. In one performance you hear about the massing of enormous armies as a Turkish bey prepares for battle. But although the muster-list of champions and their hundreds of followers in splendid war-gear seems to go on forever, even so overwhelming a force as that cannot commence its journey until Tale arrives. And how does he arrive? On a swayback, dun-colored horse besieged by flies, partnered by a dubious-looking standard-bearer carrying the proud standard upside down and an Islamic holy man who drinks like a sailor. That's one chapter in Tale's implied biography. Another performance may mention our curious hero's home village, where his mad sister runs naked while Tale himself stands in the middle of a swift-running stream to sharpen his sword on a whetstone turned by his comrades on the shore. A third performance may contribute other less than laudatory details, such as his legendary tightfistedness or his crude cursing of his commander's mother. Nonetheless, we're told formulaically and idiomatically on nearly every occasion that "there can be no journey there without him," and experience with the poetic tradition teaches that Tale will indeed prove himself the indispensable hero. Nobody is as brave or clever as he is—believe it or not. What should we make of characters like him who are introduced telegraphically in one version and only fleshed out by the audience who has heard or read more than a single chapter of the implied book? Only a frame of reference that takes account of the larger poetic tradition can make sense of Tale.

Then, too, as we shall see in the Eighth Word, oral poetry is fundamentally an ecology of genres, a verbal ecosystem. Readers separate out any organic part from its whole at their peril. I mean this in two ways. First, as noted throughout the book, every performance happens in context, as an event embedded in social life. For that reason our frame of reference must include much more than an extruded text; most of the ten homemade *proverbs* make that very point. Second, the verbal ecosystem of oral poetry contains species that depend not just on their individual social embedding but also on one another—species to species, if you like. To put it another way, part of the context for any genre is in fact the other genres that populate the same environment. Our own research in southern Serbia made this interactive balance only too evident. Alongside epic in the village repertoire of verbal art stood lyric or women's songs (themselves a variety), magical charms, genealogies, funeral laments, folktales, and speech-acts for which we could find no formal designation. Oral poetry served many needs, took many expressive forms or genres, and could not be isolated as simply one "thing" or another. Whether to take account of the overall ecology of oral poetry in a given society or to combat the text-driven assumption of separable items, diversity demands that we pay close attention to our frame of reference.

From this point we turn from precepts to illustration. The Seventh Word will consider Native American storytelling, slam poetry, the ancient Greek *Odyssey,* the south Indian *Siri Epic,* and the Old French *Song of Roland.* In the Eighth Word we'll sample magical charms, funeral laments, genealogies, and various kinds of epic from the South Slavic oral-poetic ecosystem. All of these witnesses are summoned for one purpose: to suggest the breadth and richness of oral poetry worldwide from ancient times to the present day.

Notes

1. Personal interview.

2. Concordances of various sorts, such as Bessinger 1978 (Old English) and Prendergast 1971 (the *Iliad*), are useful for such work, but more recently developed tools can be especially valuable in this kind of research. See further the *Thesaurus Linguae Graecae*, a CD-ROM with all available ancient Greek texts from Homer through 600 C.E. (<http://www.tlg.uci.edu>), and the searchable online database of Old English texts compiled by the University of Toronto *Dictionary of Old English* project (<http://www.doe.utoronto.ca>). For research on South Slavic oral epic, I have assembled a computerized concordance of 11,363 lines from the Stolac region of central Hercegovina.

3. On Andromache and Hektor in *Iliad* 6, see Foley 1999: 188–98; on Achilles and Priam in *Iliad* 24, Foley 1991: 174–89.

4. For more on this most unusual hero, see Foley 1995a: 32–41.

Further Reading

African oral epic: general overview: Okpewho 1992, Finnegan 1970; actual performances and texts: Biebuyck and Mateene 1969, Johnson 1992, and Johnson et al. 1997; context: Belcher 1999, Hale 1998

Beowulf and oral tradition: Foley 1990, 1991; Niles 1999

Coyote stories: Bright 1993

Homer and oral tradition: Foley 1990, 1999; R. Martin 1989; G. Nagy 1996a, b; Seventh Word below

Mexican folk-drama: Bauman and Ritch 1994

Oral tradition, writing technologies, and the Internet: Hobart and Schiffman 1998; O'Donnell 1998; Foley 1998b

Proverbs: Mieder 1982; Mieder and Dundes 1981

Serbian charms: Eighth Word below

Serbian funeral lament: Eighth Word below

Slam poetry: Seventh Word below

South Slavic oral epic: Eighth Word below

Zuni storytelling: Fourth Word above and Seventh Word below

Seventh Word:
Reading Some Oral Poems

Up to this point we've spent a good deal of our time unpacking the title *How to Read an Oral Poem*. Our agenda has also included formulating a repertoire of three reading approaches and summarizing some core ideas from a fresh perspective in a "Poor Reader's Almanac" of ten homemade *proverbs*. Now it's time to try a few practical applications, to use what we've developed over the first six Words on some actual specimens of oral poetry.

But first an important disclaimer, and I hope a reasonable one. No matter how many examples of oral poems we summon for this brief lab experiment, no matter how widely we look geographically or chronologically, our best efforts will always fall short of completeness. There will always remain myriad more places and times that couldn't be examined for logistical reasons. What follows, then, is certainly not an exhaustive or even a wholly representative sampler of oral poetry. Nor do I believe that such a miracle could be brought to pass within the covers of this or any other book. The Seventh Word is thus merely a suggestion of how the perspectives we've evolved can be applied to real-life instances of oral poetry.[1] It's a blueprint for an evolving project that must be continued beyond the physical expanse of this book via the *HROP* Web site[2] and, more importantly, through your own extensions to other oral poetries.

Something similar should be added about the case studies themselves. They're extremely short, even cursory, and none of them pretends to cover the oral poetry in question in anything like the depth it deserves. That isn't their purpose. Rather, each is intended only as a "way in," a place from which to start. Cumulatively, and with the aid of the additional resources that follow each unit or can be consulted on the *HROP* Web site, they amount to a passport or visa for a journey yet to be undertaken. Indeed, if the Seventh Word works properly, it will inevitably spark more questions than it answers and prompt many more applications than it can rehearse, stimulating others to fill in the blanks. In that sense it isn't an end in itself but an invitation to further reading.

Case Studies and the Grid

I've put together these case studies with two main criteria in mind. The first is to explore different combinations of categories (Oral Performance, Voiced Texts, Voices from the Past, and Written Oral Poetry) and approaches (Performance Theory, Ethnopoetics, and Immanent Art). This mix-and-match organization seems the best strategy for providing readers with a sensibly broad base from which to pursue their own subsequent readings of oral poetry. For the sake of ready reference, here's a grid outlining the categories and approaches we've covered over the First through Fifth Words.

Types/Categories of Oral Poetry

1. Oral Performance
2. Voiced Texts
3. Voices from the Past
4. Written Oral Poetry

Approaches/Ways of Reading

1. Performance Theory
2. Ethnopoetics
3. Immanent Art

The second criterion involves striking a balance between those oral poetries that are in relatively wide circulation and those that, due to the tyranny of mainstream languages, cultural groups, and publication media, are less well known or even completely unknown. This emphasis assures us of both "canonized" and "uncanonized" instances of oral poetry, thus opening the door to rereadings of familiar works, initial readings of unfamiliar works, and comparisons and contrasts along the spectrum between those poles. Our sample must be varied (Oralpoetry *is a very plural noun*), as must our repertoire of "ways of reading" (*True diversity demands diversity in frame of reference*).

In what follows we'll be pursuing various combinations of types and ways of reading. To each case study I will prefix (a) the category to which the poem or poetic tradition belongs and (b) an approach that will help us to understand it as oral poetry. Of course, we must leave ample room for variety and flexibility within all categories as well as for alternate approaches to the same poem. Nothing here is "writ in stone," nor should it be. It's my hope, however, that the cumulative exercise over a half-dozen examples—two Native American story traditions, a slam poetry event, Homer's *Odyssey,* the Indian *Siri Epic,* and the medieval French *Song of Roland*—will help sketch the beginnings of a repertoire for reading oral poetry.

* * *

Zuni and Kaqchikel Mayan Oral Poetry (Contemporary Native America)

Category: Oral Performance
Approach: Ethnopoetics

Of all cultural groups worldwide, among the most diverse must be Native American. Any designation that aims at capturing more than three hundred languages and traditions under a single heading must be powerful proof of our homemade *proverb* that "*Oralpoetry* is a very plural noun." That's the positive spin. The shortcoming, of course, is that such complexity can't possibly be captured or even reflected in this short sampler of oral poetries. We'd need to reach out over a geographical area that extends from nearly the North Pole to the tip of South America and address a chronological period approaching two millennia (but with fragmentary remains for most of it). We'd have to select evenhandedly from all available genres or types, each of them culturally embedded. Additionally, we'd somehow need to recognize that certain genres have been privileged by collectors and publishers because they have analogues in modern Western literature; they are (or appear to be) known, recognizable quantities. Correspondingly, certain other forms have been excluded by that same arbitrary and unexamined rule of thumb, and too many remain simply invisible to modern Western literary vision. How many of us are ready to consider oratory or magical charms alongside stories? Indeed, the very assumption that "stories" are a universal category makes the point. And that's not all. We'd have to come to grips with the undeniable contribution that oral traditions have made and are still making to contemporary Native American novels—presumably among the most textual and literary of species and therefore the "least oral." That presumption turns out not to be true, however; many Native American, African, and Indian novels have their roots sunk deep in oral poetry.[3] Clearly, the variety and enormity of Native American oral poetry preclude any pretension to balanced coverage.

Faced with such a challenge and yet mindful of the responsibility to offer a way into reading this rich and complex body of oral poetry, let's pursue a double strategy. In keeping with the emphasis in the Seventh Word on diversity and on including both readily available and less well known material, let's listen to two very different examples of Oral Performance in Native American verbal art.

Zuni Stories — The first is the narrative poetry of Zuni storytellers as collected, translated, and presented by Dennis Tedlock in his volume *Finding the*

Center (1972; rev. 1999). The Zuni, who call themselves the Aashiwi, inhabit an elevated plateau region of western New Mexico and maintain both a religious and a secular governmental structure. Tedlock anthologizes seven tales (*telap-naawe*) and two creation stories, scripting them ethnopoetically in a typographical code he invented for the purpose. He sets up the page to accommodate lines of from one to more than seventy syllables and to encode pause, softness or loudness, intonation patterns, extended vowels and consonants, and other performative features. These cues are meant to prompt readers—who are enjoined to actually vocalize the sounds and create the silences of the poem as they proceed—to become feeling, hearing, involved participants rather than distanced onlookers.[4]

Less familiar will be our second example of Native American verbal art, drawn from an only recently published tradition in Guatemala but very much alive for a long time as oral poetry in both Kaqchikel (a Mayan language) and Spanish. This cycle of stories concerns Hermano Pedro Betancur, a Christian missionary who traveled through the Canary Islands and Honduras to Guatemala in the mid-seventeenth century until his death in 1667. The tales chronicle his many miracles and his inner spiritual life. Brother Peter's magical interventions have thus survived in a continuous bilingual tradition for more than three centuries, and in their wake he is often appealed to in contemporary Guatemalan life as an exemplar and guide. Another manifestation of the word-power behind this oral poetry is the fact that the Vatican is presently evaluating him for sainthood. It is this figure and the oral poetry that memorializes him that María Cristina Canales and Jane Frances Morrissey collected and translated, and for which they conceived an ethnopoetic representation in their anthology *Gracias, Matiox, Thanks, Hermano Pedro* (1996), selected from a fieldwork archive of twenty-three Kaqchikel and sixty-eight Spanish story-performances. Their renderings are similar to the structural scripts pioneered by Dell Hymes and described in the Fourth Word.

Like many other Native American tales, the Zuni story "Coyote and Junco" can be read on many levels. In one sense it is an etiological narrative, the kind of story that explains the origin of a natural phenomenon or human custom. The trickster figure Coyote, who makes a mythic career out of overreaching, hears the junco bird singing a winnowing song and gets it into his head that he'll learn it to sing to his children. Old Lady Junco cooperates and teaches him not once but three times; on each occasion Coyote, whom nature never meant to sing this song, loses the tune and has to return to his teacher for a refresher lesson. But the fourth request pushes Junco too far, and she refuses. Trying to frighten her into compliance, Coyote threatens to bite her "shirt," which Tedlock identifies as "the hood-like area of dark gray or black that covers the head, neck, and part of the breast of this species" (74). Unknown to him, she's slyly inserted a rock into the "shirt," and when he bites down in anger all he accomplishes is to break off some of his back teeth. He then returns to his children, only to find them dead. The storyteller, Andrew Peynetsa, closes the tale by explaining that this is why coyotes' molars are in such bad condition.

So much for the main action and the etiology. To fill out the picture, let me reproduce the last section of Tedlock's ethnopoetic translation and ask you to read it aloud. By reperforming it, you can get inside Peynetsa's original performance and reenact it from an insider's perspective. By voicing it yourself in something approaching the way in which this oral poetry really works, you can see for yourself how *Performance is the enabling event, and tradition is the context for that event.* Your enactment will return the poem to life, and you'll be performing within the Zuni poetic tradition—as faithfully as textual and cultural distance permit, of course.

Here is Tedlock's code: capital letters indicate increased volume, new lines involve at least a half-second pause beforehand, asterisks call for at least a two-second pause, raised or lowered type indicates an intonation shift up or down, a series of dashes signals a prolonged word, and italicized phrases give nonverbal stage directions. As you begin, Coyote has just started his threatening countdown to eating Junco (71–73):

> "ONE!" he says.
> "The fourth time I, uh, speak and you don't sing for me, I'll bite you," he
>   tells her.
>
> * * *
>
> "Second time, TWO!" he says.
> "Quick! Sing your song," he says.
> When she doesn't sing, "THREE!" he says, "I'll SPEAK for the LAST
>   TIME," he says.
>
> * * *
>
> Coyote says, "QUICK! SING IT," to her.
> She doesn't sing.
> Coyote bites Junco clear through.
> He bites Junco, CRUNCH! He bites the round-rock Junco.
> Right here (*points to molars*) these here
>   all his teeth come out, the whole row of teeth comes out.
> (*in a tight voice*) "This is exactly what I wanted to do to you." "Ay! Ay!"
>   he says.
> When the prairie wolf returned to his children, by the time he got there
>   his children were dead.

Because of the one who lived this long ago, coyotes have no teeth here
(*points to molars*), that's A————LL THE WORD was short.

The emphases you heard in the louder words and phrases reflect Peynetsa's
own vocalization. Amplifying the numbers increases the drama of the counting and the force of the interjection "CRUNCH!" as well as the formulaic closure to the story. The pauses segment the telling in real time, reinvigorating the
process of oral poetry and converting the text—through your agency—back
into the event it once was. The italicized phrases restore some part of the mimetic, physical reality of the storyteller's interaction with the audience, adding a visual cue about Coyote's dental disaster (*points to molars*) and further
specifying how a certain phrase should be uttered (*in a tight voice*). In the first
edition (1972: 83), the final notation—(*laughs*)—framed the tale as, among other
things, an amusement. But even without that cue we have both common Native American attitudes toward Coyote as a trickster figure as well as Peynetsa's own comments on its lack of cosmic seriousness to guide us in understanding the story as a lighthearted diversion rather than a melancholy tale.[5] Coyote
was attempting to do something nature never meant him to accomplish.

Now let's add a few more performative cues and give you an opportunity
for revoicing part of another Zuni tale. Once more I ask you to read it aloud,
to make it Oral Performance again. Even with the handicaps imposed by translation and non-native reperformance, you'll be taking a huge step beyond settling for the textual stasis and silence to which we usually reduce oral poetry
when we commit it to texts. In this selection from "The Sun Priest and the
Witch-Woman," a young witch and her mother have convened a covert meeting to discuss killing the highest-ranking Zuni priest and replacing him with
one of their own, a young boy. Their confederate, the Witch Bow Priest (or
Witch Sun Priest), is speaking as we pick up the story in Tedlock's ethnopoetic transcription, which this time includes a smaller font for softness and rising or falling letters (as well as words) to mimic the pitch-arc of intonation
patterns (172–73):

> "If we KILLED THE SUN PRIEST
> then this man here would replace him, is that what you had in mind, is
>   that why you
> called this meeting?"
> So their Witch Bow Priest said.
>
> * * *
>
> The little boy sat there with his head down
> the little boy thought about their words with his head down.

* * *

Then it was their
Witch Sun Priest who spoke: "YES, in TRUTH, even if that's what you
think about the Sun Priest
I'm NOT WILLING:
I don't know the prayers,
          or how my words could be heard by the raw people.
This wouldn't turn out well for us.
We would be found out quickly.
Certainly
there are the Ahayuuta twins, and
they are wonderful, they are extraordinary persons.
If we made a mistake
then SURELY
we would be killed.
Then what would happen? After they killed us
could we still carry on?" so
their Witch Sun Priest said.
"So I don't agree, but
          whatever you think
whatever you think
WELL NOW, SPEAK, what's this all about?" he said.
"Yes, in truth,"
the girl said,
"I know that
my feelings are not good."

I've quoted at some length for a reason. The best explanation of how an ethnopoetic script works is the experience of giving it voice, of becoming the oral poet and sensing how it sounds and feels to embody the poem. The oral-aural landscape, to state the obvious but too often overlooked, resides in the event of reperformance—not in the prompt-book itself or, worse yet, in a third-party discussion of the effects and features it cues. *The play's the thing (and not the script).* Of course, we could observe from a comfortable textual distance that the transcription restores emphasis, de-emphasis, and silence, and that signals for intonation reveal levels of complexity in the poet's way of speaking. But such observations pale in contrast to "reading" the signals through your own vocal apparatus and physical gestures. In fact, before going on it might not be a bad idea to reperform these two brief passages. They're most genuinely a replica of Oral Performance when you make them so.

Guatemalan Stories — Ethnopoetics helps us to dissolve textual boundaries and transform poems-as-things into poems-as-events. The collection of Guatemalan stories about Hermano Pedro provides another opportunity to participate in the (re)making of oral poetry and to investigate a few related dimensions of Oral Performance. How active can an audience be in the telling of the tale? Where does the poem's composition end and its reception begin? Can more than one person actually be composing the poem? Such questions don't arise with most poetry that awaits us on the page—static, complete in itself, and ready for dissection. But they do arise with many oral poetries, complicating matters in a demanding and enlightening way.

To point toward some answers, I reproduce the opening lines of the Canales-Morrissey transcription of "Along Came a Lizard," performed by Nicolás Murcía, a Kaqchikel then in his seventies, who was egged on in a very participatory fashion by Rafael Coyote Tum, a Mayan linguist and professor at Universidad Mariano Galvéz. The tale was told in Kaqchikel and was transcribed and translated to reflect small pauses of less than a second (intralinear spacing) and longer pauses (vertical spacing with asterisks). The editors understand the entire event as "the poem," and so include the ellipses, expletives, false starts, and other natural performative phenomena that textual culture brands as blemishes to be erased. As with so many poetries outside the narrow confines of Latin-based Western languages, the line is a breath-group rather than a syllabic abstraction. Bold-face letters mark increased loudness. Once again, I ask you to voice the poem yourself and participate in its (re)making, its *poiêsis*. Here are the first eighteen lines (85):

then   **brrrup**   along came a little lizard
    [Rafael] oh
    [Nicolás] a lizard crossed his path   they say

* * *

"wait there   little sister lizard   wait there"   he
    said to her   he stopped the little lizard   the
    little lizard stopped   her dewlap inflated
        [Rafael, Nicolás] **ha** **ha** **ha**
        [Nicolás] she stood   the little lizard
            stood still
        [Rafael] uh-huh
        [Nicolás] "well now you'll come along with me"
he said to her   they say   he took out a good-sized
        piece of paper from his sack   they say   wrapped
        her up in the paper   he did   put her in his

        sack like that   "now   everything's all set"   he
        said   they say   it was a little lizard
so then he went to a store

* * *

he asked for a loan   let's say   two thousand   three
        thousand   but in those days   three thousand was
        an awful lot of money   it was a lot of money
        yeah   really   because the cost of living was
        cheaper then   everything was a lot cheaper
        he asked for two or three thousand   then he
        said "do me a favor   lend me a   a couple of
        thousand
and I'll give you as a pawn this little animal here"
        he brought out the little animal   she was all
        covered with gold
            [Rafael] oh!
            [Nicolás] and she even wiggled   she did
they say that the people thought that the little
        animal could produce gold
            [Rafael] uh-huh

As the story proceeds, Hermano Pedro uses the magic lizard to secure funds
to build a hospital. The tale closes with his animal helper being released back
into nature, its job done and the miracle concluded.

   The ethnopoetic transcription makes evident a number of qualities or features that a one-dimensional record would obscure or simply delete. Right
from the start we see that the performance is a cooperative exercise: Nicolás
Murcía takes center stage as the primary storyteller, but he's hardly alone.
Rafael Coyote Tum performs an important supporting function, productively blurring the distinction between teller and audience with his own interjected
remarks. Tum also reinforces or certifies Murcía's words (and "words") with
periodic affirmations like "uh-huh" and "oh!" at points of narrative segmentation throughout the performance. We might compare the role of the *naa-
munaamuna* ("encourager"), so integral a participant in the performance of
West African epic, who chants "indeed," "mmm," "true," or the equivalent at
the end of each and every line spoken by the bard.[6] Numerous other oral poetries also feature this type of interaction, often referred to as "back-channel-
ing" or, in African American verbal arts, "call and response." For our purposes
Tum's contribution serves as ready evidence of how deeply involved and influential listeners can be, how—whether explicitly or implicitly—they are effectively composing along with the poet. It's only a matter of how they di-

vulge their role in the joint enterprise, and whether a transcription reveals it. In our special sense of the term, *reading* oral poetry is typically more a dialogue than a soliloquy. To reperform many such poems, you'll need a partner.

We can identify a few additional features brought out by the Canales-Morrissey performance-text. Murcía—and many other storytellers in the Hermano Pedro tradition—construct their tales in large, stanza-like "words" with internal pauses. These "words" are breath-groups, as noted above a much more widespread metric internationally than our treasured syllable-counting. On a smaller scale, the frequent interjection of phrases like "they say" and "he said to her" amount to oral-aural punctuation. Like Homer's lines of speech introduction, they serve about the same purpose as quotation marks in texts; as such, they shouldn't be over- or underinterpreted. We hear the same sort of oral-aural signaling in the informal register used by many American teenagers as they narrate incidents to one another (more seldom to adults). In this highly patterned way of speaking, the interjection "like" marks the onset of a quotation, as in the exchange:

> I'm—like—How'd you find that parking space?
> And he's—like—I had to go around the block maybe twenty times.

Finally, even this short passage from "Along Came a Lizard" displays a number of features associated with oral poetry that are made more obvious by spacing, lineation, and other ethnopoetic cues. Among them are parallel structures, repetition or recurrency, and the equivalent of cinematic jump-cuts in which the audience needs to fill a cognitive gap by providing its own transition from one situation or perspective to the next.

At root both the performative and the structural versions of ethnopoetics aim at the same goal: making the reader a part of the audience. Tedlock has crafted the Zuni story-text to reawaken its sounds and its silences by projecting them back through the reader. This strategy makes for an intimate and personal as well as a more realistic experience. It uses reperformance to dissolve textual distance, to make oral poetry present and immediate. Canales and Morrissey include some of the same sorts of signals, but their primary focus is re-creating the idiomatic structure that serves as companion to the ideas and sounds of the Hermano Pedro tale. Reperforming "Along Came a Lizard" means sensing the lines and "words" in which the poetry takes its distinctive shape, playing off one phrase or perspective against another, looking (and hearing) beyond the smooth skin of its textual surface to the traditional musculature that supports the oral poem's art. In both cases the advantages of an ethnopoetic libretto over the usual kind of flat, reduced text are best grasped by actually speaking it aloud, by giving voice to what we find on the page, by embodying the poems. In both cases ethnopoetics goes a long way toward making Oral Performance deserve the name.

Further Reading

Ethnopoetics: DuBois 1998; Hymes 1981, 1989, 1994; Tedlock 1983, 1999

General background on Native American: Krupat 1989, 1993; McDowell 1998; Ramsey 1999; Swann and Krupat 1987; Toelken 1998; Wiget 1996

Mayan and the *Popol Vuh:* Tedlock 1993, 1996

Oral tradition and the contemporary Native American novels: Brill de Ramírez 1999

Translation: Evers and Toelken 2001; Swann 1992

* * *

Slam Poetry (Contemporary North America, Europe, and the Middle East)

Category: Voiced Texts
Approach: Performance theory

> ". . . these poetry slams, in which various young men and
> women in various late-spots are declaiming rant
> and nonsense at each other. The whole thing is judged
> by an applause meter which is actually not there, but
> might as well be. This isn't even silly; it is the death of art."
> —Harold Bloom

> "The points are not the point, the point is poetry."
> —Allan Wolf [7]

As we discussed in the Four Scenarios that opened this book, slam poetry is a widely practiced contemporary oral poetry that has spread quickly in urban contexts in North America and to a lesser extent overseas. Its trademark brand of competitive performances of original poetry can be experienced today in most major U.S. cities and many smaller ones, and a national-level championship for both individuals and teams is held each year. Poets do write their poems, and sometimes their works reach a conventional printed form. But that's not the primary mode. These poems are meant for live performance before an audience, for highly charged, face-to-face interactions where the audience loudly shouts its approval or disdain—often during pauses within the performance—and judges evaluate each competitor's presentation according to a point system. That's the space and the moment in which this poetry lives.

What follows is a perspective on an actual slam at the Nuyorican Poets Café (NPC). Located at 236 East 3d Street between Avenues B and C in lower Manhattan, it comes complete with a many-sided history of verbal arts in performance as well as a proud, insistent present that features slam poetry. Seven nights a week the NPC hosts theater, live music, hip hop, and film; it also features poets reading their work aloud in the tradition of Beat generation bards like Allen Ginsberg. On Friday nights, however, it becomes what emcee Nathan P calls "the Mecca for slam poetry." The Dead Poets Team Slam that began late on Friday, March 30, 2001, and continued well into the next morning took place in the twenty-sixth year of the NPC's reign.[8]

To understand what went on that night, you had to be there. Since you weren't, I'm going to invoke performance theory—or "Being there" as we nicknamed it in the Third Word—to help you understand what it was to be a member of an actively participating audience. That's the key idea here: participation. From the perspective of performance theory, and aided by a few photographs available on the *HROP* Web site,[9] I'll try to make you part of the audience.

At the Nuyorican — Picture 150–200 people mashed into a space maybe 50 feet across and 40 feet from front to back, not counting the double-closet area of the bar, itself full of the comings and goings of patrons and performers. A DJ provides hip hop and alternative rock as spotlights glare unremittingly on a tiny stage graced only by a mouth-high microphone and a black music stand atop a faded oriental rug. Brick walls tower to a 20- to 25-foot ceiling, giving a vertical roominess to what's otherwise the busiest and most congested of verbal agoras. Into the arena enters Nathan P [**Photo 1**], a wiry, simpatico black man of perhaps 25–30 happy to send himself up with self-deprecating one-liners even as he steers a complex, multilayered event with what seems like effortless dexterity. "I'm just your emcee," he cheerfully complains, "not your maître d'. Some woman came up to me a few minutes ago and said 'Table for four, please.' I don't do that." Squeezed together as people are, his story has a warm, welcome resonance. He'll continue to shape the proceedings, ever so subtly, in the chinks between individual poem-performances, between rounds one and two, and anywhere else he's needed. His spots are the interstices between more foregrounded moments in the slam ritual.

Nathan P explains the rules governing tonight's activities. Two teams will compete, one made up of NPC regulars and the other a put-together team from folks associated with the People's Poetry Gathering 2001 (PPG), a three-day celebration of worldwide poetries, ancient to modern, sponsored by City Lore and Poets House.[10] Thus the good-natured challenge—regulars from the Mecca versus non-NPCers. Nathan P goes on with his explanation: four people to a team, two rounds, a total of sixteen performances, with the sequence of contestants to be determined by the individual team (which of the four chooses to go first, etc.) and by captains' draw (which team leads off round one). Later on, in an example of the audience involvement that's ever at the core of poetry slams, he'll put the second-round order to a voice vote by the patrons. An unusual aspect of tonight's event: the first round will be devoted to performing "poems by dead poets," while the second will follow the customary track by featuring the slammers' own creations.

A number of satellite events whirl around the planetary center of the Dead Poets Team Slam, heightening anticipation even as they flesh out the ongoing drama. Some of these can be observed at slams around the country, from venue-based and city competitions to the annual national championship,[11] while others are NPC-specific rituals. At the Nuyorican the first reading is done by the "spotlight poet," roughly equivalent to the opening band at a rock concert. In this case that role was played by Thomas Lynch of Michigan [**Photo 2**], a well-published poet and funeral director who read aloud from his books of poetry for about thirty minutes. Notice that I said "read aloud." He wasn't slamming but purveying the spoken word in another register, voicing his literary creations in a mode and spirit familiar to coffeehouses in general—and the NPC in particular—for decades. Where the experience diverged from the academic ceremony wasn't so much in his own performance but in the no-holds-barred reaction of the audience, who though muted during the presentation itself were noisily enthusiastic in showing Lynch their appreciation immediately after each poem. They weren't polite, they were genuine. And the spotlight poet basked in their acclaim as he helped ready them for what lay ahead. You could feel the energy rising, looking for release.

What happened next was what regularly kicks off slams: the "sacrifice poet"—tonight it's Nathan P himself—is offered up [**Photo 3**]. The purpose of this "demonstration" performance, part of the ritual around the country at every level, is simple. Someone who's not involved in the actual competition performs a sample slam poem to warm up the judges and the audience, helping to set the calibration for scoring the real thing that will soon follow. Often, as in this case, the sacrifice, far from being a throwaway, provides one of the evening's more memorable moments.

Slam is a competition, like so many other poetry duels throughout history and around the world.[12] It's important to emphasize, however, that the competition is a vehicle, not the sole purpose or overriding goal. The contest frame keeps everyone, poets and audience alike, in the moment, intensely engaged in what's emerging. Of course, it's fun to win, and at the nationals and other large events winning can bring trophies and titles as well as cash. But these things are not the driving force behind slam; being part of the ritual in as immediate a way as possible is the aim. As one of the epigraphs above puts it, "The points are not the point, the point is poetry."

But slam still needs a system to buttress its sustaining fiction and select its winner(s). So, well before Nathan P stepped onto the floodlit stage, he selected five two-person judging teams from among the audience and gave each pair an adjustable numerical placard. Scoring goes from 0 to 10, with discrimination by tenths welcomed in order to break potential ties. Of the five scores the highest and lowest will be discarded, making 30 points the maximum total for a single performance in tonight's competition. And what are the criteria for scoring, which for most performances varies more than you'd expect? Nathan P deadpans: "If you hear a poem and it makes you think about doing your taxes—and the poem isn't *about* taxes—that's a zero." A perfect 10 lies at the opposite end of the spectrum, and veteran audiences know that chanting "Ten! Ten! Ten!" just after the poet finishes might well influence the judging. Audiences learn a bag of expressive tricks, too.

So the judges are selected and introduced, the rating cards distributed, the audience warmed up, the sacrifice poet sacrificed in the name of the larger ritual and the common poetic good. The competing teams have determined the order in which they'll perform for the first round and plotted their overall strategy. All the preliminaries are over. It's time for the main event.

The team captains' drawing has resulted in the PPG side going first, with alternating performances to ensue. Nathan P presents each poet, adding a few comments about where they hail from originally as well as where they live now, prompting spontaneous explosions of territorial allegiance among the audience. As in any battle, territory counts. There'll be many more outbursts of identification and advocacy as the slam proceeds.

These initial eight performances will present other people's poems and therefore, strictly speaking, they won't be Voiced Texts. The Voiced Texts will follow in round two when poets perform their own compositions. The contrast between performing other people's words and enacting their own "words" turns out to be instructive, as we shall see. But like other parts of the whole—other acts or scenes in the larger drama—the dead poets' works are slam.[13] Each slammer now takes the stage in turn, ready to bring verbal art to life in this communal celebration of spoken-word poetry.

First up, Juan Martinez [**Photo 4**] of the PPG team, identified as a student at Bard College, and Aya DeLeon [**Photo 5**], from Oakland but now a member of the NPC group. They perform consecutively, enacting favorite poems by dead poets. Martinez doesn't attribute his selection, while DeLeon acknowledges hers as authored by Gwendolyn Brooks. Virtually no numerical blood is drawn in this opening bout; Martinez earns a cumulative 22.3, DeLeon a 25.5.

The judges, most of whom haven't attended a slam before (thought to be no hindrance to evaluating this poetry of inclusion and anti-elitism), are feeling their way. The audience will happily and demonstratively show their displeasure at the scoring whenever they feel the urge, but in general, both now and throughout the night, they're highly appreciative of and empathetic with the performers. Quite clearly, it's *their* event and ritual as well as the performers' and emcee's.

The next three bouts pass quickly, but not without incident and unexpected developments. The PPG team's Sparrow [**Photo 6**], as the next competitor identifies himself, announces his chosen author as William McGonagall, whom he labels the "worst poet in history." After suffering through the interminable and splendidly awkward "Bridge of Tay," delivered with mocking drama and punctuated by audience groans and outright shouts of protest, no one is likely to disagree with his evaluation.[14] He earns a 10.2, based on scores ranging from 0.4 to 7.1. Opposite Sparrow is Yolanda Wilkinson [**Photo 7**], originally from Virginia but now a resident of the Washington Heights area and a member of the NPC championship team that represented the Nuyorican at the 2000 national competition in Providence, Rhode Island. Her reputation has preceded her, and is certainly borne out tonight: a uniquely animated performance of Dr. Seuss's *Green Eggs and Ham*—which not incidentally shows how vital enactment can be and how slam isn't in any way limited to a prescribed tone or style—brings down the house. The audience begins the "Ten!" chant, and the judges agree: two 10's and a 29.2 total score. NPC has pulled ahead substantially, but the score is secondary at most. The crowd remains in the moment, concentrating on what's immediately before them rather than allowing themselves to be distanced by an overconcern for points.

Dan Ferri's [**Photo 8**] up next for the PPG, and he's chosen the "Fiddler Jones" speech from Edgar Lee Masters's *Spoon River Anthology.* Ferri is a sixth-grade schoolteacher and a pioneer in Haiku slam; he also appears in the film *Slamnation* (Devlin 1998), so he's a known quantity to some of the audience. Grimacing under the spotlight, he earns a respectable 23.7. But Ferri is topped by the NPC poet, Dwaywah Frazier [**Photo 9**], a journalist and performance artist who, Nathan P explains, agreed to step in at the last moment. She was slated to be the sacrificial poet, but when one scheduled NPC member failed to show up she was asked to join the home team. That's why Nathan P sacrificed himself. At any rate, Frazier reads more than performs Langston Hughes's "Harlem" to a warm reception and a score of 25.8. The first round closes with PPG's Marj Hahne [**Photo 10**] performing e. e. cummings's "Marge" for a 24.6 and Jonathan Reeve's [**Photo 11**] selection from Allen Ginsberg's "America" for a 26.8.

Strong as these performances are, there's a feeling of ever-increasing expectation among the audience that dampens them just a bit toward the end of the first round. Maybe it's got something to do with looking ahead to the second round, to the time when the slammers will cut loose and do their own poems, when a celebration of other people's words brought back to life will give way to the poets' own art in real life—no filters, no resuscitation, just raw, immediate, always-demanding enactment. The second round will consist of Voiced Texts, poems that fulfill their potential only in performance, only when they escape the page, get embodied via slammers' voicing, and modulate into events rather than things. In the sense we've been developing throughout this book, the second round will feature "words" as well as words.

Intermission between rounds brings to the stage Victor Hernández Cruz, a longtime supporter of the NPC and an accomplished poet, to read from his published works. Like his opposite number Thomas Lynch he isn't slamming, but he's nonetheless part of the slam ritual. Some audience members take the opportunity to replenish their refreshments, but most listen pretty intently to Cruz. It's a different sort of listening, though, just as it's a different sort of performing. Audiences as well as poets have different spoken-word gears.

As the main event resumes, Nathan P asks the audience whether they want the contestants to maintain the first-round sequence or reverse it. The voice vote heavily favors reversal, so Jonathan Reeve [**Photo 12**] leads off the slammers' presentation of their own work. And a memorable beginning it is, easily subject to radical misinterpretation outside the context of the present instance and ongoing tradition of slam, which project certain convictions about the role of poets and the nature of their constituency. Reeve asks the hundreds of people anxiously awaiting his "word" whether they like Henry James. They don't, for the most part. This prompts a perfunctory apology to those who do, and with that the poet launches energetically into his ode entitled "Buttfucking Henry James." He meanders graphically and with painful physiological precision through the first part of the poem, which depicts him sexually assaulting not only the late Victorian mainstay but Romantic poets like Wordsworth, Keats, and Shelley. This isn't a homosexual love fantasy; it's about who's in charge, who's the master and who's the mastered. It's easy to get outraged, even if you don't much like Henry James, because the action is so violent and gross. We audience members cringe and moan, pushed painfully outside our comfort zone. We strain to write it off as humorous dissing of establishment poetry, an almost justifiable siege on the smug bastion of the academically insulated literary tradition. But it's difficult, really difficult, for many of us.

Just as the overwhelming crudeness threatens to sink his rhetoric, Reeve instantly changes gears to an affirmation of poetry as living art, as performed words, as the voice of people extending a hand to each other rather than insisting on holding one another at arm's length. The shift is quicksilver brilliant. It's also self-reflexive. People end up cheering the very process in which they're participating—poetry as an inclusive not an exclusive art—and the judges jump on the bandwagon with a 27.4. Make no mistake about what's happening here: slam is saying that worshipping the ancestors isn't enough, singing someone else's song (no matter how contemporary and vital) isn't enough, dead poets aren't enough, books and texts aren't enough. Reeve's poem and more generally the evolving slam movement are demanding nothing less than a living performance tradition, an oral poetry.

It was serendipity that the audience voted to reverse the order for this second round of performances. That reversal put Reeve's "word" first, marking an unambiguous change of tone, content, and effect as the slammers moved from dead poets' works to their own. It's as if you stepped off a curb unawares. In place of someone else's carefully molded reflections, here comes the onslaught: socially committed subjects, rough language and rougher delivery, uncut crystalline metaphors. Marj Hahne [**Photo 13**] ponders "Lies We Tell Ourselves" and Dwaywah Frazier [**Photo 14**] tells of unchartable "Journeys," while Dan Ferri's [**Photo 15**] untitled reverie makes memory material by recalling the coins jingling in his father's pocket on a summer night. All three are powerful and wrenching, and all three engender an intimacy that can't be constructed outside the face-to-face reality of a performance. Their scores are comparable—26.3 for Hahne, 26.9 for Frazier, 28.7 for Ferri—but that hardly seems the point anymore. The ritual has taken full hold with the Voiced Texts of the second round, and the competition is ever more transparently a vehicle for more meaningful strivings. No one's really keeping score, except as a way to thank the poets for making and remaking their world.

There's always room for humor and flat-out fun within the slam ritual, and the next two contestants show their rapt constituency two ways to send up the contemporary scene gently but no less effectively. Yolanda Wilkinson's [**Photo 16**] meditation on "Snack Crackers" takes as its cosmic subject the lowly triscuit, following this modest emblem of a marketing-blitzed society from its absence in the dictionary to its multifunctionality in too many daily lives. In the process she exposes instances of mindlessness and distressingly automatic behavior by the dozen, demonstrating that social criticism doesn't have to resort to heartbreaking stories, sharp-tongued political commentary, or jumbo abstractions in order to pierce the cultural hide. The judges award her a 26.9, but I think she deserves a lot better and join the strenuous chorus of boos as Nathan P announces the scores. The shoe was on the other foot with Sparrow's [**Photo 17**] "Harmonica," very much his own composition, which follows just afterward. It may well have been overrated by the judges, who registered two

10's, a 9.9, 8.3, and 6; once the highest and lowest are thrown out (as some thought should be done with the poem itself!), the cumulative score was 28.2. I'll quote the poem in its full splendor and let you decide: "Bill said, 'Don't harm Monica.'" His award of 2.3 points more than Wilkinson received underlines at least two of our observations: slam offers safe harbor for unpretentious fun, and scoring isn't really the point.

It's left to the final pair of contestants to close out the contest, and Aya DeLeon [**Photo 18**] of the NPC team seizes the moment and won't let go. Her "Icon" samples a famous line from Martin Luther King's Washington Monument speech of 1963, using rhyming variations on "I have a dream"—scheme, etc.—as jumping-off spots for targeted instances of social injustice. Bending King's words this way and that, she illustrates how contemporary society has deformed the ideals he championed, overlooking core issues of freedom and dignity in favor of shallow devotion to lesser values. The last few syllables weren't out of her mouth more than a half-second before the audience, roiling with visceral approval all "word" long, started up the mantra. "Ten! Ten! Ten!" they shouted, and three of the judging pairs concurred. Discarding one of the 10's and a 9 and adding a 9.9, Nathan P announces a 29.9 to the noisy delight of everyone present, including both slam teams. It was the highest score of the night, and well deserved. Juan Martinez [**Photo 19**] closes the proceedings on a somber note with a very personal poem about what it means to be used by another person. With his 27.4 the slam is concluded.

Well, almost concluded. While the final scores were being tabulated to see who would win the $10 per person team prize, Monique Baptiste [**Photo 20**], a student at Rutgers University, read her poem, "Angry Black Woman Syndrome." She framed her biographical observation by telling the audience that she was pretty much past the anger now, but that didn't milk any of the power or humor out of her sometimes outrageous and always entertaining remarks. The scores for the slam eventually came in, and to no one's surprise—and also to no one's purely egocentric delight or rank disappointment—the NPC team was victorious. More to the point, both teams crowded up on and around the stage, celebrating the aftermath of the ritual, charged up by what they had accomplished for and with the audience [**Photo 21**]. The performance was over, the Dead Poets Team Slam now a memory. Enactment had ceased, at least until next Friday night at the Nuyorican.

Slam as Performance — How does performance theory help illuminate the event I've just tried to re-create for you? Back in the Third Word, we began our discussion of that approach or way of reading by asking a simple, straightforward question and giving a direct, unevasive answer:

Q: What difference does performance make?
A: Performance is part of the meaning.

Beyond the textually governed kind of exchange to which we're accustomed lies the possibility of communicating in a different mode, of speaking an alternate language. The very act of performing—and for that matter of serving as an audience—moves slam poetry off the page, out of the book, and into the arena of face-to-face, emergent art. You can't mark your place, brew a cup of tea, and curl up on the sofa to resume the experience; you can't isolate a captive ode between covers and peruse it at your leisure under whatever reading conditions you choose to impose. Poets can't offer up their works as handsome icons enshrined in the politically sanctioned medium of print, any more than they can protect themselves by abandoning their creations on your doorstep and scurrying back into anonymity. Presence and interaction can't be avoided; they're the name of the game.

Everything that happened that night of March 30, 2001, at the Nuyorican helped to frame the event, to give it meaning. From the moment Nathan P took the stage and opened the ritual, through the spotlight and intermission poets, and most essentially via the contestants who waged war with words (but only symbolically and for the greater artistic good), the enactment took on a life of its own. To borrow a concept from Immanent Art, everyone there willingly entered a performance arena that they assisted in establishing and maintaining. Within that arena certain expressive rules defined the texture of the experience, rules familiar to many but by no means all of the audience—though even newcomers quickly got the drift. Like the laws that govern other species of language, these rules were less important as abstractions in themselves than as channels for some very focused social dynamics. As happens every night around the country, the kingdom of slam again held sway—just as it has and will whenever and wherever this tradition of competitive oral poetry is invoked and reinvoked. To a degree, March 30, 2001, at the Nuyorican was not only the "same" event as other Friday nights in that space but also the "same" as other slams in other cities that same night or other nights, or the "same" as the prior year's national competition in Providence or any other such event in any other city at any time. Virtually speaking, slam isn't one particular venue or moment but a frame of reference outside the clutches of place and time.

And how is this virtual arena invoked? Another way to ask the same question is to inquire about the keys to performance, the cues that alert performers and audiences and make slam what it is. Here, as with any oral poetry, we need to broaden our notion of keys beyond the original six features suggested by Richard Bauman, who himself cautioned against expecting universals. That night at the Nuyorican made it plain that the set of rules governing the competition served as a major key, linking this particular event to the ritual that also plays out in so many other times and places. All elements—the choosing of judges, the ordering of teams, the introductions, the scoring, and not least the audience's multileveled and active participation—were signals that created the experience, gave it recognizable shape, taught everyone present how to understand what was happening. Was every person exactly "on the same page" with the Dead Poets Team Slam? Of course not: prior experiences and myriad other factors will always necessarily make for a healthy variety in reception. But the rules helped to frame the event and create the performance, which was part of the meaning.

We also wouldn't be going far afield to observe that some of the features of the NPC slam (and of other slams) can be translated into Bauman's original terms. *Special codes* and *special formulas* were evident in the poets' language and gestures, in emcee Nathan P's self-sacrifice and whimsical hosting, in the patterns surrounding the scoring process, and in the audience's chants for 10's and other participatory actions. *Figurative language* and *parallelism* abounded in the slammers' own poems; they also took on individualized aural emphasis in the voicings of dead poets' works. Every aspect of the slam ritual was in effect an *appeal to tradition,* whether implicit or explicit, even when the poem itself was transparently antitraditional. Because of these cues—no matter whose system of terminology we use to describe them—the event of slam poetry happened. Because it was immediate and face-to-face, it left no choice but to join the audience. Although there's clearly no substitute for actually being there, I hope this re-creation of the NPC Dead Poets Team Slam has helped you imagine that you were. If so, welcome to the performance arena.

Further Reading

History of the Slam movement: "Timeline" (Glazner 2000: 235–37); "An Incomplete History of Slam" (<http://www.e-poets.net/library/slam/diaspora/html>)

National Poetry Slam: Poetry Slam International Web site (<http://www.poetryslam.com>)

Nuyorican Poets Cafe: Algarín and Holman 1994; Roach 2000; Nuyorican web page (<http://www.nuyorican.org>)

Rules: Glazner 2000: 13–14

Textual collections: Bonair-Agard et al. n.d.; Glazner 2000

Video performances: Devlin 1998; Hemstreet et al. 2000; film involving slam, Levin 1998 (winner of 1998 Camera d'Or prize, Cannes Film festival), Stratton and Wozencraft 1998 (screenplay and filmmakers' journals)

*   *   *

The Odyssey *(Ancient Greece)*

Category: Voices from the Past

Approach: Immanent Art

Most of us need no introduction to Homer's *Odyssey*. Whether through hearing the tale during childhood storytelling or reading it ourselves at some stage, we're well enough acquainted with at least the main outlines of the plot. For that reason—as well as an ulterior motive that will soon be divulged—I choose to start by sketching the outline of another story, one that will sound curiously familiar. This "other story" is hard to pin down: it exists in hundreds of versions from central Asia to western Europe, from the Balkans and Russia to the Turkic-speaking nations along the Silk Roads, from medieval England to modern-day Balochistan. It's so broadly distributed across space and time, in short, that it must be extremely old.[15] Of course, if we remember how late in our species-year even the ancient Greek texts appear (December 19 or afterward), we can see that there's more than ample time for such a story to have crisscrossed the faces of Asia and Europe. Stories travel easily as oral poetry, taking ready advantage of bilingual speakers and intercultural contacts.[16] At any rate, here's the tale, which has been dubbed the Return Song.

A young but already accomplished hero is called away suddenly to take part in a major military expedition. He leaves behind his wife (either pregnant or with their child already born) or fiancée and joins a composite fighting force under the command of a regional or national leader. As a result of the war, he is detained for many years, held prisoner by a powerful enemy until an equally powerful female figure intercedes. She or her male counterpart manages to free him, and the hero begins an extraordinarily difficult journey homeward, during which he is attacked or threatened by various inimical figures. Often he barely escapes with his life. This hero eventually reaches his home community in an impenetrable disguise and proceeds to test the loyalty of his family, servants, friends, and colleagues by falsely reporting his own demise and gauging their reactions. He also enters an athletic competition against his mate's suitors, who are intent on taking over his household, and, although his depleted physical condition makes it seem unlikely, he defeats all comers. Soon his wife or fiancée will see through his disguise, recognizing him via some sign only she can interpret. At that point the suitors flee or are put to death and the hero resumes his position as husband/fiancé, father, and master of the household.

Or maybe he doesn't. As we look across the variety of stories from different times and cultures that follow this basic blueprint, we see two roads diverging. One of them—let's call it the route toward Penelope—leads to a happy ending, the result with which circumstance has made most of us more familiar. The other path heads in exactly the opposite direction: toward an unfaithful wife/fiancée who has plotted against her mate and has perhaps already replaced the long-absent hero with someone else. Let's think of that road as the route toward Clytemnestra. In the well-collected traditions, those like South Slavic that preserve not one but hundreds of Return Songs, both outcomes are common. What's more, they're exhaustive; all the Return stories follow either one pathway or the other. The particular heroes and heroines may change, as may the commander of the composite force, the specific nature of the hero's trials, the assortment of athletic contests, the place-names, the list of characters whose loyalty is tested, and so on, but inevitably the story tracks toward a single determining moment: the mutual recognition between the two mates and the revelation of whether the hero has returned to a Penelope-type or a Clytemnestra-type. Everything hangs in the balance until that secret's out in the open.

Two additional details will help us assimilate this story to the *Odyssey* and read it via Immanent Art. First, the story *conventionally* starts in the middle, with the hero mired in captivity and unable to reach his homeland. It's only later that we learn about how he got there—through a flashback, like Books 9–12 of the *Odyssey*, during which the hero tells the Phaeacians of his troubles since leaving Troy. This "inside-out" sequence and flashback aren't flaws or departures from the logical order; they're expected strategies for the Return Song. That's how you tell this kind of tale.

Second, the real fulcrum of the narrative turns out to be the heroine, not the hero. Once embarked on such a journey, the male protagonist in this kind of story will always reach home eventually; it may take many years, and he may have to overcome a host of obstacles, but he will finally arrive. That much is certain and expectable. But it's by no means certain whom he'll find when he gets there. The female protagonist remains *conventionally* in doubt, ever a mystery, inexplicable in her inscrutability even to those closest to her. And why not? It's precisely that principled guile that has held the suitors at bay during her husband's long absence. She can't afford to cave in trustingly to a man claiming to be her missing mate until she is certain he's the one. And that's where the recognition trick comes in.

What does Immanent Art have to say about this situation, both as a general story-pattern or "word" in itself and with special application to the *Odyssey*? How can we proceed if we have only one Return Song from ancient Greece? There are a couple of clues. One of them is the constant reference that the *Odyssey* makes to the alternate outcome of this type of song, contrasting the triangles of Odysseus-Penelope-Telemachos and Agamemnon-Clytemnestra-Orestes no fewer than nine times over the course of the poem. Another is the cryptic description we have of a lost epic, the *Nostoi*, which may well have portrayed the alternate ending to the Return Song pattern. Still a third is the testimony of Agamemnon's ghost in Book 24 (lines 192–202), who speaks of a "pleasing song" about Penelope versus a "song of loathing" about Clytemnestra. All of these clues hint at Homer's and his tradition's awareness of the other outcome, the discovery of an unfaithful wife. Most of all, however, the close congruency between the international paradigm of the Return Song and the sole surviving exemplar from ancient Greece, the *Odyssey*, urges the comparison.[17]

Reading the *Odyssey* from this comparative perspective solves any number of problems that have nagged literary scholars for centuries. First, the matter of its nonchronological order of events and the overworked bromide that epics must "begin in the middle" need revisiting. The *Odyssey* doesn't begin in the middle; as a Return Song, it begins idiomatically, where it should. The flashback and "skewed" sequence of events are in fact the norm for this kind of oral poem. Anything else, including straight chronology, would be unidiomatic. As competent readers, we must expect both the "inside-out" order and the flashback in which the hero rehearses his fate.

Second, the argument over when or whether Penelope knew this or that should be recast into an active appreciation of her stubbornness and, yes, even duplicity. From the point of view of the Return Song as an international story-pattern, it's the woman—not her husband or fiancé—who determines the story's path. It's she who controls the narrative crossroads. Her heroism consists precisely in delaying the inevitable, refusing to acknowledge impending realities, sticking to her skepticism. It's that very uncertainty that has gotten her this far, and it's that same cleverness that will determine Odysseus's identity beyond doubt by posing the riddle about their unique bed. We may imagine that Penelope's name had powerful mythic resonance in the Greek tradition, and that no one doubted that she would prove herself as she did. On the other hand, her individual actions and qualities play out over a traditional map of expectation that points toward two opposite destinations. As always, the art of oral poetry draws from both individual and traditional sources (*Read both behind and between the signs*). She is Penelope *and* she is a Return Song heroine; both identities are important to "reading" her.

Reading the traditional implications of the *Odyssey* also means paying attention to levels of "words" other than the story-pattern. The approach through Immanent Art concerns itself equally with phrases, scenes, and story-patterns, seeking as far as possible to open up the traditional resources of "words" no matter how large or small. In the Sixth Word, for example, we traced the idiomatic meaning of "green fear" as supernaturally inspired fear, and in the Fifth Word we saw how the Lament scene functions as an active cue for interpreting the interaction between Andromache and Hektor in the sixth book of the *Iliad*. We've also highlighted the indexical nature of naming formulas—"swift-footed Achilles," "much-suffering Odysseus," and the like—in various places throughout this book. As additional examples of how traditional structures mean, I now offer two small bytes of phraseology and a pervasive narrative pattern, all of which play a role in both of the Homeric epics. If we listen to their idiomatic overtones as well as their literal values, they will help us read.

The first witness couldn't seem more insignificant. The small phrase "But come . . ." in either the singular (*all' age*) or plural imperative (*all' agete*) handily fills a metrical slot at the outset of the Homeric line, but hardly appears to mean much more than any reputable dictionary would stipulate. It's well to remember, however, that *The best companion for reading oral poetry is an* un*published dictionary.* Over each and every one of its 154 instances in the *Iliad*, *Odyssey,* and Homeric Hymns this unassuming phrase idiomatically signals (1) a change in direction within a speech and (2) a change in mode by introducing a command or prayer in the form "Come do something" or "Come let us do something." The audience fluent in the Homeric register won't gloss over this miniscule "word" as a throwaway but will understand it as a rhetorical signal that helps prescribe what's to come and how we're to react. In *Odyssey* 1 (224) it divides and integrates Athena's two-part speech as she follows her brief compliment on Telemachos's lineage with some challenging questions about the suitors' out-of-control behavior in Ithaca. At the other end of the poem (24.171), the same cue provides a traditional transition between two distinct but interrelated moments in a crucial speech by Penelope. First she rebuts the disguised Odysseus's criticism of her stubbornness, and then she orders the old nurse to do the impossible—to make up the olive-tree bed outside the bedchamber. As such, "But come . . ." shows a high degree of communicative economy, with a very small part standing for a much larger, more detailed whole. It is a tiny sign, to be sure, and a quite general one, but it effectively points the way toward a deeper, truer reading.

The second sound-byte, again just two of our words and one of Homer's "words" in length, is the frequent expression "sweet sleep." The most common form of the phrase in Greek is *glukus hupnos,* which regularly combines with a verb to fill the second half of a hexameter line. Oral-formulaic theory understands "sweet sleep" as a metrically convenient way to name "sleep," nothing more or less. But Immanent Art asks whether this recurrent byte might also harbor some additional implication, something poetically as well as mechanically useful to the composing poet and his audience or readership. And indeed, if we gather together all of its occurrences, an idiomatic meaning does emerge. When characters give themselves over to the inevitability of sleep, they open up a double possibility: the sweet release that will result in (often much-needed) refreshment or, just as likely, vulnerability to great danger. Within the Homeric register "sweet sleep" is like a fork in the road; it presents the two alternatives without choosing between them. That choice, and the resolution of tension that will accompany it, are left to the unfolding of the story. At *Odyssey* 9.333, for instance, Odysseus recounts how he and his comrades planned to attack the Cyclops "when sweet sleep might reach him." The Cyclops's rest may appear to be simply a wine-induced slumber, a respite offering refreshment, but it will also leave him vulnerable to eventual blinding. It's a sleep that releases Polyphemos but also costs him dearly, and Homer is able to economically portray both sides of that reality with a single modest-sized stroke. Irony takes root from traditional implication.

The final "word" to be examined here is a scene that recurs no fewer than thirty-two times in the *Odyssey* and three times in the *Iliad*. It may be very brief or hundreds of lines long, but the Feast always includes a host and guest(s), the seating of the guest(s), and some set of actions that constitute feasting. That much is expectable, but what always precedes and follows the ritual is not—unless you happen to be fluent in the Homeric register, that is. No matter who hosts or who attends, no matter where the event occurs or under what special conditions, the feast conventionally leads from an obvious, preexisting problem to an effort at mediation of that problem. Some initial disruption gives way to a solution or at least an attempt at solution. Such are the traditional implications of this typical scene.

A few examples will illustrate how this immanent meaning comes into play, how *Oral poetry works like language, only more so*. When Athena arrives in *Odyssey* 1, posing as Odysseus's old friend Mentes, she finds Telemachos and the household in sorry shape. The suitors have ransacked the place, and the boy seems powerless to stop their depredations. After the feast, however, just when the well-schooled audience or readership should expect some improvement, Athena advises Telemachos to undertake his mini-odyssey to Pylos and Sparta. It is partly as a result of this trip that he matures from a helpless boy to a more self-sufficient man who will attempt to take charge of his father's affairs and eventually join in visiting revenge on the usurpers. Or consider the two feasts conducted by Circe in *Odyssey* 5. In the first of these she hosts Hermes, who after they break bread delivers Zeus's message that Odysseus must finally be freed. Circe, intransigent until now, accedes. In the second feast she hosts Odysseus himself. After their ritual runs its course, she warns the hero of the hardships that lie before him and the next day helps him build a raft, donates provisions, and passes along some tips on star navigation. In both cases a feast provides a narrative bridge from problem to mediation. Odysseus is still far from home and Poseidon's terrors await him, but the traditional signal promises progress toward Ithaca at last.

Reading the *Odyssey* as oral poetry can open up new riches in the epic. More specifically, the lens of Immanent Art can disclose perspectives that textual parallax has obscured or even caused to vanish. Sometimes the traditional implications of story-pattern, typical scene, and phrase simply reinforce what we can discover through other approaches. We should expect and welcome such congruency. Sometimes, as in the examples cited above, awareness of how the traditional register means can help us understand this remarkable work in more depth. If we can better grasp Penelope's brilliant ambiguity, more faithfully understand what hangs in the balance with "sweet sleep," and learn what to expect when a feast begins, then the effort we expend to learn Homer's special poetic language will be well rewarded. Our gains will always be measured and partial, since we'll always be non-native speakers working with fragmentary, fossilized records of a once-living tradition. But we can read the *Odyssey* better if we realize and put into practice the powerful truth that *The art of oral poetry emerges* through *rather than* in spite of *its special language.*

Further Reading

Formulaic phraseology: Parry 1971; Edwards 1986, 1988; Foley 1990: chap. 4, 1999: chap. 7
Homer and Immanent Art: Foley 1991, 1999
Homer and oral poetry: Lord 1960; G. Nagy 1996b; Foley 1997; R. Martin 1998
Return Song: Foley 1999: chap. 5
Typical scenes: Edwards 1992

* * *

The Siri Epic *(Contemporary India, Karnataka Province)*

Category: Oral Performance
Approach: Performance theory

In December 1990 a team of Finnish and Tulu folklorists under the direction of Lauri Honko completed a videotaped recording of a 15,683–line performance of the *Siri Epic* by the singer and possession priest Gopala Naika. Eight years later a three-volume monument to that performance appeared, containing a complete text in the original Tulu with a facing-page English translation (Honko et al. 1998a, b) and a companion volume that provides a rich context for the event as well as important discussions of comparative oral epic and a digest of previous fieldwork projects (Honko 1998). Together this massive record constitutes a benchmark for studies of oral epic performance.

Most readers of *HROP* will be unfamiliar with the *Siri Epic*. To give some idea of its movement and scope, I excerpt from the introduction to the first volume (Honko et al. 1998a: xv–xvi):[18]

> The Siri epic is named after its main protagonist, an exemplar of womanhood and a fighter for the female and familial values in a particular matrilineal society with predominantly male executive power. The story covers three generations of remarkable women, Siri and her descendants, and thus belongs to the category of biographical epic. Only one man, Siri's son Kumara, rises to the level of the female protagonists, the seven women who are transformed into divinities at the end, when the great narrative of the past is transformed into a religious institution of today. Most other men, with the possible exclusion of the wise grandfather type, are not depicted as heroes but in rather critical terms, as sources of tension and conflict in human relations.
>
> That heroes are heroines and that violence has no role in the epic, set the Siri story apart from most epics in India and elsewhere. The epic tension, a necessity for a great narrative, is created through confrontations between gods and humans, men and women, and, quite importantly, between women themselves. Religion and rural caste society are part and parcel of the story. Yet the focus is on the fate of the individual and her emancipation, and even when conservative values prevail, the epic criticises social injustice and introduces social innovation.

So the *Siri Epic* is more than a story. In fact, the extent to which this oral epic serves a social, religious function in the lives of the Tulu people in general and of Gopala Naika in particular cannot be overestimated. As opposed to holding oral poetry at arm's length, as we Western text-consumers do when we segregate it as "entertainment," the poet, followers, and audience quite literally embody the tale's characters and actions in separate ritual gatherings. The fieldwork team documents in great detail how participants are possessed by the divinities Siri and Kumara in a festival that lasts from late evening until the following dawn.[19] During this complex and multilayered event, possession grips scores of women and fewer men, as the myth underlying the *Siri Epic* becomes an active and directive frame of reference. Very importantly for our purposes, this is an event wholly detached in form and purpose from Gopala Naika's one-man oral epic performance recorded on videotape by the Honko team. They are two distinctly different expressions—the one a single narrator's solo rendition within the Tulu epic genre and the other a group experience involving rites of passage, possession, and an entire ritual drama. Nonetheless, both events draw their meaning from the story of Siri and her children. Both are anchored to the same mythic fastness.

For our present purposes we will concentrate on the oral epic poem, and most closely on its performance. But we'll also have something to say about alternate performance contexts and the meanings they engender toward the end of this section. Indeed, the power of these various contexts illustrates how *True diversity demands diversity in frame of reference.*

Performance theory maintains that "being there" makes a difference to the nature of any communication. It also holds that performance is keyed by tell-tale signals used by the poet to alert the audience, to instruct them how to "read." Several of Bauman's keys are present in the *Siri Epic* as regular features of the discourse, among them special formulas, figurative language, and an appeal to tradition.[20]

Special formulas are especially obvious and functional. The formulaic phrases used to summon the main heroine Siri, for example, echo through the narrative in much the same way as do Homer's (and his tradition's) "swift-footed Achilles" or "goddess gray-eyed Athena." Here are a few of her coded names: "Siri of Satyamaalooka" ("Siri of the great world of truth," far the most common), "Siri of Addolige," and "Siri of Bañjolige." The latter two describe her as connected with mythical places, but that's not really the point. All three of them are tried-and-true pathways to the same traditional reality, examples of the "special formulas" that remind the audience and readership what sort of communication is underway and bring the protagonist to center stage in idiomatic fashion. Geography—even divine geography—is less important than the word-power of convention.

Such phrases can serve other purposes as well. Some are extremely modest, like the speech introduction or closure that shows its stability and also its flexibility in the following pair of instances:

> To the reply a reply, to the response a response the Brahman gives: (5213; a speech follows)

> Thus to the reply a reply, to the response a response
> Siri of Satyamaalooka is giving in the assembly court. (4372–73; a speech precedes)

Likewise, with great regularity Gopala Naika describes "the beauty of his/her coming," using this uncomplicated phrase as a kind of traditional index. Once again, there seems to be no special, focused overtone associated with this composite "word"; it's applied to a full spectrum of characters and events regardless of the nature and purpose of their journey. We read it best, that is, as neither merely literal nor simply structural, but rather as the modest traditional idiom it is. It plugs the character in question into the idiomatic network.

Or consider the small prayer "Naraayina oo Naraayina," which uses one of the god Vishnu's names and recurs with great frequency. Far more than simply a line-filler or a spiritual expostulation, it regularly marks a boundary between episodes or cantos, much like a paragraph break or other textual signal for ending-plus-transition. Or take one of many cases in which the whole proves significantly greater than its parts. The individual words "sooya" and "maaya" literally name the human world and the other world, respectively; that's what you'll find in a dictionary. But taken together as a phrase or single "word" in performance, "sooya, maaya" amounts to "an expression of bewilderment" (890). These simple bytes of diction, used regularly by Gopala Naika as he makes his traditional poem, show how *The best companion for reading oral poetry is an* un*published dictionary*.

Two additional examples of special formulas will help furnish a sense of the spectrum of meaning encoded in such keys. Especially resonant are phrases or "words" such as "fire of the child's mouth" (3020, e.g.) and the exclamation "Alas, what a sin! Alas, what a shame!" The former indexes the ravenous hunger felt by a pregnant woman due to the metabolic strain of gestation, as well as looks forward to the desire-feast that is socially and spiritually prescribed as its ritual remedy. As such, the phrase also implicates the reality of pregnancy and the woman's life-pattern of birth, betrothal, puberty rite, wedding, and childbirth, and does so in a powerfully economical way. Gopala Naika "speaks volumes" through these few syllables, drawn from the wordhoard of the traditional register.

The same can be said for the latter couplet—"Alas, what a sin! Alas, what a shame!"—that recurs throughout the *Siri Epic* to signal cataclysmic changes of fortune. In the Ajjeru subepic, for example, Siri, returning from her clothes-washing to find Kumara's cradle empty, marks the seriousness of the situation with this phraseological sign (3700). She repeats the same telltale exclamation a few lines later when she cannot locate Ajjeru, her child's caretaker while she is gone, in his customary place on a sleeping cot (3714). Indeed, this formula recurs dozens of times in many different narrative situations, as when Siri's co-wife Saamu Alvedi bemoans her "sister's" lack of a place to give birth to her second child (7753). Whatever the particular circumstance, "Alas, what a sin! Alas, what a shame!" frames the problem as a life-threatening or at least socially disastrous one, embedding the uniqueness of the individual moment in a timeless traditional context. Such is the word-power of that key.

Other signposts or cues also guide the reader, signaling performance and focusing reception. *Figurative language* abounds in the *Siri Epic,* from start to finish, but perhaps no sound-byte is more resonant than the simile. By their nature, similes are the furthest thing from utilitarian devices: they don't advance the narrative but rather dwell lyrically on a moment or person or event. In oral poetry like the Tulu epic, or indeed like Homer's *Iliad,* they serve another end as well. In addition to their own lyrical beauty, and apart from the particular poem in which they're embedded, they add luster to the oral performance. Using an expectable strategy, one associated with the telling of the Siri myth at great narrative length, they affirm the connection between this performance—happening here and now—and the tradition of performances from which it stems. If we picture the poet's performative strategies as a collection of verbal "keys" on a circular ring, the simile must be one of the readiest ways to unlock the wordhoard. Here's an example of such an extended comparison, remarkable both for its individual artistry and for its indexical force. In speaking of Saamu and Siri, co-wives to Koḍsaava Alva, the singer conceives of them as follows (7941–45):

> . . . Saamu and Siri were,
> Naraayina, like twin stars arisen in the sky,
> like two young serpents born in a serpent-dwelling.
> Naraayina oo Naaraayina oo.
> Like Raama, Lokṣmana, like the children born in the belly of one
> mother.

Similes illustrate how trademark stylistic devices can also key performance.

A third key that presents itself very prominently in the *Siri Epic* falls under the heading of *appeals to tradition.* Via this signal, either implicitly or explicitly, performers cite the source to which this (or any) instance refers. Before Gopala Naika begins singing the Siri epic narrative itself, he introduces it with a series of three invocations. These are substantial and important preludes, stretching altogether to fully 563 lines and in their content illustrating once again how the story is woven into the religious experience of the society and especially of the individual singer. They're the furthest thing from a detachable artifact. The first invocation, called "The Installation of the Seat" (1–256), consists of invitations to a variety of spiritual beings and prayers for human needs. The second and third, "The Seating of the Divine Assembly" (257–470) and "To the Divinities Salute!" (471–563), name the invitees and the places from which they have come to be present at this feast.

But what function do invocations actually serve? They aren't part of the story itself (at least from our external point of view), so are they truly necessary or simply an optional embellishment? Fortunately, the fieldwork team was able to determine answers to such questions with some precision, and their comments, based on the singer's own observations, are revealing (Honko 1998: xlii): "The invocations are, as Gopala Naika insists, part of the 'whole' epic, not so much plot-wise but as a religious commentary on the ranking of epic personages among divinities of various kinds." Only if we insist on tearing the *Siri Epic* out of the natural context in which it exists, only if we insist on making a performance into a text, only if we insist on a blatant misreading based on irrelevant models, do the invocations become inessential. Whatever we may think of his practice from our often irrelevant perspective, it's well to remember that this is how the singer chooses to begin. It's he who decides to start his performance with this version of the appeal to tradition, which does its job by acknowledging and celebrating the story's most essential network. The invocations are a good lesson in at least two respects: they illustrate the social and religious embedding of the narrative and they show us that "preliminary" material—not unlike the proems to the South Slavic epics and Homer's *Iliad* and *Odyssey*—are indeed part of the performance. Why? Because the singer and his tradition make them so.

But do things always work out this way? Is the story always told in this fashion? Granted, the power of performance to determine what goes on is substantial and irrefutable. Typically, oral performance varies within limits, but that variability isn't willy-nilly; it's programmatic and rule-governed. Just so, the fieldwork team presents evidence that Gopala Naika's epic narration has a discernible consistency to it, as glimpsed both within the videotaped *Siri Epic* and by comparison to an earlier dictation.[21] As a performance genre, the epic reveals a fundamental traditional regularity. But what if the Siri story also existed in alternate performance contexts?

In fact, Tulu epic stories do show a variety of performative contexts, and what happens in the particular arena depends on the applicable rules. The fieldwork team lists no fewer than nine distinct performance arenas, and each of them conditions what takes place within its boundaries.[22] Among the different possibilities are: small parts of the epic (never the whole) sung by men during ancestor worship, selections intoned during men's work songs (palm-tree tapping) or women's work songs (plucking rice paddy seedlings), and appropriate excerpts sung by women on the day before a wedding. Each is sui generis, using the epic material in a way all its own. The *Siri Epic* thus serves the community as a "mythical charter."[23] Under its more-than-textual authority, diverse performance contexts focus the implied Siri story in a variety of ways according to the particular social and religious event. Thus the fieldwork team reports the separate, free-standing dramatization of a scene from the epic involving the twins Abbaya and Daaraya and the board-game of *cennε*, for example, as well as the panoply of ritual activities involved with the festival at Nidgal cited in note 19.[24] To borrow a term from another of our three "ways of reading," the Siri story remains immanent to each of these other performance contexts, active via implication in each milieu, even as the contexts themselves change. The variety of real-life settings and the distinctive rules that govern each context are further evidence for the determinative role of performance. "Being there" certainly does matter.

Further Reading

Context (*Siri Epic* and theory): Honko 1998; Rai 1996
Structure and meaning: Honko 2000b; Honko and Honko 2000
Text and translation: Honko et al. 1998a, b
Other Indian oral epics: Blackburn et al. 1989; Parthasarathy 1993; J. Smith 1991
Women's oral traditions from South Asia: Raheja 1997

* * *

The Song of Roland *(Medieval France)*

Category: Voices from the Past
Approach: Immanent Art
The *Song of Roland* chronicles the death of Charlemagne's nephew Roland and the decimation of their comrades and troops at the Battle of Roncevaux in the Pyrenees. The story stems from an actual historical event, securely dated to 778, while its earliest and finest poetic recasting is the Oxford manuscript apparently written some three hundred years later. The *Roland* is one of about a hundred surviving Old French epics, or *chansons de geste,* that fall into three major groups or families: the cycle of the King (Charlemagne), the cycle of William of Orange, and the so-called Epics of Revolt. Behind these manuscript-prisoned epics stands a tradition of oral composition and transmission by singers of tales, called *jongleurs,* although clerical and scribal activity intervened in various ways between oral performance and written record. The name Turoldus appears in the Oxford manuscript of the *Roland;* some see him as its author.

Except for these few precious facts, little is beyond dispute. Most pertinently for us, the precise relationship between the Oxford *Roland* and its originative oral tradition cannot be determined. Paul Zumthor has suggested an ever-evolving train of oral performances and texts, a continuous process he calls *mouvance,* as the complex genesis of poems like the *Roland.*[25] If he's right, then the fieldworker's two-part presumption of a performance converted into a text may be a vast oversimplification. Whatever the case, because the Oxford *Roland* both derives in some fashion from an oral tradition and retains structures and textures typical of oral poetry, we must be careful not to misread it as a silent, tradition-less text. Given these considerations, and mindful of avoiding the baby-with-the-bathwater error, we assign the *Roland* to our category of Voices from the Past. We know it only as a manuscript dating from about 1100, but it's without doubt an oral poem.

If that's the case, so what? How do we read it? The first step is to choose an appropriate "way of reading," and to various degrees all three approaches we've studied would qualify. Performance Theory works best when we have reliable information about just how an oral poem was performed—not poetic, idealized description from within this or a parallel poem but firsthand, unembroidered observation of what really went on within the tradition.[26] We seldom have such ethnographic information for Voices from the Past, and the *Roland* is no exception to the rule. Still, although scholars have jousted for decades over the performance context of Old French *chansons de geste* that have reached us in manuscript, we shouldn't neglect what evidence or theories exist concerning oral performance in medieval France. Questions about the *jongleur*'s own divisions or "sessions" in the performance, the role of the instrument (the *viele*), and the performance keys typical of Old French epic are certainly worthy avenues of inquiry.[27] Likewise, ethnopoetics offers a chance to re-script the received manuscript according to what we can discover of its natural make-up, to highlight the terms in which the poem presents itself. Here the features of assonating decasyllabic lines, stanza-like *laisses,* and larger divisions demand our attention. Even if these initiatives don't lead to final answers, they'll help lift the poem off the page and give it voice.

But let's ask primarily how the approach through Immanent Art can help us read the *Roland.* Scholars like Jean Rychner and Joseph Duggan long ago established the existence of oral-formulaic "words" in the poem. The hundred-odd surviving *chansons de geste* collectively show that Old French epic tradition depended heavily upon formulaic diction and typical scenes as building blocks. Formulas tend to be a decasyllabic line in length (not unlike the *guslar*'s line-long "words"), and the recurrent scenes follow regular patterns. But these tale-telling bytes are more than well-formed pieces in the *jongleur*'s Lego set; they also carry the weight and force of idiomatic meaning. Some are modest and workaday bytes, like the boilerplate introductions to speeches; others resonate with associations. Together they constitute a register with traditional implications, and it's our responsibility to learn to read that register as best we can.

Take the formal lament for the dead as an example.[28] The seven instances of this scene in the *Roland* are each based on the same sequence of six elements: a link between finding the corpse and initiating the dirge, direct address of the fallen warrior, a prayer, a statement of praise, external signs of mourning, and inward grief. Immanent Art sees this pattern not as a necessary evil or a straight-jacket forced on the poet by the demanding circumstances of composition in performance, but as a special case of language, a focused way of speaking. The six-part skeleton provides a guide not only for the poet but also for the reader or audience, a shared signal that has endemic expressive advantages for all involved. Of course, each recurrence of the lament varies somewhat, with one devoted to Roland, two to Oliver, one to Turpin, and three to a large group of knights. Speakers change as well, as do numerous other aspects of setting and placement within the story as a whole. Indeed, it's that very plasticity that gives this and other traditional structures their strength and word-power. In short, we recognize a familiar gambit: the same variation-within-limits strategy that lies at the basis of all language and so fundamentally at the core of many oral poetries—which *work like language, only more so.* The reader uses the outline to process the details, the familiar frame to enclose the individual portrait.

What difference does it make to speak the *Roland* poet's language instead of defaulting to ours? We can answer that question most succinctly with another question: what difference does two-way fluency make to any verbal exchange? At the very least, it enables a basic level of communication. Just so, at the very least these large "words" create a performance arena by alerting (and re-alerting) the reader or audience to the register and overall context in which the poem takes voice. They offer an invitation to enter the performance arena and to communicate with unmatched economy. "Expect a certain style," they caution, "and understand the language on its own terms. Don't take it simply at literal face value." Moreover, these large "words" may foster exchange in other, more focused ways. Depending upon the reader's fluency in that way of speaking, they can also bear traditional implications of many different sorts. If both the poet and the audience or reader are speaking the same language, then the opening strains of a lament will signal the actions to come. The first few notes forecast the melody to follow. The map points the way. In this fashion the situation-specific uniqueness of each dirge can play out against the generic traditional background. We can *read both behind and between the signs.*

The same is true of smaller "words," that is, of the frequently recurrent formulas that the *Roland* poet employs to tell his tale. By using the poet's and tradition's cognitive units for our own reading (by seeing the forest as opposed to its trees), we aren't subscribing to a mechanical disassembly of the *Roland.* Rather we're viewing the formulas for what they are: manifestations of an ongoing, idiomatic language that correspond not to one another but to verbal predispositions. Because they recur rather than repeat, they serve as signals bearing more-than-literal meaning. Patterned language need not be a hindrance; it can offer unique expressive advantages.

We can gain a perspective on that distinction by confronting a famous problem in *Roland* studies. Here's the line in question: "Roland is worthy and Oliver is wise" ("Rollant est proz e Oliver est sage" [line 1093]).[29] One strain of literary criticism holds that this proverbial-sounding verse crystallizes a salient contrast between the two heroes, epitomizing the typological opposition between Roland the heroic and rash versus Oliver the equally heroic but more judicious. This two-word capsule characterization—*proz* versus *sage*—does in fact seem to match their contrasting battlefield behavior: while Oliver urgently counsels his comrade to sound the oliphant, or horn, to call for aid from Charlemagne's troops, Roland's pride keeps him from doing so until it's too late. According to this train of thought, Roland the "worthy" should have listened to his foil, Oliver the "wise," and line 1093 embodies their distinguishing qualities in miniature.

But as apt as this perspective may appear, it amounts to a misreading of the line on at least two levels. First, what follows this supposed "chestnut" goes a long way toward erasing the supposed "worthy" versus "wise" distinction by emphasizing their sameness:

> Both have amazing courage,
> When they are on horseback and armed,
> They shall not avoid battle even if it means death;
> Both counts are worthy and their words noble.

On a second level, the dynamic opposition of Roland and Oliver in this verse dissolves when we consider that it depends on words instead of "words." The minimal unit in a formulaic diction is customarily a formula, but "worthy" and "wise" fall below that minimum. However faithfully we as modern text-advocates may respect the boundaries of dictionary items and white space, we can't insist on imposing irrelevant frames of reference on oral poetry. We can't deconstruct "words" beyond their ability to mean. Whereas such smaller units make sense to a poet and readership who are trading in that verbal currency, they don't qualify as meaning-bearing signals in the traditional register of the *Roland*. In the end, the literary perspective on line 1093 singles out parts of a "word"—the logical equivalent of syllables or phonemes—as evidence for reading, and that just isn't sustainable. Furthermore, "Roland is worthy and Oliver is wise" is a unique line in the poem; there's absolutely nothing to support the hypothesis that any of its possible senses—of either its parts or its whole—is in some way proverbial. If we want to paint a portrait of Roland versus Oliver as rash versus wise, we'll need to look elsewhere for evidence. Line 1093 won't fit the bill.

Instead of trying to balance oral poetry on the head of a textual pin, Immanent Art seeks to read poems like the *Roland* on their own terms. Consider a formulaic phrase that recurs four times and is clearly involved in a network of associations. Here are the four instances:

With them came Count Roland
And worthy and noble *Oliver.*　　　　　　　*E Oliver, li proz e li* gentilz.
(174–75)

"His nephew Count Roland will be there, I know,
And worthy and reliable *Oliver.*"　　　　　*E Oliver, li proz e li* curteis.
(575–76)

"Yesterday the brave knight Roland was slain
And worthy and honorable *Oliver.*"　　　　*E Oliver, li proz e li* vaillanz.
(3185–86)

"My nephew, whom you will never see again,
And worthy and reliable *Oliver.*"　　　　　*E Oliver, li proz e li* curteis.
(3754–55)

The first point to stress is that in these lines it's Oliver—not Roland—who is presented as "worthy" (*proz*). Moreover, it's Oliver—not Roland—who is characterized in that way recurrently and formulaically. As opposed to a unique line that we have to dissect in order to ferret out evidence that finally isn't admissible, here we have an idiomatic attribution of "worthiness" not to Roland but to his supposed foil, Oliver.

Two additional aspects of this group of lines are worth noting because they illustrate fundamental principles of the register: variation within limits and networked implications. The italics indicate how this multiform phrase operates; it amounts to a "word" with one substitutable increment, a two-syllable adjective. At the surface of the poem it looks much like an algebraic equation, with one constant and one variable. The constant is "And worthy and . . . Oliver," and the variable is either "reliable" (twice), "noble," or "honorable." At least, that's a quick and easy way to glimpse the multiformity, the variation-within-limits character of the register. In reality, the linguistic processes underlying the fluent speaking of a register are not so mechanical. Language never is. But viewing the group of four lines as a substitution system helps to illustrate formulaic structure and to give us some perspective on the minimal unit of the decasyllabic line.

How about the four contexts in which this "word" appears? In the first (175), the emperor Charlemagne is convening his council of warriors to discuss the enemy King Marsile's treacherous offer to convey extraordinary riches and become a Christian convert if Charlemagne will only halt his Spanish campaign and go back to France. The second instance (576) occurs during the French knight Ganelon's treacherous counseling of Marsile to delay his attack on the French army until Charlemagne returns home, leaving behind his vulnerable rearguard under the command of Roland, Oliver, and others. By the time of the third recurrence (3186) the tragedy has happened, and the enemy prince Baligant and his son Malprimes are discussing the Saracen victory and the impending battle against Charlemagne. Finally, in the fourth instance (3755) Charlemagne asks his barons for a verdict on Ganelon's treason, which led to the deaths of Roland, Oliver, and so many others. The wide variety of these contexts shows how generally applicable traditional diction can be. Instead of being made only for a single, specific narrative nexus, this formulaic line obviously serves a panoply of different events, from "home-team" councils both before and after the great battle to enemy plotting by two different sets of adversaries.

What's more, the single line "And worthy and . . . Oliver" doesn't exist in a vacuum. It's linked in every case to mention of Oliver's comrade-in-arms Roland (lines 174, 575, 3185, and 3754) and to rest of the Twelve Peers, Charlemagne's inner circle of warrior-barons. The particular role played by Oliver and these other characters shifts radically—from offering counsel to being cited as potential victims to being acknowledged as the spur for Charlemagne's return attack to being mourned as Ganelon's prey—but their heroic collective remains unfractured even in death. The men who perished together so gloriously at Roncevaux have attained the kind of poetic afterlife we see in many oral narratives around the world, from the Homeric *Iliad* to the Tulu *Siri Epic.* Charlemagne himself was not among that rearguard force, nor does he appear in the small catalogue that recurs four times; to him is left the responsibility for vengeance. Oliver, Roland, and the others live on in oral poetry as an integral band of warriors, celebrated and memorialized individually, to be sure, but also remembered and portrayed collectively. They are preserved as a "word" in the *Roland,* and at their center lies a "word" about Oliver.

Whether the structure in question is formulaic diction or a typical scene, whether "worthy Oliver" or a formal lament, Immanent Art calls for attention to both idiomatic content and individual instances. At every level, the poet weaves together the warp of traditional structure, complete with its implications, and the woof of situation-specific context. At every level, both aspects of the process are central if we want to read in the poet's (and poetry's) own terms. For the *Roland* as for other oral poems, Immanent Art prescribes attention to both the story and the register in which that story is told, heard, and read.

Further Reading

Background and overviews: Brault 1978b; Taylor 2001; Vitz 1998

Editions: Brault 1978a (scholarly), 1984 (student-oriented, with facing-page English translation)

Medieval Hispanic epic: Duggan 1974, 1989; Webber 1986a, 1986b; Zemke 1998: 202–7
Oral-formulaic structure: Duggan 1969, 1973; Rychner 1955, 1958
Translations: Brault 1984; Burgess 1990; Goldin 1978; Harrison 1970

A Repertoire for Reading Oral Poetry

Together with the Four Scenarios that began this volume and with what's upcoming in the Eighth Word on the varied ecosystem of South Slavic oral genres, this Seventh Word has aimed at two targets. First, I have tried to hint at the enormous diversity of oral poetry around the world and throughout history. I say "hint at" because that's all we can aspire to do in such a limited space. The *HROP* Web page offers more leads, but the best possible reaction to the inevitable brevity of the sample here is for readers themselves to extend this volume's observations and principles to oral poetries with which they are acquainted. If oral poetry dwarfs written poetry in both size and variety—and it most certainly does—then that would seem the only viable strategy, the only way to continue building an answer to the question that has fueled the overall presentation: "How do we read oral poetry?" This initiative in turn implicates a spectrum of activities from collection, edition, and translation of Oral Performances and Voiced Texts all the way to rereading Voices from the Past and Written Oral Poetry. On the one hand we begin with fieldwork and events, and on the other we seek to reinvigorate poetry that has too long languished as mere texts. The very heterogeneity of our subject—its refusal to be pigeonholed by quick and easy definitions—will keep us busy and engaged.

I've also aimed at demonstrating the corresponding diversity of frames of reference necessary to the reading task. We can't go on appropriating oral poetries like colonial magistrates annexing territory for the crown. Simply put, they're someone else's territory. What's necessary at this point is to learn to read oral poetries on their own terms, not ours. The three approaches used in *HROP* offer a start, but let me caution against global applications just as carefully as against assuming a flat, uninteresting universality among the verbal arts of different cultures. If faithfully done, each reading will itself be a performance, an act that permits methodological variation within limits, that adjusts as it needs to for the sake of what it proposes to examine. Each act of reading will inevitably be different, even unique, though it may apply a familiar perspective and achieve recognizably similar results.

To close the Seventh Word with this emphasis on accommodating diversity within a repertoire for reading, let's turn once more to the Poor Reader's Almanac of *proverbs* from the Sixth Word. Here they are in schematic form:

Proverbs

1. Oral poetry works like language, only more so.
2. *Oralpoetry* is a very plural noun.
3. Performance is the enabling event, tradition is the context for that event.
4. The art of oral poetry emerges *through* rather than *in spite of* its special language.
5. The best companion for reading oral poetry is an *un*published dictionary.
6. The play's the thing (and not the script).
7. Repetition is the symptom, not the disease.
8. Composition and reception are two sides of the same coin.
9. Read both behind and between the signs.
10. True diversity demands diversity in frame of reference.

The five case studies can help put some flesh on the bones of these maxims. *Oral poetry works like language, only more so* reminds us that we're dealing not with a thing or a product, which language never is, but with a process. Texts may hypnotize us into thinking that the oral poetry they encode is static, but it isn't. What's more, that process brings into play an extensive network of more-than-literal meanings—the "more so" of this first *proverb*. We saw that Homer's "green fear" and *Siri Epic* poet Gopala Naika's "Alas, what a sin! Alas, what a shame!" both encode more than any available lexicon can capture, and that's of course the reason that *The best companion for reading oral poetry is an* un*published dictionary.* Likewise, we learned how a formal lament pattern underlies a variety of discrete situations in the Old French *Song of Roland,* framing a panoply of individual moments in terms of a shared pattern. It and so many other patterns and phrases are the best evidence that *The art of oral poetry emerges* through *rather than* in spite of *its special language.* From this it follows that for oral poets *Repetition is the symptom, not the disease.* Their recurrent language isn't slavishly limited or redundant, but connotatively explosive. Behind their spoken (and even written) poems lies the living expressive force of idiom, not the dead letters of cliché.

The Native American stories, whether from Zuni or Kaqchikel, taught us how to read via reperformance. That act of embodiment, which moves beyond textual encoding to living presence, exemplifies the reality that *The play's the thing (and not the script).* What's more, because ethnopoetics seeks to restore performative values that have accrued within a tradition of poem-making, it underlines the fact that *Performance is the enabling event, tradition is the context for that event.* Slam poetry, which doesn't really exist except in performance defined by a widely practiced, traditional set of expressive conventions, makes the same argument, as do the performance traditions of the Tibetan paper-singer and the South African praise-poet whom we met in Four Scenarios. Not incidentally, this *proverb* also sheds light on the false dichotomy of "traditional versus individual," one of the most pernicious and stubborn viruses to afflict the study of verbal arts, especially oral poetry. In short, we needn't make the impossible choice between the two or even indicate a preference: both belong to an indissoluble synergy. To put things in the form of an eleventh *proverb*, *Without a tradition there is no language; without a speaker there is only silence.*

Nor can oral poetry do without an audience, whether that audience is composed of listeners living in the moment or of far-removed readers aiming at the best fluency they can muster under the conditions. Slam poets ply their trade within a mesh of rules, sometimes explicitly articulated by the emcee, as in the Nuyorican Dead Poets Team Slam described above, but always in force whether announced or not. Homer's *Odyssey* survives only in manuscript, but calls on its reading audience to recognize the idiomatic underpinning of the Feast, the Return story-pattern, small bytes of resonant diction, and much more. The most basic lesson for the audience, then, is to do what the poets do—to speak the same language. And why? Proverbially put, because *Composition and reception are two sides of the same coin.* If we acknowledge the reciprocity of composer and audience, we can begin to understand "what else" readers of oral poetry must do, how they owe it to the medium to make themselves aware of the "more so" of idiom. At the same time, every performance—live or captured only on the page—will be unique; each poem and poet and audience and venue will be in some fashion unlike any other. For that reason, because we must be equally concerned with idioms and with the way they play out in the real time of the oral poem (or risk a reading that lacks depth), our vision must remain stereoscopic. We'll need to *Read both behind and between the signs.*

That Oralpoetry *is a very plural noun* can hardly be in doubt at this point. The First Word, not to mention the Four Scenarios and the Seventh Word, have provided copious evidence of its innate and bottomless diversity. If one hundred or fewer true literatures have ever existed and we struggle to contain their differences, then how much broader and deeper are the verbal arts of human culture at large? The real thrust of this *proverb* is thus not so much to reiterate that reality but to advocate that each oral poetry—whether Zuni narratives, Kaqchikel stories, slam poetry, the *Odyssey,* south Indian epic, Old French *chansons de geste,* or any other form—should be treated with respect for its uniqueness as well as for its convergence with other oral poems. Ways of reading must adapt to ways of speaking. That's another way of saying that *True diversity demands diversity in frame of reference.*

Notes

1. To the collection of examples below should be added the oral poetries addressed in Four Scenarios as well as the ecosystem of South Slavic oral poetry described in the Eighth Word. I have not included in this Word any separate examples of reading Written Oral Poetry, primarily because the methods are so similar to those applied to Voices from the Past. See further the example readings of the *Odyssey* and *The Song of Roland* below, as well as the discussion of Written Oral Poetry in the First Word.

2. See further <http://www.oraltradition.org>. The Post-Script to this volume briefly considers the possible future role of electronic media and hypertext in the more-than-textual representation of oral tradition.

3. For Native American novels, see Brill de Ramírez 1999; for African novels, Obiechina 1992 and Balogun 1995. Arundhati Roy's *The God of Small Things* (1997) is a prize-winning contemporary Indian novel that depends heavily on oral traditions associated with the *Ramayana* (in folk as well as Great Tradition versions).

4. Tedlock's methods and aims were discussed in the Fourth Word; see further Foley 1995a: esp. 67–75. For cultural and poetic context, see Tedlock's "Introduction" to the second edition (1999: xxi–xliv). For selections from the original Zuni performances as well as oral renditions of the English translations, see the Electronic Poetry Web site at the State University of New York at Buffalo (<http://epc.buffalo.edu/authors/tedlock>).

5. On the fascinating figure of Coyote among the many Native American peoples who tell his stories, see esp. Bright 1993. About a possible lesson encoded in the story, Peynetsa says (Tedlock 1999: 74): "It just teaches how the coyote is being very foolish. It doesn't teach anything like a human being might do."

6. See, e.g., Johnson 1992: 20–101 (a text of a performance of the Mali epic *Son-Jara;* explanation in Johnson 2000: 240).

7. The Bloom quotation is cited from Bonair-Agard et al. n.d.: 178, the Wolf quotation from Glazner 2000:11.

8. For more on the NPC, see its Web site (<http://www.nuyorican.org>) as well as Bonair-Agard et al. n.d. and Roach 2000; information on current and upcoming events is also available by telephone at 212–505–8183.

9. In what follows, the boldfaced photo designations between brackets indicate photographs of performers and audience that I took during the slam. They can be accessed on the *HROP* Web site.

10. On the gathering itself, see *Peoples Poetry Gathering* as well as the Web site at <http://www.peoplespoetry.org>. See also the home pages for City Lore (<http://www.citylore.org>) and Poets House (<http://www.poetshouse.org>).

11. On the National Poetry Slam, see esp. the Poetry Slam International Web site at <http://www.poetryslam.com>; also *Words on Fire,* the program for the 2000 event in Providence, Rhode Island.

12. See further Miner 1993, which offers brief descriptions and references to poetic contest in ancient Greek, Arabic, Celtic, Latin, German, Japanese, and other traditions.

13. According to National Poetry Slam rules, each poet must present only his or her own works. In this as in many other aspects, however, local rules allow great latitude.

14. A short biography of the poet, together with selected poems, is available from

the William Topaz McGonagall Appreciation Society in Dundee, Scotland (<http://www.taynet.co.uk/users/mcgon/default.htp#poems>).

15. For more details on the comparison, see Foley 1999: 115–67. On Return Songs in various traditions, see Foley 1999: 298, n. 2.

16. On a bilingual *guslar* able to perform epic songs in both South Slavic and Albanian (although preliterate in both languages), see Kolsti 1990.

17. The *Odyssey* is the sole surviving *epic* exemplar. See also the *Homeric Hymn to Demeter,* which features a double-cycle return involving Demeter and her daughter Persephone (Foley 1995a: 175–80).

18. See Honko 1998: 605–33 for a detailed synopsis of the entire epic.

19. See Honko 1998: 454–98 on "The Siri Festival in Nidgal."

20. *Special codes* are also present, for example in the special epic language used by Gopala Naika; the same is true of *parallelism,* evident in both the verse and scene structure of the performance. I do not find any occurrence of *disclaimer of performance,* but, as noted in the Third Word, any and all of Bauman's keys are tradition-dependent and genre-dependent rather than universal. Each oral poetry has its own set of constitutive signals.

21. Between October 1985 and March 1986, Gopala Naika dictated a version of the *Siri Epic* piecemeal to Chinnappa Gowda, who was later to become a member of the Finnish-Tulu project team. On that version of 8,538 lines, as opposed to the continuous, live videotaped performance of 15,683 lines that took place in December 1990, see Honko 1998: 257–60.

22. Honko 1998: 249.

23. Honko 1998: 447.

24. Honko 1998: 498: "The Siri festival in Nidgal turned out to be a lesson in ritual discourses. There was much less linear narrative singing of the epic than we had expected, even less than in the house daliya. Instead we found the presence of the mental text and the basic myth in everything that was said and done during the ritual lasting from late evening until dawn."

25. On the special mobility that is *mouvance,* see Zumthor 1987, 1990: esp. 203–8.

26. But see Bauman and Briggs 1990 for applications to a wide variety of performances and texts.

27. For a comprehensive history of critical ideas about oral performance, see Taylor 2001: 36–41; on music, see Brault 1978a: 111–12 and the references therein. Some of Bauman's keys to performance, such as special formulas, are recoverable from the manuscript. Of special interest is Brault's discussion of the "gestural script" (1978b:111–15), which involves suggestions about mimetic movements and emphases that the epic poet may have used in performance.

28. See Duggan 1973: 160–85 for a complete analysis with documentation.

29. I cite the original and quote English translations from Brault 1984, the most readily available source for both and a fair, usually literal translation in its own right. The only exception to this policy occurs below with lines 176 and 3186, whose translation I have regularized (to make the English as consistent from instance to instance as the Old French).

Eighth Word:
An Ecology of South Slavic Oral Poetry

Oral poetry doesn't exist in a vacuum. Only its forced exile into texts creates the illusion of separateness or detachability. In real life all verbal activities are inseparable from their speakers, receivers, and contexts, and nowhere is this principle more vital than with oral poetry. To appropriate a biological metaphor, oral poems inhabit an ecology of verbal art. Neither poems nor performances nor genres can be isolated without doing violence to that ecology, without changing them into something they aren't.

This premise is a cornerstone of *How to Read an Oral Poem*. We've emphasized the importance of context from the cover photo and Four Scenarios onward. Regardless of what he may seem to be doing as we watch him through contemporary Western eyes, the Tibetan paper-singer is "reading" his poetic tradition, not the sheet of (blank) white paper or newsprint he extends before his eyes. The South African praise-poets who chronicled Nelson Mandela's reemergence after decades of imprisonment were using a genre of chieftain-praise that draws strength from deep, nourishing roots in their culture. Slam poets write for a single overriding purpose: performance in an arena where audiences are enmeshed in every step of the process and where well-crafted, arresting social commentary is the language spoken and heard. Homer—or the tradition of oral poets who came to be indexed by that legendary name—framed his tales in a resonant register that bristles with connotation, that means far more (and far differently) than even the best lexicons can suggest. Likewise, the examples cited throughout the First and Second Words as well as in the three "ways of reading" Words and the Poor Reader's Almanac provide additional evidence on the crucial significance of context, as do the case studies featured in the Seventh Word. For oral poetry, the environment or setting is undeniably part of the meaning.

To illustrate that premise from another perspective, we now shift gears. In the Seventh Word we directed our attention *inter*culturally, across six different oral poetries stemming from different places and times. Our aim was to suggest the natural diversity of oral poetry itself, as well as the diversity of approaches available to read its more-than-textual contents. Now, in the Eighth Word, we'll adopt an alternate but complementary perspective. Here we'll be reading *intra*culturally, looking within a single area to sample forms from approximately the same time and from one or a few closely related cultures. In some cases the oral poems we'll be examining exist alongside one another in the very same village or group of villages; in others they derive from different geographical parts of the former Yugoslavia or from different ethnic groups.

A few notes on procedure will get us started. First, we won't be limiting our selection of poetic forms or genres to those that later get ratified as literature. To put a realistically positive spin on it, our brief survey will be just as interested in charms, genealogies, and laments, sometimes misunderstood as minor or "primitive" forms, as it will in the supposed master-genre of epic. And here's a salient point, only too unthinkingly swept under the rug by our highly textual culture. Oral poetry does more than "ventilate the senses." It does more than simply entertain or, for that matter, simply instruct. Oral poetry is a crucial cog in the revolving wheel of culture, a verbal support system for social activity and identification, a partner to effective cultural citizenship. In this section we'll be seeing firsthand how oral poems can cure disease, or weave a fractured community back together, or record family history, as well as celebrate historical heritage or ethnic pride. Oral poetry is a socially embedded, functional brand of verbal art. Not *Ars gratia artis* ("Art for the sake of art") but *Ars gratia vivendi* ("Art for the sake of living").

To reverse the usual order of privilege, then, we'll start our ecological survey with the so-called minor genres. That means we'll begin with magical charms, moving on in sequence to funeral laments, then to genealogies, and only finally to epic. This strategy places the little-known or unknown before the well known, the speech-acts of women before the speech-acts of men, the sparsely collected and virtually unpublished before the extensively collected and widely published, the genres largely without literary progeny before the textually seminal genres, the "functional" before the "entertaining" or "instructive."

Second, I'll be drawing from a limited number of sources, all of them as close to actual Oral Performance as possible. Examples of the first three genres— charms, laments, and genealogies—come directly from fieldwork jointly undertaken by Barbara Kerewsky Halpern, Joel M. Halpern, and myself in the 1970s and 1980s. We were investigating the role of oral tradition across the broad face of Serbian peasant culture, focusing on one well-defined area within the former Yugoslavia: the region in southern Serbia known as Šumadija, or "the forested place," and in particular the villages of Orašac and Velika Ivanča. As for the fourth genre, oral epic poetry, I turn to the field collections made by Vuk Stefanović Karadžić in the mid-nineteenth century and by the Halperns in the 1950s, and also to the Milman Parry Collection of Oral Literature at Harvard University, which houses what is without doubt the largest and most varied archive of South Slavic epic anywhere in the world.[1] The Karadžić collection, made via oral dictation to writing collectors during the heyday of Serbian epic more than a century ago, is the leading source for the shorter Christian subgenre of epic. Although epic had nearly disappeared from the region in which our fieldwork team was based, the Halperns did manage to record the classic narrative of the "Widow Jana" in the late 1950s. The field expeditions conducted by Parry, Albert Lord, and Nikola Vujnović, mainly in the mid-1930s, form the basis of the Harvard archive, which is especially rich in the longer Moslem variety of epic. Thus my choice of witnesses: an across-the-board profile from two Serbian villages in which we worked and the most extensive and representative archives of South Slavic epic available.

Third, I make no claim whatever to universal or final pronouncements here. In fact, I actively dismiss the very possibility. Given the historical complexity of the Balkan region in general and of the former Yugoslavia in particular, caution must be our watchword. In the past few decades alone, languages and peoples have changed names, territories have been reassigned, and ethnic connections have been broken and reestablished many times over. Today the empty shell of a nation-state lies abandoned by many of its prior citizens. Fragmentation has been so radical that we hardly know what to say in place of the outmoded term "Serbo-Croatian." Oral traditions and folklore, never neutral media in the Balkans or anywhere else, have been appropriated politically by various interests and factions for their own particular purposes.[2] In fact, summoning one of our *proverbs*, we can observe that it's precisely because "Oral poetry works like language, only more so" that such material has proven so politically useful. More attention needs to be paid to this phenomenon. For present purposes, however, we'll focus on these four South Slavic genres as verbal art in cultural context, as windows on the role of oral poetry in a given region, as varied perspectives on a complex verbal ecology. If we're successful, we'll at least get a glimpse of the fundamental role of oral poetry in the fabric of social life.

Healing the Body: Magical Charms (*Bajanje*)

It's not that aspirin and other over-the-counter medicines were unknown in Orašac, nor were people unaware that some maladies called for professional medical care in Belgrade, eighty-two kilometers to the north. With the regu-

lar transit of people and information between the village and the urban me-
tropolis, mediated by more frequent converse with the nearby market town
of Arandjelovac, all of these modern wonders had their place on the menu of
interventions. But in certain cases, *bajanje,* the art of healing by charms, was
the remedy of choice. As one man put it, "For some things, what do doctors
know? Injections, injections—and nothing! For some things, you have to cure
with charms."

When our fieldwork team began to search for *bajanje* and people who performed it, we ran into a number of roadblocks. The art of healing with incantations proved a jealously guarded secret—we weren't sure exactly why at
first—and there seemed to be no apparent pattern to its practice or to the dis-
tribution of its practitioners. These difficulties soon revealed themselves as
stemming much more from our faulty presumptions than from any other
source. In time, our initial puzzlement matured into a good lesson in learning to navigate the overall cultural ecosystem of oral poetry. We discovered we
were looking for the wrong things in the wrong places.

First, with a single exception, performers of magical healing charms, called
bajalice, turned out to be post-menopausal women. What's more, conjurers
customarily learned their spells before the onset of puberty. In the patrilocal
scheme that underlies Serbian village society, that meant that a young girl
would receive charms from her grandmother (skipping her mother's generation), marry out of her natal village into her husband's family village, and not
actually begin performing the healing remedies for decades. Not only did a
space of perhaps thirty to thirty-five years intervene between acquisition and
initial performance, then, but *bajalice* in any one village, having married in
from elsewhere, shared no continuous tradition among themselves. In place
of the sisterhood of healers we expected, the village ecology presented a competitive group of independent contractors. And there were other consequences.
Unlike men's genres, women's oral poetries showed a crazy-quilt pattern of
transmission. Add to that complexity the fact that *bajanje* was seen as a precious part of a woman's dowry, something she brings to her husband's family, and it's easy to see why charms were so zealously guarded. When we asked
to hear and record some examples—and it became clear we weren't in need
of treatment—the usual and logical response was "Why?"

With a new and much improved frame of reference we set about trying to
learn more about charms as oral poetry. After some negotiation it was agreed
that Barbara Kerewsky-Halpern, whose two daughters of marriageable age had
accompanied her to the village, would be considered a *baba* or grandmother
(though in fact neither daughter was yet married), and that we could collect
sample charms from their practitioners on that peer-to-peer basis. Needless to

say, I was ignored in the process; this was a woman-to-woman transmission. There was also an understanding that we wouldn't redistribute the charms, so that this concession to our unusual request didn't threaten to disturb the "balance of word-power" in the village. Although we were never allowed access to *vračanje,* or black magic, those women who commanded a repertoire of healing charms to combat skin disease, infertility, postpartum problems, and so forth were willing to speak their incantations for the tape recorder.

And what a remarkable way of speaking it turned out to be. Using words that even they struggled to define, the conjurers intoned their healing poems with amazing rapidity in a low, sotto voce whisper. They employed an eight-syllable verse-form, the characteristic vehicle for the women's genres as opposed to the men's decasyllable. Some of the *bajalice* felt that implements such as a coal scuttle with a burning ember, a knife, and a piece of silver should be placed alongside a kneeling patient. Others assured us that they simply speak the spell into the ear of the person to be cured wherever they happen to be, whether kneeling or standing and whether alone or in a crowded room. Here's an excerpt from one of Desanka Matijašević's performances of "The Red Wind," a charm to dispel the skin disease erysipelas:[3]

> Out of there comes the red horse,
> the red man, the red mouth,
> the red arms, the red legs,
> the red mane, the red hooves.
> As he comes, so he approaches,   5
> he lifts out the disease immediately;
> he carries it off and carries it away
> across the sea without delay—
> where the cat doesn't meow,
> where the pig doesn't grunt,   10
> where the sheep don't bleat,
> where the goats don't low,
> where the priest doesn't come,
> where the cross isn't borne,
> so that ritual bread isn't broken,   15
> so that candles aren't lit.
>
>   * * *
>
> Into the wolf's four legs, fifth the tail,   45
> Out of my speaking has come the cure!

This highly patterned exorcism probably appears quite opaque, and there's a good reason for that. This is a narrow, highly specialized register, meant to accomplish only one particular thing and, unless one happens to be fluent in its mysteries, it will make little sense. Let me offer a thumbnail context for the *bajalica*'s words, which at the same time constitute a very powerful single "word." She starts by enlisting a heroic ally, a man on horseback (lines 1–8), to help rid the world of the intrusive red disease and take it back to where it originated and where it properly belongs—in the "red" world. Like her other helpers, including maternal figures like a mother hen and cow (not mentioned in this excerpt) who parallel her nourishing function, the man and his horse are themselves red. This coloring identifies them as denizens of that other world to which the illness must be returned. The color itself is systematically coded: if the disease to be banished were jaundice, the conjurer would summon yellow-colored helpers; if it were anthrax, her allies would be black. So it goes for the nine skin diseases treated with this charm; each of them is thought to be carried into our world on one of nine colored winds and disposed of by summoning a correspondingly colored agent. That's the folk epidemiology behind the administration of this charm.

The binary otherness of the "red world" emerges in the capsule (9–16) that follows the horse and rider section. What lies across the sea is a place so unlike our world that cats don't meow, pigs don't grunt, and in general animals don't sound like animals should. The "where X doesn't Y" unit can be expanded to include other domesticated creatures, such as chicks, roosters, hens, and horses, all of them behaving as they shouldn't. However many members it may feature in a given performance, however, the force of this capsule is the same: the "red" disease must go back to its rightful location, where even the most natural of sounds is wholly lacking. As if to underline that assertion and move toward the cure, Desanka Matijašević then extends the contrast to Christian ritual (13–16). The sphere from which the disease emanates is so completely opposite to our existence that even the priest and the cross have no place in it, nor do the panspermia loaf or candles associated with the Orthodox rite. The "red" universe is an anti-world, and the intrusion of disease is seen as a cosmic imbalance that needs to be set right.

The final agent (45–46) who assists the conjurer is also the strangest, not just a garden-variety wolf but a demonic beast who according to folk belief mediates between worlds. Barbara Kerewsky-Halpern and I were unaware of its special identity and function when we first heard the performance and even later when we began to edit and translate the charm. The wolf seemed initially just as puzzling as some of the vocabulary items that weren't recorded in any available lexicon. But then serendipity struck. On opening up the *Srpski mitološki rečnik* (*Serbian Mythological Dictionary*) some months later, the solution materialized right there in front of us. To illustrate the word *vuk*, or "wolf," Š. Kulišić had appended a line drawing of the mythical wolf-figure penned by the artist Milić of Mačva. It showed a huge and monstrous beast stretching out over a deep chasm. Its hind legs stood in a small village settlement with a half-dozen buildings surrounded by a bucolic countryside, while its forelegs rested in a wasteland marked only by a burning tower of bones. As if to map the action onto the digestive tract, the artist showed the animal vomiting a bone toward the pyre; clearly, whatever intruded into the peaceful, wholesome world of the village was both highly undesirable and difficult to send back. But the wolf stood there as a magical conduit between worlds, the folk equivalent of the "wormhole" of science fiction that allows instant passage from one galaxy or universe to another. The *bajalica* was using the *kurjak,* as she called him, to help restore these two separate universes to the status quo. The wolf was much more than a wolf, just as *bajanje* is much more than a detachable poem.

In fact, *bajanje* figures crucially enough in village life that there's substantial ecological pressure to maintain access to spells' curative power. Along those lines we learned how such pressure once resulted in a unique transmission, an exception that proved the rule of who gets to perform *bajanje.* Our next-door neighbor, Vojislav Stojanović, let slip that he knew a charm to restore a cow's milk production. It involves an elaborate transfiguration of an offending snake, whose bite is thought to be the source of the animal's drying up, as the conjurer's "word" changes the serpent first to her sister and then to the Virgin Mary. This turns out to be a frequently used spell, so its "owner" and administrator was much in demand. Given the customary gender and life-cycle requirements for *bajalice,* however, we were initially bewildered as to how he learned it and, even more, under what conditions he was licensed to continue practicing it. We had noticed that other people might know a few lines from this or that charm: for example, Desanka Matijašević's six-year-old grandson glibly prompted her when, nervous about performing for the tape recorder, she lost the thread of her speech-act. But being able to mouth a couple of octosyllabic verses wasn't nearly the same as actually serving as a functioning conjurer. Men couldn't do that. Vojislav Stojanović shouldn't have been doing that. Things didn't add up—unless you knew the context.

It happened that this male *bajalica* was the only person present during his aunt's final hours. On her deathbed she had two choices: to let the "snake" charm die with her (she had not passed it on to anyone) or to convey it to her nephew. Restricted to these two alternatives, she chose to transmit it to Vojislav, who for the purpose of this spell and this spell alone became a full-fledged *bajalica.* He made no effort to learn any additional verbal magic, nor did anyone offer to teach him. From the point of view of the overall ecology of oral poetry in general, and of the word-power of *bajanje* in particular, he was "standing in" as a conjurer, as a substitute for this charm only. Within the expressive economy, he was taking up the slack for life's unexpected developments, keeping this important form of veterinary medicine alive for the sake of the community. Stepping back a bit, we can perhaps see that this unparalleled instance isn't so much a violation as a validation of the rules. Continuity, functionality, word-power; there's considerable ecological pressure to nurture all of these cultural investments, and that can't be done without both a performer and an oral poem—no matter what the performer's gender and no matter what the poem's specific contribution. As the "extra" eleventh *proverb* developed in the Seventh Word put it, *Without a tradition there is no language; without a speaker there is only silence.*

Healing the Spirit: Funeral Laments (*Tužbalice*)

Throughout recorded history and in many places around the world, laments for the dead have occupied an important niche in the ecology of oral poetry. Such dirges are prominent in Homer's *Iliad* and in modern-day Greece, for example, and have been especially well collected and studied in Finland. The former Yugoslavia is thus hardly alone in the ritual significance it places on what are called *tužbalice,* sung by women of any age in the octosyllabic meter that supports female performance in Serbian villages. The ongoing traditional practice of formally mourning the deceased again demonstrates, but from a different perspective than that of the magical charms, how oral poetry can serve a vital social function.

Perhaps the most revealing way to introduce *tužbalice* is to recount briefly how, as a well-meaning but predisposed citizen of a modern Western culture, I initially misconstrued their substance and context. As our fieldwork team tried to assemble a cross-section of Serbian village oral poetry, we became aware of the tradition of formal laments. Long experience in Orašac and the surrounding area had educated my colleagues, Barbara Kerewsky-Halpern and Joel Halpern, about the essentials of this practice. They knew that *tužbalice* were always composed and performed by women, usually the closest female relative of the deceased, and had listened to performances and recorded samples over two decades. They had learned about the lament's recurrence at regular intervals for many years after the subject's demise, as well as observed the prohibition against playing back the tapes in the village.[4] They had watched and heard the ritual wailing in the village cemetery among the gravestones. They had constructed a ready frame of reference to accommodate this form of oral poetry, and they generously shared it with me.

As we made plans for fieldwork on this genre, however, I first objected to the idea of barging in on what seemed to me a private ceremony, and was particularly horrified at the thought of inserting our tape recorder into what had to be the most intimate of settings. Collecting charms or lyrics or epics was one thing, I contended, but how could we justify invading some poor woman's ritual space at such a trying time?

What I completely failed to realize was the unambiguously public nature of the proceedings. This is no self-absorbed, clandestine act but rather a straightforwardly social event in which the mourner performs for an audience—the community who visits her to show their support. The collective and nourishing nature of the enterprise is no fantasy or illusion; it's concretely imaged in the generous spread of food and drink that the lamenter conventionally lays out before her on a table cloth, a visual invitation to any and all to join her in weaving the community back together. She and they have suffered a grievous blow, to be sure; they've lost a family member and friend, and the separation is permanent. The lament encodes the overpowering sadness of that separation, and does so repeatedly over a series of performances that lasts for years. But it also links this death and its consequences to other such losses, creating a traditional context for the singular event, contextualizing this and other deaths as expressions of a natural, recurrent rhythm. The lament for the dead typically finds its way into canonized literature only as a lyric echo of real life, a subsidiary aspect of a larger plot or drama. But in a Serbian village the *tužbalica* is much more important than that; it's equipment for living, and as such it contributes crucially to the overall ecology of South Slavic oral poetry.

To give an idea of how *tužbalice* work, let me quote the entire seventy-four lines of a poem collected and translated by Barbara Kerewsky-Halpern.[5] This particular lament was composed and performed by the mother of a young boy, Milorad (also affectionately called Mile, Mićane, and Miško), who was killed along with some of his friends in a freak accident as they returned from a local St. Peter's Day fair. As they were running across an open field during a thunderstorm, a bolt of lightning struck them down.[6]

> Good morning, young men,
> Oj, where are you this early morn?
> Early morn, where did you spend it?
> For we had so hoped
> that you didn't reach here,　　　　　　　　　5
> and we had so hoped
> that our Mile was late [getting home].

Dear luck, we all hoped,
where your mother embraces a stone,
a sad stone, [already] seven years.   10
At your house, my Mićane,
all quietly sit, without girls or little children.
I can't [go on], I lack the strength, I lack
        the heart.
You dug out my heart,
dug it out and carried it off.   15
But then to see an even worse grief,
flashing lightning unexpected.
A great, Mile, a great sorrow
that Mile brought us grief
because you brought [it] on yourself.   20
If only we had not had sorrow
from this accursed war;
we had just begun to get settled again.
But then to see an even worse grief,
another grief unexpected.   25
Oj Mićane, my hero,
speak out, my happiness!
Look, your sister has come.
"My beauty," she says,
"I want, mother, to see [where my
        brother lies]."   30
You, Miško, did not stay at home,
at the hearth, your heart.
Darinka looks after the house for you
and after your grieving parents.
Your sister has come to beg you   35
to give her in turn your blessing.
Here some letters are destroyed;
who destroyed this?
May God destroy his luck
as [He destroyed] you, my Mićane!   40
Your name is destroyed
and it's a sorrow, son, for me
and for our young people.
The young people lead the *kolo;*
they permitted and saw   45
that the letters were destroyed.

Woe is me, my Mićane,
who destroyed the letters?
Woe is me, my joy Miško,
the officials here told us   50
that they will repair this.
I, poor one, did not know
where it was greatly destroyed.
But Darinka says to me,
"It isn't, mother, all that much but
          just a little,   55
and [some] letters are fainter [than others]."
Milorad, my wonderful joy,
this hot sun is burning,
but for you it is not hot.
Your youth is destroyed,   60
and the branch cut off.
And, Miško, I want to ask you:
Has Peko arrived [there]?
Does his wound ache terribly?
Tell me, householder, household head—   65
have his orphans remained?
Have your companions, Miško,
returned to their homes?
Did the young Polekšić fellow
die? Woe to his mother!   70
O my Suljo, my "live wire"!
Into the marshes, suffering,
into icy dark water,
the "live wire" is killed!

The performance arena for *tužbalice* always provides a powerful frame of reference for all involved. People are conventionally caught up in the mourner's grief, in both its immediate poignancy and its long-range social therapy. But this particular event was unusual, even unique. As opposed to the natural, timely exit of an older adult whose life had run its course, the loss of Milorad and his friends seems inexplicable, a decidedly unnatural fracture of the prevailing rhythm of the life cycle. By placing this unique situation in a traditional context—which is precisely what the *tužbalica* does—we can sense the extraordinary confluence of ritual and instance, the meshing of frame and contents. Milorad's mother struggles to contain her son's demise within the species of oral poetry that her society licenses for this purpose. She enters the performance arena of formal lament, composes and recomposes within the designated register or way of speaking, and makes her best attempt to integrate this unexpectable reality into her (and her society's) experience. That's what these dirges do: they offer a ready vehicle to support social life. We can justifiably see them as verbal art, of course, but we also need to recognize that their role in the overall expressive ecology is fundamentally practical. They're just one more way in which *Oral poetry works like language, only more so.*

We could use any of our "ways of reading" to further elucidate the *tužbalica* for Milorad, which in this instance was one of a group of such laments. Performance Theory could interpret the ensemble wailing that preceded each one-woman lament, each mother's practice of clasping a black-and-white photograph of the loved one to her chest as she performed, or the supportive behavior of extended family and neighbors. Based on the original acoustic recording, Ethnopoetics could score the oral poem for reperformance, helping readers to understand how the genre works by encouraging them to reperform the lament themselves. Immanent Art could emphasize the more-than-literal coding of the formulaic language and the symbolic function of the gravestone, which, like the gravestones of Homeric heroes, comes to stand for the overall life and achievements of the person memorialized—the concrete part symbolizing the intangible whole. That helps explain the speaker's intense worrying over the weather-based erosion of Milorad's name from the marker, for example. Deterioration of the material sign, no matter how natural and inevitable, threatens his disappearance from village and kin memory. Soon only the oral sign may remain.

But whatever tack we take in reading this lament, the central point is its role in the village ecology of oral poetry. It was composed in performance, yes; and it doubtless shows verbal artistry. But it also enlists these qualities in serving an essential social purpose. The lamenter is shaping reality in a fundamental manner, and she's using oral poetry to accomplish that feat. To read this oral poem, we need to read the culture.

Tracking Identity: Genealogies (*Pričanje*)

We don't usually think of genealogy as a freestanding genre. If our notion of a family lineage ever gets beyond a tree diagram to something verbal, we usually conceive of genealogies as part of something else—the "begats" of the biblical Genesis, for example. Similar kinds of lists are also customarily seen as contributors to a larger, more important design, such as the famous "Catalogue of Ships and Men" in Book 2 of the *Iliad* or its analogues in any number of South Slavic or central Asian oral epics. In contemporary Western culture we tend to prefer the textual, granular facts suspended in a database; catalogues, whether familial, regional, or national, tend toward bare-bones representations. We write family names and life-cycle statistics on the inside covers of cherished books, or print (and recycle) telephone directories, or reclaim lost friends and communities via Internet search engines. All of these methods keep identity alive, at least to a degree and very much at arm's length.

In Orašac and more generally in Serbia, another mode of genealogy has until recently served this important social purpose. Instead of relegating their family histories to one of our paper or electronic data-sets, Serbian villages have "deposited" this crucial aspect of identity into what they call *pričanje* (literally, "narrating, telling"). This oral poetic species is an important inhabitant of the overall ecology of oral poetry, since it bears the responsibility of preserving the story of lineage from the legendary originator of the family forward. That is, if your name is Stojanović, meaning "son of Stojan," then the genealogy begins with that first Stojan and works forward to the present day. If your name is Matijašević, then the first person recalled is Matijaš and the job is done only when the speaker reaches his own generation and then his progeny. Since lineage membership plays a crucial role in the village social organization, there can be no doubt of the significance of this genre's contribution. It's nothing less than an identity charter.

Genealogies are spoken, not sung, but they employ the same decasyllabic meter as the epic. The eldest male in the given lineage or extended family is the depository and performer of *pričanje*. Fieldwork established that as of the mid-1970s there was little call for old men to tell such "kin-stories," and this once-thriving species of poetic genealogy was beginning to weaken or even disappear from the village ecology even at that point.[7] Reasons for its demise affected the whole oral-poetic ecosystem to an extent, and included factors such as younger people's disinterest in traditional ways and their outright abandonment of the village for jobs in an urban setting. Significantly, the intrusion of new media and the fact of increasing literacy seemed to have had less of an effect. Performance arenas collapse just as readily when the audience leaves as when the poets find other things to do. But whatever the reasons, things were changing, and it's now no doubt very difficult to locate and collect *pričanje*.

Fortunately, for both intracultural and intercultural purposes, Barbara Kerewsky-Halpern succeeded in collecting a full genealogy from Mileta Stojanović, patriarch of his lineage, in 1968. During their long experience in the Šumadijan region, one of the Halperns' chief goals had been a series of demographic analyses. They gathered and analyzed information in order to paint an accurate picture of social life and its evolution over a 25-year period. Fundamental to their method was a thorough survey of births, marriages, and deaths, with the derived family tree eventually configured in the standard anthropological code of circles for women and girls and triangles for men and boys. This economical notation supports quick and easy mapping of any lineage. Marriage and birth patterns emerge at a glance: one can see immediately how row after row of generations march through the life cycle, marrying and producing offspring who then continue the process. Since 1954 the Halperns had collected data by interviewing numerous informants, as well as by examining the written records kept by the village priest, and they used their findings to plot the demography of Orašac. These investigations and the maps that schematically summarized them led to sophisticated mathematical profiles.

But our fieldwork team, committed to understanding the role of oral poetry in all aspects of village life, came to realize that a map was one thing and the story from which it stemmed was quite another. Prompted by Robert Creed, Kerewsky-Halpern went back to her field notes and recordings to study the form as well as the content of Mileta Stojanović's poetic and narrative response to her decidedly unpoetic demographic questions. Here's the first section of what he told her: the initial forty-seven lines of an oral poem (1980: 305–6):[8]

> Grandpa's dear, you will sit there!
> Sit down so I can relate everything to you.
> Long ago they, our ancestors, came;
> Stojan came even before the Uprising.
>
> * * *
>
> Ej! Old Stojan had three sons: 5
> these were Petar, Miloje, Mihajlo.
> Of sons Petar had four:
> Miloš, Uroš, Nikola, and Stefan.
> Daughter, do you know my grandfather Nikola?
> Of sons Miloje had three: 10
> these were Vučić, Matija, and Lazar.
> Mihajlo had just the same, three:
> Radivoje, Radovan, Radoje.
> That Miloš, he had two sons:
> these were Milutin and Andrija.   15
> Then Uroš had three sons:
> Tanasija, Vladimir, Djordje.
> Like so, daughter, the eldest is Djordje,
> And the youngest did not remain living. . . .
> My Nikola he had four: 20
> Antonija, Svetozar, and Miloš,
> and the third, Ljubomir my father—

may God forgive his soul!
Stefan, look here, had no sons.
Come now, Vučić, he had three: 25
Radojica, Andrija, Ljubomir.
And Matija had only one,
who was called Blagoje. . . .
Ej! Radovan, that one from the third brother
had Petar, Miloje, Radomir.   30
Now Radoje: only one, Dragomir;
Radivoje: Velimir and Branko.
Pay attention, now, I'm counting my brothers!
Well, Uncle Milutin had a trio:
Živomir, Pavle, and Velimir.   35
There are no descendants from them!
Now Andrija: Svetozar, Velisav.
And by Djordje and Tanasija
only Veljko remained as a mature man;
Dragoljub, Svetislav, and Dragoslav—   40
all were killed in the war.
Svetozar likewise had no luck,
nor Živomir, nor Miloš, nor Vitomir;
by them there are no male children at all.
But Dragiša, thank God, had [one].   45
Come now, here I am, Mileta!
Then my brother Milosav.

How does Mileta Stojanović's kin-poem work? First, this is a record of genealogy within a patriarchal, patrilocal society, where descendants and prop-
erty are tracked through the father's side and women marry into their hus-
bands' villages and raise their families there. It's therefore not surprising that
under such conditions *pričanje* portrays the story of the lineage exclusively in
terms of male precursors and progeny. Starting with Stojan, the source of the
Stojanović kin-group, Mileta next proceeds to Stojan's three sons—Petar,
Miloje, and Mihajlo—and then to their sons. This same pattern continues
through the genealogy, reflecting the cultural importance of extended-family
relations outside the nuclear family. When Mileta says, formulaically and rhetorically, "Pay attention, now, I'm counting my brothers!" (line 33), he uses the
South Slavic word *brat,* which covers cousins, uncles, and nephews as well as
biological, nuclear-family siblings. Where independent testimony from church
records was available, it became clear that he organized each set of siblings
according to descending age. The full genealogy covers no fewer than 105 peo-

ple over six generations. What emerges is a "family photograph" with much greater depth and breadth than is typical of such portraits in contemporary Western cultures.

Interestingly, *pričanje* shares some expressive features with another species in the overall oral-poetry ecosystem, the epic. For example, both genres can begin with a prologue (*pripjev*) that sets the performance arena and cues the audience as to the nature of what will follow. Mileta Stojanović speaks directly to Barbara Kerewsky-Halpern, who prompted this performance by inquiring about demographic information, instructing her to assume the position and role of audience. With that exchange the performance frame is established. Then, in phraseology that closely parallels epic prologues, he intones "Long ago they, our ancestors, came," locating the starting-point of his narration at the legendary beginning of the lineage. Epics from this and other regions often start with some version of a similarly proverbial cue, such as "Long ago it was, now we are remembering it." To emphasize just how ancient that time was, he adds that "Stojan came even before the Uprising," referring to the First Serbian Revolt against the Ottoman Empire in 1804. That epochal event began a new chapter in Serbia's history; to place something before that moment is not merely to date it, but to thrust it back into the mythical mists of the past, to a time beyond the reach of factual history. This too is an epic impulse.

As noted above, *pričanje* has now largely disappeared from the village ecology of oral poetry. But while it flourished, it provided a way to embed a person within his lineage, to situate individual identities within a large group of relations over a long period of time. It told the story of "who I am" and "who we are" from the beginning of kin-time to the present day. Genealogy was not an aspect of some larger form, a catalogue to ornament an epic, but a freestanding genre in its own right. Like charms and laments, it served a practical social purpose—one that we cannot afford to call mundane if we are to understand the true scope and the heavy responsibilities of oral poetry in various cultures around the world. Fundamentally, *pričanje* shows us yet another way in which *Oral poetry works like language, only more so*.

Living the Heritage: Epics (*Epske pjesme*)

We're familiar with epic, or at least we think we are. If comparative studies in oral tradition have proved anything over the past twenty years, it must be that "epic" means different things to different cultures. Unwarranted presumptions, the eternal thorn in the side of oral poetry studies, blinded us for quite some time. At one point scholars were convinced that the genre didn't exist anywhere in Africa, until it was pointed out that what didn't exist there was *Homeric* epic, an idiosyncratic type of long narrative that we had falsely assumed was an archetypal form. We've since learned that epics from around the world may incorporate dance, visual aids, co-performance with another bard, a bewildering variety of melodic and percussive instruments, and on into the night. Then too, as we saw in the Seventh Word with the *Siri Epic,* the attached mythology can gain expression in a variety of other genres and performance arenas. Nor is length a reliable common denominator. Comparative studies show that, internationally speaking, the 16,000 lines of the *Iliad* and the 12,000 lines of the *Odyssey* are actually toward the shorter end of the spectrum. Oral epic, like oral poetry itself, has revealed itself to be endlessly diverse. We don't know epic nearly as well as we think we do.

A major reason for our presumed familiarity with epic is its survival into literature. With Dante's *Divine Comedy,* Spenser's *Faerie Queene,* Ariosto's *Orlando Furioso,* Milton's *Paradise Lost,* and other stalwarts in the European canon, not to mention the classical benchmarks of Homer's cornerstone poems and Virgil's *Aeneid,* epic won a prominent and permanent place in the Western literary constellation. Great individual authors took up large-scale issues like national and political identity, sacred history, and human suffering and resiliency, modeling their grand creations on works that had already gained a foothold in textual culture. This kind of epic serves the society in which it appears in only the most abstract and high-minded way. Once it exits the ecosystem of oral poetry and becomes self-sufficient as a textual monument, epic can discard its responsibility to be practically functional in favor of fulfilling the "entertainment and instruction" credo of most literature. This is most certainly not to denigrate literary epic, but it is to warn that South Slavic oral epic poetry may not look very familiar at all.

And what in fact do we find there? A two-part answer will give some idea of the variability of the genre even within the former Yugoslavia. First, in the region of Šumadija and elsewhere we encounter Christian epic, that is, a subgenre sung chiefly by Orthodox Serbs and generally reaching no more than three hundred lines in length. The classical era of Serbian epic was the early and middle nineteenth century, the same period during which the Grimms and so many other European scholars were seeking their national and ethnic roots in folk poetry. As part of this movement, Vuk Stefanović Karadžić and his network of assistants collected *epske pjesme* from a veritable army of *guslari.*[9] Karadžić was to publish four volumes of this performance-collection during his lifetime, and more has reached publication posthumously. Many of the poems from his original volumes have been translated and have won international acclaim as finely crafted expressions of national and ethnic history.

Christian epic focuses chiefly on an array of semihistorical figures, events, and topics, none of them more fundamental to Serbian identity than Prince Marko and the Battle of Kosovo. Marko's adventures are particularly noteworthy for their symbolic portrayal of a spirited people caught in an oppressor's grip. An actual historical character whom the poetic tradition "King Arthurized," the epic Prince Marko is the unwilling Serbian mercenary of the Turkish tsar, an always restive vassal who hated the Ottoman Empire even as circumstances forced him to do its bidding. Living a virtually schizophrenic identity, Marko delights in his role as the insubordinate warrior whom his superiors can't do without, the infidel who merrily enjoys wine during the Islamic holy month of Ramadan, the outrageous underling who unapologetically plunks his riding boots on the tsar's holy prayer-rug. Through stories that celebrate his bravery and heroic accomplishment against all odds—but also portray his incendiary temper and inability to deal with virtually any woman other than his mother—we see a double focus emerge. Marko is both a representative of the best his people have to offer and a warning against intolerance, racism, and misogyny. He's their best hope and their worst nightmare, all at once. Tales chart both his adventures and his misadventures, reflecting the triumphs of the downtrodden while not ignoring the pitfalls lurking in the darker corners of human nature.[10] The double focus is a functional feature of this particular brand of Christian epic; it contributes to the overall ecology in both direct and subtle ways.

The Kosovo cycle of Christian epic functions in a parallel fashion. Memorializing King Lazar's heroic demise at the hands of the infidel Ottoman force led by Sultan Murad in 1389, it chronicles a supreme Serbian devastation. But its roots go deeper than that. Lazar was one of the three surviving competitors for the throne of Serbia, along with Tvrtko, the king of Bosnia, and Marko, who was to assume such a prominent place in epic poetry. It was Lazar who assembled the armies of his son-in-law Vuk Branković, Tvrtko, and others into the composite force that met the Turks at Kosovo on St. Vitus's Day. Over the course of the Kosovo poems Lazar is pictured as shifting his focus from the temporal to the spiritual, in some cases actively choosing a heavenly rather than an earthly kingdom. In "The Downfall of the Serbian Kingdom," for instance, what seems at first to be a falcon arrives from Jerusalem with a message. It turns out to be Saint Elijah bearing a letter from the Virgin Mary asking him to decide between these two alternatives. If he chooses the earthly kingdom, his armies will triumph; if he opts for the heavenly realm, he must build a church and prepare to die. Forsaking the concerns of this world, Lazar chooses the latter. From that decision onward the slaughter is foreordained.

In addition to expectable poems about the actual fighting and its immediate consequences, compelling songs about other aspects of the cataclysmic loss add a human, pathetic dimension to the oral poetry that chronicles these events. Among the most celebrated of these is "The Kosovo Maiden," in which a young woman searches the battlefield in the aftermath of the slaughter, ministering to the mortally wounded with water, red wine, and bread. The religious overtones of her actions are clearly audible. Eventually she encounters Pavle Orlović, maimed beyond hope of recovery, who asks her what she's doing there in the midst of so much carnage and misery. She replies that she was promised betrothal to Milan Toplica by his blood brothers Miloš Obilić and Ivan Kosančić and by the bridegroom-designate himself. She then describes all three heroes in very similar terms and tells how each of them gave her a keepsake (a spotted cloak, a golden wedding ring, and a golden veil) as his pledge to fulfill the promise. It's left to Pavle Orlović to convey the sad news of the death of Milan Toplica and the others and to break the spell of her romantic reverie, returning them both to the brutal reality of what surrounds them. With "The Kosovo Maiden" we're provided a window on how the tragedy extends well beyond the exposed space of the battlefield into even the most protected spheres of social life.

Traditional poetic structures are everywhere in both the Marko and the Kosovo cycles of Christian epic. While Marko lives, his adventures are related in "words" of typical shape and implication: formulaic diction, ring-structure, thematic units, and many other expressive strategies are evident in virtually every poem.[11] They resonate idiomatically, adding depth to each poem by traditional reference. When Marko dies, the singer Tešan Podrugović portrays his demise by reversing the familiar scenes of Arming the Hero and Caparisoning the Horse. One by one, the great Serbian prince destroys his weapons and his faithful equine companion, Šarac. Indeed, "The Death of Prince Marko" wouldn't be half the poem it is without the traditional background that provides a ready context for these last heroic rites. Marko lives heroically and independently, and he exits in just the same fashion.

Things proceed similarly with the Kosovo songs. In "The Downfall of the Serbian Kingdom," the arrival of a falcon, itself a heroic symbol, forebodes a battle of consequence. The message, or *knjiga,* always announces a turning point in South Slavic epic narrative, and the alternative it presents is usually framed in the classic "either-or" pattern that is a feature of the poetic register in hundreds of songs. The notation of early morning that begins "The Kosovo Maiden" is likewise a convention for starting a poem (a strategy we met earlier in the funeral lament), and often accompanies the well-known pattern of an unmarried young woman tending to a wounded warrior. As part of that ministering, the young woman typically learns something striking that will deeply affect her subsequent life, and "The Kosovo Maiden" is certainly no exception to the idiomatic rule. In a similar fashion her descriptions of the heroes are variations on a single theme, and collectively they constitute the kind of catalogue that very frequently appears in the epic.

All of these structures and implications amount to another illustration of our *proverb* that *The art of oral poetry emerges* through *rather than* in spite of *its special language.* The Kosovo myth has remained vital for centuries, and the epic poetry surrounding it and conveying its historical and nationalistic sentiments is no small part of that survival. Nor does the heritage wane with the advent of print: the Christian epic stories of Marko and the Battle of Kosovo have served for many decades as a staple of public education from elementary school onward. Given the recent ethnic depredations at this same Kosovo, which were defended by their perpetrators in part through appeal to tradition, we can see how oral epic poetry can indeed foster "living the heritage." For better and for worse, these poems have long been a vital and integral species in the regional ecology of oral poetry.

In 1954 the village of Orašac yielded up another piece of the puzzle that was its own local ecology. Joel Halpern and Barbara Kerewsky-Halpern tape-recorded a performance of *Udovica Jana* (*The Widow Jana*) from the *guslar* Aleksandar Jakovljević.[12] Typically for the Šumadijan region, the singer was not a professional but a farmer who performed chiefly for his family and groups of friends and neighbors at occasional gatherings. For all intents and purposes the epic tradition was on its last legs in Serbia when Jakovljević, then 64, performed for the Halperns. Nonetheless, both the singer and the audience maintained that the song in question was well and widely known among villagers; it was a popular choice. Their enthusiastic reception may seem curious once we grasp what transpires in this small story, which belongs to the densely populated "unfaithful mother" category of Christian epic poetry.[13]

Here's how the story goes. The widow Jana awakes with the dawn (by now a familiar cue for South Slavic oral poems of all sorts) and is immediately approached by a man whose given name of Halil reveals his non-Serbian ethnicity and Moslem faith. Halil apparently wants her to take up with him, though an official marriage is doubtful given their opposite ethnic and religious affiliations. Although by all cultural criteria she should refuse his advances outright, Jana states that she'd be willing except for the responsibilities associated with her two sons, Niko and Nikola. This impasse leads to a plan, hatched by the mother herself, to send the boys on a trumped-up errand to the river Koran to fetch water. She instructs her paramour Halil to hide himself nearby and kill her sons when they arrive. What saves the boys' lives is intervention by the stock "nurturing sister" figure, here called Jelica, who overhears the plot and alerts her brothers to the ambush. Warned of the treachery, they turn the tables on Halil, dispatching him swiftly and bringing his head to their mother. She flees, but is eventually caught and executed by two horses who "draw and halve" her. It is a violent and gruesome ending to a violent and gruesome story, and it may well leave us wondering just what sort of heritage is being celebrated here.

The answer's not far to seek. Halil's shameless approach to Jana and their dastardly plan to rid her of the encumbrance of her progeny—all gross violations of the rules that structure social life in the region—are effectively countered using family resources. If we understand one major aspect of the living heritage of *The Widow Jana* as reaffirmation of kinship and affinal harmony, then the poem becomes a memorable illustration of how society and family respond when things fall apart. A maternal death-plot, unthinkably unnatural in real life, is derailed by a compensating and natural force: a sister's "foster-mother" commitment to her brothers. We see the competing forces in microcosm near the end of the song, as Jana and Jelica lead two separate *kolo* dances, each woman expecting different news from the river Koran. With the boys' appearance Jana's *kolo* dissolves, along with her socially and familially nonviable plan. At a symbolic level, we can read the story as an affirmation, as evidence that even the most heinous wrong can and will be set right. The "unfaithful mother" songs are an interesting species within the poetic ecology, in that they celebrate not momentous events or renowned figures in cultural history but everyday social and kin-based structures that affect everyone in the village. And don't be put off by Jana's short-lived blight on the flower of motherhood: what matters is the response she triggers, not the unsustainable crime she threatens.

For our final species of South Slavic oral poetry, we must leave the village of Orašac, and indeed all of Serbia, in order to travel to what is today Bosnia, homeland of the so-called Moslem epic. It was this "more Homeric" form of epic, much longer and more elaborate than its Christian counterpart, that Parry and Lord sought to record for comparison with the *Iliad* and *Odyssey*. In the Fifth Word I told a short version of the story of their explorations as they sought to prove Parry's thesis of Oral-Formulaic Theory in the living laboratory of then-Yugoslavia.[14] It would be irresponsible, for at least two reasons, to leave even this preliminary discussion of South Slavic oral poetry without a nod toward this kind of epic. First, in order to give a fair sense of the overall ecology and especially the species called epic, we need to take account of both major members of that species, the Christian and the Moslem varieties. Second, it has been the Moslem epic on which so much has been based in comparative research over more than 150 additional traditions. Let's be as explicit as possible. Parry and Lord derived the supposed universals for "oral poetry" directly from their fieldwork collection and its overlap with the Homeric epics that have reached us only in manuscript. All verbal art from oral tradition was in effect balanced on the head of a pin. Even if we now know that Oralpoetry *is a very plural noun* and that no single set of definitions can do anything but muddy the waters, we need to know where this initial—and enormously influential—approximation came from.

Moslem epic derives from the Ottoman court, particularly of the sixteenth and seventeenth centuries, an environment that provided long-term, professional employment for singers of tales and an opportunity for epic to prosper in an extended form. As the empire waned, this tradition moved into the *kafane,* or coffeehouses, frequented chiefly by adult males. Especially during the holy month of Ramadan, when fasting until sundown is the rule and men gather there afterwards to eat and drink, the more modern context also encouraged longer performances and more extensive repertoires. All of this contrasted sharply with the Christian song-performances, which tended to take place less frequently and less regularly. The result was two quite different strains of epic poetry: the Moslem variety could reach thousands of lines in length, while the Christian subgenre seldom surpassed two to three hundred lines. Each was a creature of its own performance arena, which in turn was formed and sustained by ethnicity, cultural history, and religious affiliation.

Parry and Lord's fieldwork took them to six regional centers in Bosnia: Novi Pazar, Bijelo Polje, Kolašin, Gacko, Stolac, and Bihać. Lord was to use material from all of these areas to support Oral-Formulaic Theory in his seminal book, *The Singer of Tales;* the official publication of the Parry Collection, *Serbo-Croatian Heroic Songs,* has presented samples of their recordings, so far chiefly from Novi Pazar and Bijelo Polje. Indeed, from the latter of these two regions come the remarkable performances by Avdo Medjedović, the most accomplished *guslar* they encountered. Medjedović's *The Wedding of Smailagić Meho,* dictated over the period July 5–12, 1935, to Parry and Lord's native assistant Nikola Vujnović, runs to 12,311 lines, about the length of the *Odyssey.* This was no fluke: another of the same *guslar's* performances, *Osman Delibegović and Pavičević Luka,* sung for acoustic recording on aluminum disks on July 17–20, 1935, reached 13,326 lines.

But mere length tells only one part of the story. Taken together, the Moslem epics present a grand myth-scape of brave (but not always trustworthy) heroes, magnificent (and often daring) heroines, revered cities and strongholds overseen by ruthless beys and tsars, epochal and bloody battles, edge-of-your-seat spy missions, grand wedding assemblies, and a seemingly unlimited supply of hair-raising adventures. In addition, the singers command a number of story-patterns—such as Return, Wedding, Rescue, and Siege of City—that

Ibro Bašić, a *guslar* from Stolac in the former Yugoslavia. Photo
by A. B. Lord. Courtesy of the Curators of the Milman Parry
Collection of Oral Literature. Copyright President and Fellows
of Harvard University.

serve as flexible molds for composing oral epics and readily recognizable maps
for reading them (*Composition and reception are two sides of the same coin*).
Each story-pattern underlies and helps plot any number of different, individualized stories. All of this adds up to an enormous constellation or network
of epic, much of it just below the explicit surface of any given story. It's that
large-scale network that each and every performance implies and idiomati-

cally taps into. Like the other genres we've examined, Moslem epic depends heavily on its context.

The rich implications of Moslem epic tradition are thus both a blessing and a curse. If a reader is reasonably fluent in the singer's register and cognizant of the background against which the performance takes place, the result is a full and resonant experience. But pity the poor reader who—like most of us— is not a native speaker of the poetic language (or even of the "standard" language) and lacks much of the implied background. In the West we grow up with Athena, Achilles, and Zeus, but how many of us have even heard tell of Zlata, Djerdjelez Alija, Tale, or Mustajbey of the Lika? Given the cultural shortfall, we'll want to take pains, as recommended above for other South Slavic genres, to become as fully aware of the context as possible.

In the Post-Script that follows the Eighth Word, I'll offer some suggestions on using the new electronic media to create a truer representation and experience of oral performance in general, and of South Slavic oral epic performance in particular. These "textual aids" will include audio versions of the songs and electronic editions of example poems in hypertext, both to be made accessible on the Internet. For the moment, let me reprint a draft headnote to my forthcoming paper edition of *The Wedding of Mustajbey's Son Bećirbey*, a Moslem epic from the Parry Collection, as a reminder of some of the context we need to read it.

> This performance by Halil Bajgorić, a *guslar* from the village of Dabrica in the Stolac region of central Hercegovina, is a classic example of a Wedding Song in the Moslem tradition of South Slavic epic [cross-reference to other Wedding Songs]. Sung for the records on June 13, 1935, it tells the story of how Mustajbey, duplicitous leader of the loosely confederated beys and pashas who ruled over the borderland or Lika, sought to marry his only son Bećirbey to the fair Zlata, only daughter of the champion of Kanidža. What stands in the way, quite expectably, is an irruption of the Turkish-Christian enmity so typical of the reign of Sulejman the Magnificent (ruled 1520–66), during which period most of the epic narratives are set, in the form of the Christian ban Baturić contesting the marriage and provoking what always seems to accompany a grand wedding in South Slavic epic—namely, an equally grand battle. Marriage and battle are linked traditionally via the storytelling idiom, and culturally by the ritual bride-stealing motif that survives today in rural villages (sometimes using a Mercedes Benz rather than horses, however). The free-agent hero Djerdjelez Alija travels to Mustajbey's territory in order to serve him and is appointed the nominal leader of troops assembled from far and near, though the young Bećirbey himself and the trickster figure Tale also play important roles in the outcome.

Halil Bajgorić, a *guslar* from Dabrica in the former Yugoslavia.
Photo by A. B. Lord. Courtesy of the Curators of the Milman
Parry Collection of Oral Literature. Copyright President and
Fellows of Harvard University.

The epic singer Bajgorić employs his own idiolectal versions of traditional language and narrative patterns shared among *guslari* from this region, with particular attention to the typical scenes of Arming the Hero and Catalogue of Heroes (as represented in letters of invitation and subsequent arrivals), and features a rich portrayal of Tale's inimitable comic antics. [Included here will be an excerpt from Nikola Vujnović's conversation with the singer Bajgorić.]

Like other genres, Moslem epic is a formidable species of oral poetry. If we enlarge our idea of the ecosystem of South Slavic oral poetry beyond the villages of Orašac and Velika Ivanča and beyond Serbia to the larger sphere of the former Yugoslavia, we'll need to take account of its role.[15]

Let me close by posing a question and proposing an answer. There's a stark disparity between the poor Moslem farmer or tradesman who until recently sang such epics in the coffeehouse and the subject matter of the epics themselves. Of course they're "good stories," especially if you've learned some of the background history and social context. But what personal connection could such peasant men possibly feel to Ottoman opulence that lay four centuries in the past, to broad-canvas issues of power politics and superhuman feats of derring-do, to a royal and privileged way of life that had little or nothing in common with their own modest situation? Why, in short, did they continue to sing these songs?

Here's one answer. Conversations with *guslari* offer evidence that, in spite of superficial discrepancies, the Moslem epics really did remain a living heritage—but at a different level from other genres. They certainly provided no healing magic, they didn't reintegrate a community fractured by death, and only occasionally did they provide any reliable genealogical data (and then certainly not for local families). Nor do Moslem songs mime contemporary social structures and values, except by accident. Their role is closer to the Marko or Kosovo stories of Christian epic, in that they serve as an elegant and ready reminder of what once was, reaffirming a historical identity implicitly claimed as the singers' (and audience's) own. To sing and to hear such stories was not to fly in the face of everyday reality but rather to frame today within the glories of yesterday, to provide some roots. Keeping that nourishing heritage alive—no matter how anachronistically—is also a worthy ecological contribution.

Speaking in Poetry: An Unclassified Species

Not every species our fieldwork team encountered in the Šumadijan verbal ecosystem was well known, much less well documented. Not every speech-act could boast a recognized identity as a way of speaking, even among villagers themselves. A case in point was a "comment" made by Milutin Milojević, a *guslar* from Velika Ivanča, who uttered the following four lines just after I took his photograph near the end of our session:

Ja od Boga imam dobrog dara,	Yes, from God I have a fine gift,
Evo mene mojega slikara;	Here comes my photographer;
Kogod' oće, ko me lepo čuje,	Whoever wishes, whoever hears me well,
On mene lepo nek slikuje.	Let him take my photograph well.

I include the original South Slavic in this instance to illustrate some remarkable features of Milojević's response. First, he sang four decasyllabic lines that follow all of the rules governing the epic verse-form.[16] Second, these lines derive from the epic register; we can find systemic relatives—though not identical siblings—throughout the poetic tradition. Third, he added the acoustic flourish of rhyming couplets, hardly a requirement of this verse form but a dextrous elaboration. Fourth, he accomplished all of this fluently and without hesitation; he was simply composing and delivering his short poem within the epic way of speaking.

When we add to this account the fact that Milojević had never had his photograph taken before that moment—indeed that he'd never seen a camera before—we can gain some idea of just how fluent he was in the epic register. What's more, he had to manufacture some vocabulary items to cover photography: *slikar* (line 2) literally means "painter, artist" and in his village lexicon the verb *slikati* named the painter's act. All in all, this is a stunning example of the flexibility and word-power of South Slavic epic diction in the hands of a talented speaker. Milojević succeeded in pushing his specialized language to do something it wasn't ever "meant" to do.

Similarly, Ljubica Branković, a *bajalica* or conjurer from Orašac, responded inimitably when we naively asked how she managed when she forgets part of a charm. Her answer came in the form of two octosyllabic verses:

Što upamtim ja upamtim;	What I remember I remember;
Što ne upamtim ja sasnim noć'.	What I don't remember I dream at night.

Note that her reply is a poetic byte, a "word" in our special sense of the term. She frames it in eight-syllable lines, the meter of the women's genres in this part of Serbia, and the two lines are syntactically balanced, acoustically patterned, and set up as a semantic contrast.[17] Once again we have a speaker pushing a poetic register beyond what it was fashioned for, using her fluency in a well-defined way of speaking for a unique purpose.

So what's the upshot of Milutin Milojević's and Ljubica Branković's unexpected responses? Literary theories of genre can't explain such utterances, which lie far outside the realm of formal speech-acts. Nonetheless, these sorts of events and the facility that makes them possible are real and must be recognized as part of the oral-poetic ecosystem in a Serbian village. Modest and informal though they may be, they're living species in the local ecology of oral poetry, which *works like language, only more so.*

A Diverse Ecology

It's easy to forget that every living species exists in and depends on its ecology. Without that sustaining environment, replete with organisms of varying description and a context that keeps them alive, nothing can survive. But as text-consumers we've made a cultural project of forgetting these simple truths as they apply to verbal art in oral tradition. We're brought up with a text-centered, literary disposition, taught to impose extrinsic cognitive categories: first we separate the organism from its environment, isolating it from other organisms and the context that nourishes them all; then begins the vivisection. Too often we base our *reading*—and that process starts as early as fieldwork and continues through edition, translation, and publication—on a crippling agenda that guarantees misreading. Armed with prejudices that originate and flourish with the support of mainstream media, we select and dismiss genres according to indefensible criteria: the known or paralleled over the unknown or unparalleled; forms with literary descendants over forms that lack that pedigree; distanced, armchair entertainment and instruction over social function. The small group of oral genres that survive such winnowing are dead on arrival.

In the Eighth Word, as throughout *How to Read an Oral Poem,* I have tried to counteract this knee-jerk reflex by advocating a wider, more inclusive view of oral poetry, this time within a single ecosystem. The four genres featured— magical charms, funeral laments, genealogies, and epics—collectively teach at least two lessons that can be transferred to other such ecosystems. The first is that oral poetry can and does serve its society of origin in myriad ways. Some of these forms may seem homelier or less profound from a literary perspective, but once we've recalibrated our idea of what poetry can do, that bias will disappear. We'll understand the enormously broader and more interesting role of poetry in human culture. Second, it follows that we have a responsibility as readers to make ourselves as aware as possible of the full ecology of oral poetry. We need to be curious about all the species that populate a given environment, not just a special, preselected few: as our *proverb* reminds us, Oral-poetry *is a very plural noun.* It simply won't pass muster to artificially foreshorten the horizon of oral poetry, either by shrinking its natural diversity or by setting some arbitrary limit on strategies for reading that ever-shifting, highly varied "more-than-a-canon." In the end our perspectives for reading must reflect and serve oral poetry's own manysidedness: *True diversity demands diversity in frame of reference.*

Notes

1. See the Parry Collection Web site at <http://www.fas.harvard.edu/mpc>.

2. See esp. Gordy 1999: 103–62.

3. Quoted from Foley 1995a: 117–19. The acoustic record and an original-language transcription of this charm can be accessed at the *HROP* Web site.

4. In a striking illustration of the perceived word-power of this genre of oral poetry, people in the village cautioned against playing back the recorded tapes lest the re-created lament cause someone else to die (Kerewsky-Halpern 1981: 53).

5. Kerewsky-Halpern 1981: 57–58. See the entire article for remarks on the context and setting of the lament, and the *HROP* Web site for the original Serbian text.

6. I offer a few cultural and poetic notes as glosses to the lament:

> *Lines 1–3.* Many South Slavic oral genres, among them lyric and epic songs, often begin with such a notation of diurnal rhythm. It amounts to a rhetorical cue for starting a speech-act.
>
> *Lines 9–10.* Milorad has been dead seven years, in other words. Laments are sung at regular intervals, and details such as "seven years" must be modified to fit the evolving situation. The gravestone is a powerful symbol in Serbian village culture (see lines 37–56 below), and the graveyard is a much more public and more frequently visited place than in most North American and Western European societies.
>
> *Lines 21–23.* This probably refers to World War II, which wrought greater devastation on Eastern Europe in general and on Serbia in particular than is usually recognized in the West. But the background of Balkan instability, which for Serbs is a deeply felt reality (e.g., the Battle of Kosovo in 1389), provides a deeper context. For poetic purposes, it is the rhetorical link between Milorad's death and war that matters.
>
> *Lines 28–36 and 54–56.* Both the society and the oral tradition create a special place and identity for sisters. Conventionally they serve as nurturers for their brothers, as dependable caretakers and protectors even when their mother has deserted or is plotting against the boy(s); see the discussion of *The Widow Jana.* Darinka is continuing to play that role even after Milorad's death; she also manages to comfort her mother about the erosion of her brother's name on the gravestone.
>
> *Lines 46ff.* The emphasis on "letters" (*slova*), which might seem unusual in an oral genre performed by a preliterate person, is actually quite common in South Slavic and other oral poetries. Performers can and do celebrate the power of written coding without themselves using it; letters take on a kind of symbolic

meaning in such circumstances. Consider the writing ("signs," *sêmata*) on Bellerophon's tablet in Book 6.168–78 of Homer's *Iliad;* on what they are and how to read them, see the Second Word above and Foley 1999: 1–5.

Lines 62–70. Milorad's mother asks about the other boys who were killed by lightning. It's well to remember here that she was performing alongside the mothers of the other boys, first in ensemble wailing and then separately with individual laments.

7. See the partial genealogy recorded by Joel Halpern and myself from the dispirited patriarch of the Maksimović lineage (Kerewsky-Halpern 1980: 320, n. 24).

8. I have occasionally rearranged word-order or otherwise slightly modified Kerewsky-Halpern's translation, which was intended as a companion to the original Serbian version, in order to foster easier, more fluent understanding for readers working only from the English translation. See her article (1980: 304–5) for the original Serbian text. Note that Mileta Stojanović addresses her as "grandpa's dear" (*blago dedi*) and "daughter" (*ćero*), with these synthetic kinship labels marking the special intimacy of their relationship.

9. On this remarkable linguist, anthropologist, and collector of oral poetry, see Wilson 1986. A survey of his published editions and of other editions of South Slavic oral epic is available in Coote 1978.

10. On the factual and fictional sides of Marko, see Popović 1988. For more on the traditional structure and implications of the Marko poems, see Foley 1991: 96–134.

11. For examples, see Foley 1991: 96–134.

12. For a full transcription and translation of the performance, along with contextual material, see Foley and Kerewsky-Halpern 1976. The text, translation, and acoustic records are available at the *HROP* Web site.

13. To my knowledge there is no English-language scholarship on this song-type; for native scholarship and examples, see further Foley and Kerewsky-Halpern 1976 (12–13, nn. 10, 11). It should be added that the following perspectives on *The Widow Jana* and its generic counterparts derive from a combination of those sources with interviews conducted in the region by our research team.

14. For the longer version, see Foley 1988.

15. We'll also need to take account of many other genres, too numerous and varied to mention here. Let me emphasize once again that I aspire not to exhaustive or even perfectly representative coverage but simply to providing some initial insights and a "way into" these materials. I hope others will expand these ideas further into South Slavic oral poetry and to other oral poetries as well.

16. Specialists will notice that the fourth line is a syllable short, but the colon structure, zeugmata, and other features are intact.

17. As with Milutin Milojević's poem, the latter line of this couplet seems to show variation from the norm, with nine instead of the expected eight syllables. In this case, however, a performance adjustment intervened: Branković spoke the first five syllables as if they were four, compressing the first half of the line into the customary tem-

poral space. As noted in the First Word, one of the most basic challenges we face in reading oral poetry is to conceive of the poetic line as an utterance and an event rather than a spatialized textual artifact.

Further Reading

Charms: Kerewsky-Halpern and Foley 1978; Foley and Kerewsky-Halpern 1978; Conrad 1983; Foley 1995a: 99–135; Kent 1983 (Czech)

Epic (Christian): Holton and Mihailovich 1997 (translation of Karadžić collection); Pennington and Levi 1984 (translation of Prince Marko songs); Matthias and Vučković 1987 (translation of Kosovo songs, including "The Downfall of the Serbian Kingdom" and "The Kosovo Maiden"); Koljević 1980 (historical context and criticism)

Epic (comparative): Beissinger et al. 1999; Honko 2000a; Foley 1990, 1991; Coote 1978

Epic (Moslem): *SCHS* (edition and translation of Parry collection), Foley 2003 (edition and translation); Lord 1960; Foley 1999: 35–135

Funeral laments: Kerewsky-Halpern 1981; Lee 2002 (South Slavic and Old Testament); Alexiou 1974 (ancient and modern Greek); Arant 1981 (Russian); Foley 1991: 168–74 (ancient Greek); Honko et al. 1993: 565–613 (Finnish)

Genealogies: Kerewsky-Halpern 1980; Halpern et al. 1983; Wagner 1983

Post-Script

Pre-script, Para-script, Post-script

For eleven and one-third months of our species-year, homo sapiens was by definition a pre-script species. That is, we fashioned and maintained our societies, as well as all of the cultural, historical, legal, and everyday machinery that made them work, entirely without the written word. According to the terminology advocated in this book, we used "words" instead of words. And we can state that fact without qualification, since words as we know them today—as print-bytes in a dictionary, as strings of letters with spaces at either end—didn't exist. Eleven and one-third months or 94 percent of our historical existence depended wholly on an alternate technology, the technology of oral tradition.

Since the appearance of Egyptian and Mesopotamian inscription at the close of the fourth millennium B.C.E., on December 10 or day number 346 on homo sapiens' calendar, script has been an available culture-making tool. That means it's been available in some quarters as a partner for oral poetry, which as we've seen interacts with writing and texts in fascinating ways. Of course, script wasn't an overnight and universal success: it made inroads gradually and differentially, initially serving as a vehicle for record-keeping in many societies. And we shouldn't overlook the fact that there are many societies today—at the dawn of the third millennium C.E.—that use writing and texts sparingly if at all. In the course of our inquiry into "What is oral poetry?" and "What is reading?" we discovered that the abstractions of orality and literacy are too blunt to be truly diagnostic. Oral and written modes of composition and expression can and do coexist not only within the same society but even within the very same individual. Since December 10 we've been a para-script species.

Now, with the advent of electronic media and especially the Internet, some of us are in some ways entering a post-script age. Note how carefully and non-

categorically that observation is phrased. Let me caution immediately that I
don't mean to identify or imply any sort of evolutionary sequence of airtight
units or stages. I'll advocate no evolution toward higher forms, no ladder of
civilization, just the emergence and interaction of new ways to communicate.
Even the most wired of societies and individuals still scratch symbols on textual surfaces, and today's increasingly computer-driven world still includes
many cultures for whom oral tradition is the chief technology. Because those
intersections are likely to continue indefinitely, a pull-down menu of expressive options is the fairest and most representative model. Oral tradition, writing, and e-communication aren't segregated; they interact in myriad ways and
are forever creating new possibilities. The myth of the media monolith—something versus something else in a battle to the technological death—is nothing
but reductive of human complexity. Instead of analyzing (from Greek *analuein,*
to "unloose, undo") the one away from the other, we'd do better to look into
their dynamic coexistence.

Pathways

Indeed, we can profit substantially by recognizing the uncanny similarity between much oral poetry and the Internet.[1] Although they may seem media-
generations divorced from one another, forever separated by the great bulk of
books and journals that fill our libraries, the truth is that both depend on links
rather than items, on connections rather than spatialized, warehousable objects. Homer tells us as much when he praises Demodokos and all oral epic
singers because "the Muse has taught them the pathways" (*Odyssey* 8.481), or
when he has Phemios beg for his life by citing the bardic credential that "the
god implanted all sorts of pathways in my mind" (*Odyssey* 22.347–48). And
we can hardly walk into an office, library, or home that isn't plugged into pathways that promise access to a whole world of information. That's what the
digital god gave us.

This isn't empty talk. The Greek word I translate as "pathway" is *oimê,* the
most fundamental meaning of which is "way, road, path." Homer and his tradition are conceiving of their epic songs not as polished gemstones in settings,
not as tidily edited and arranged papyrus scrolls, and certainly not as the se-
quenced bunches of bound pages that serve as our default notion of a work of
verbal art. They're seeing oral poetry as a linked system of *oimai,* of pathways,
which the epic singer follows here and there during the journey that is his performance and his poem—not unlike using the resources of the Internet.

The advantages of this congruency are empowering. For one thing, we can
quickly jump the fence created by texts and get a glimpse of what's out there.

If the singer's and audience's experience of an oral poem is more like a web-surfing expedition than a forensic examination of a textual corpse, then we gain a familiar, culturally embedded analogy for oral poetry. Poets travel the networks of their traditions, one time veering in one direction, another time choosing a different route. Multiple possibilities open up before them at every fork in the road. Those involved in Oral Performance can tailor the song to the present audience by selecting this or that option. Those performing Voiced Texts will follow a blazed trail, to be sure, but it will diverge in instance-specific ways every time they set out. Voices from the Past, even when frozen into singularity, can reveal at least part of the network of implications to which they traditionally refer. And Written Oral Poetry, the most textual of our flexible categories, can likewise divulge some of its pathways to the patient reader.

The key to these possibilities is to recognize that—like the Internet we browse, learn from, and purchase on—oral poetry amounts to a linked series of pathways. Manifold destinations await us; alternate outcomes beckon; no single trajectory is "correct"; each experience is different. In both media the object or goal is in fact never an object, and getting there is more than half the fun.

Cyber-editions and E-readers

In this spirit I propose taking advantage of the congruency and using the "new medium" to better image the nature and dynamics of the "oldest medium." Specifically, I plan a hypertext edition of oral poetry that builds into its innards the aspects of oral tradition that electronic media are uniquely suited to represent. Think of how the physical reality of the book has constrained us. We experience oral poetry in fieldwork, let's say, and record it on video or audio tape. Of course, as a result of this recording it's already a collection of texts rather than the experiences behind them, but we then add insult to injury by cramming some reduction of its complexity between the covers of a mass market paperback. That's the time-honored ritual for making oral poetry manageable.

So now everybody can have one, but what's really left in this cenotaph? We customarily choose one single version as the "main text" and relegate all other versions to lesser status, maybe ignoring them altogether. And we delete everything else that doesn't translate to the textual medium: the visuals (except for possibly a few photographs), the audio (including all of the linguistic and paralinguistic dimensions), the music (except for a transcription only specialists can read), and the overall performance environment. Perhaps the most crippling of deletions is any sense of a fluent audience for the oral poem, whom we replace with nonfluent text-consumers via a sort of eminent domain.

To get a sense of what improvements cyber-editions of oral poetry might

offer, consider first the general shape of a book-edition. In addition to an epitomized text, front and center stage, editors often include alternate versions or
variants of certain lines or passages, always offstage. The *apparatus criticus*
(critical apparatus) can include cultural and historical backgrounds, commentary on problematic points, a glossary, a bibliography, and other aids to reading. Of course, the book medium demands that all of these aids be document-
based and segregated from the text itself, so that flipping pages back and forth
or concentrating on one section at a time are the only methods of accessing
them. Context has to fit the reading medium or suffer the consequences; it's
strictly limited in nature and held at arm's length. The main focus remains on
the textual reframing of the experience. That's the way oral poems are remade
into texts, which then create audiences on their own revisionist terms.

But what if we were able to restore some of the experience of oral poetry,
something of the event-context that has been peeled away during the textualization process? Let's think of three kinds of strategies: (1) ancillary files, (2)
audiovisual support, and (3) the interactive edition itself. All of these would
fall under the blanket concept of an *apparatus fabulosus*—not a critical but a
story-based apparatus.[2]

The first of these reading prostheses is the easiest to conceptualize and construct. Instead of burying historical and cultural backgrounds in an introduc-
tory essay, such material can be linked in hypertext to appropriate spots and
moments in the oral poem. E-readers can navigate to and from such ancillary
files as they wish. Does the South Slavic *guslar* mention the Turkish tsar Sulej-
man the Magnificent? Then refer users to a brief history of the Ottoman
monarch's reign and its significance for the passage in question. Does the poet
recount the readying of a horse at great length? Then offer the option of immediately consulting a brief entry on the material culture surrounding that
process, with further links to a glossary explaining grooming procedures,
snaffle-bits, saddle girths, and the like. Material culture, history, biography, and
other factual dimensions can be glossed quickly and precisely via appropriately situated links.

Similarly, the linguistically inclined reader could pursue the question of
word usage. Does the *guslar* resort to other than standard dictionary forms?
What dialects are represented and why? What anachronisms appear in the singer's epic vocabulary? Anything that book-based editions do in notes or appen-
dices or separate volumes can be made as readily accessible as a single click.
Furthermore, e-readers may choose to follow a pathway or not, according to
their interests and as they see fit, giving them the opportunity to shape their
own reading each time they sit down to their desk(top)s, mouse in hand.

But the support system for reading need not end with conventional documents. Both audio and video "texts" of the performance can be made just as accessible as the kinds of things we normally commit to paper and print. Instead of languishing in inaccessible archives, those acoustic and visual resources could be brought into play via a link on the edition's home page. Suddenly, instead of having to be content with a secondhand representation and report, you can actually watch or hear the performance. Gopala Naika's 1990 version of the *Siri Epic,* which resulted in such a superb book-based edition, might appear in whole or in part through a pathway to the videotapes shot by Lauri Honko and his Finnish-Tulu fieldwork team. A night at the Nuyorican Poets Café could come alive visually and aurally through the same mechanism. Field collections of ballad, lyric, epic, or whatever that were made before the advent of portable video equipment could reemerge as an audio reality at the click of a home page button. Of course, viewing or hearing these more-than-page-bound facsimiles doesn't insert the reader back into the original audience. Those events happened, usually without any of us present, and can't be wholly re-created in order to include us. But video or audio will allow us to step into the poetic tradition to a greater degree, to see and hear a few of those many cues that vanish when a performance becomes a book-bound edition.

The third reading strategy that cyber-editions support is the most central: an interactive image of the oral poem that restores some of its multiformity, ecology, and idiom. To focus our observations, I'll address one particular case—Halil Bajgorić's performance of *The Wedding of Mustajbey's Son Bećirbey,* collected June 13, 1935, by Milman Parry and Albert Lord and mentioned near the end of the Eighth Word. But with suitable modifications to take individual traditions, performers, and media into account, similar kinds of cyber-editions could be fashioned for Voiced Texts, Voices from the Past, and Written Oral Poems, as well as other Oral Performances.

As for multiformity, an e-edition offers the opportunity to understand variation within limits and avoid the absolute epitomization of any one version. Fossils would give way to living organisms, textual products to dynamic processes. Since hypertext makes segregated textual items immediately available, other versions of any oral poem can be brought electronically into play. More to the point for our purposes, the optional links can be configured according to "words" rather than words. E-editions can thus readily reflect the terms in which the poem was composed and transmitted instead of imposing an alternate cognitive setup. As a result, they make for increased fidelity to oral poetry, simply because the activity they encourage is more faithful to the way the poem and its tradition work. As our *proverb* has it, "composition and reception are two sides of the same coin."

Ecologically speaking, any user of such an e-edition could read *across the tradition,* following a particular phrase or typical scene or story-pattern through myriad other situations.[3] Imagine the possibilities: you could examine any "word" you wish elsewhere within or outside this particular performance, as well as track its role in other versions by the same singer, other versions by different singers, or even wholly different songs. All other instances of a "word" would be immediately available, perhaps on a split screen, without ever leaving the version one happens to be reading. Should it become necessary or desirable to shift versions, you could do that as well. Once the cyber-structure is built, the only limit on reading across the tradition would be the number of versions and other songs in the data-base.

Reading Bajgorić's performance in "byte-sized chunks" thus provides the e-reader a sense of its multiformity and ecology, giving a hands-on tutorial in variability and the relations between any single performance and the tradition in which it's networked. But cyber-editions can do even more: they can help to restore the lost dimension of idiom, of traditional implication, of the "more so" in our *proverb* stating that "Oral poetry works like language, only more so."

Take a few examples. Suppose a first-time reader encounters the phrase "black cuckoo" (*kukavica crna*). Instead of letting the "word" pass by as a metrical cipher with no special connotation, the e-reader could move the cursor to the phrase and generate the pop-up notation "a woman who has lost or is about to lose her husband." Editions have never included a glossary of traditional implications, so this information would be an improvement over the norm even in the unwieldy format of the conventional book. But if finding that information and grasping its importance were as quick and easy as a pop-up definition, e-readers could factor in idiomatic meanings without interrupting their engagement with the ongoing story. Later on, some of them might decide to investigate the phrase further, essentially to improve their reading comprehension for this and subsequent reading episodes. Whatever the general or particular goal, the e-edition's network of linked pathways would support its achievement.

Numerous other "words," characters, and situations could also be given expressive life by a cyber-edition of *The Wedding of Mustajbey's Son Bećirbey.* Consider Tale, the redoubtable anti-hero on the swaybacked horse. A pop-up gloss could offer a hint of his crucial role in major battles, as well as include a link both to a longer summary and to each of the actual narrative situations into which this unlikely hero makes his entrance. Click a button opposite typical scenes of Readying the Horse and Arming the Hero, and you're offered a bare-bones sketch of the usual ritual (so that you can judge what's expectable and what's unusual about any particular instance), the heads-up advice that such scenes idiomatically lead to long journeys and danger (so that the narrative map unfolds before you), and of course a catalogue of pathways to all other such scenes in the database (so that you can enjoy a tutorial on these "words" at your leisure). Even whole story-patterns—like the Wedding song or the ubiquitous Return song—can be foregrounded in a cyber-edition. By making explicit the cues and patterns that are always implicit in South Slavic oral epic, e-editions can help to increase our fluency in the language spoken by the singer. They can make us a better audience.

In short, then, this Post-Script champions harnessing the "new technology" to more realistically represent the "oldest technology." These two communications media might seem worlds apart; indeed, our species-calendar places them fully five millennia or twenty-one species-days apart, and that's unquestionably a very long time. And yet both media depend fundamentally on pathways, *oimai* that get you from one site to another. Would it be too facetious to suggest that Homer's URL for "supernaturally induced fear" is <http:// www.greenfear.org> or that Halil Bajgorić's net address for "a widowed or soon-to-be-widowed woman" is <http://www.blackcuckoo.org>? Because oral poetries use pathways to access multiformity, ecology, and idiom, it is greatly to our reading advantage to construct cyber-editions that do analogous sorts of things. Odd though it may initially seem, it is in fact the most recent technology that gives us the best opportunity to understand how the first technology works. Perhaps post-script and pre-script aren't so far apart after all.

Notes

1. For a full discussion of this analogy, see Foley 1998b. I am only too aware that the "shelf-life" of technological innovations is always mercilessly short, and that the specific terms in which this argument is presented will need continuous updating. Hopefully, however, the basic comparison and analogy between oral tradition and cyber-communication will remain recognizable.

2. Thanks to my colleague Barbara Wallach for inventing "apparatus fabulosus" in response to my search for a suitable term.

3. Here I use the approach called Immanent Art to illustrate ecological realities, but e-editions could also be coded for keys to performance (Performance Theory) or performative and structural features (Ethnopoetics).

Bibliography

Abrahams, Roger D. 1962. "Playing the Dozens." *Journal of American Folklore,* 75: 209–18.

———. 1970. *Deep Down in the Jungle: Negro Narrative Folklore from the Streets of Philadelphia.* Rev. ed. Chicago: Aldine.

Alexander, Ronelle. 1998. "South Slavic Traditions." In Foley 1998a: 273–79.

Alexiou, Margaret. 1974. *The Ritual Lament in Greek Tradition.* Cambridge: Cambridge University Press.

Algarín, Miguel, and Bob Holman, eds. 1994. *Aloud: Voices from the Nuyorican Poets Cafe.* New York: Owl Books.

Arant, Patricia. 1981. "Aspects of Oral Style: Russian Traditional Oral Lament." *Canadian-American Slavic Studies,* 15: 42–51.

Baker, James N. 1993. "The Presence of the Name: Reading Scripture in an Indonesian Village." In J. Boyarin 1993: 98–138.

Balogun, F. Odun. 1995. "*Matigari:* An African Novel as Oral Performance." *Oral Tradition,* 10: 129–64.

Barton, David, and Mary Hamilton. 1996. "Social and Cognitive Factors in the Historical Elaboration of Writing." In *Handbook of Human Symbolic Evolution,* ed. Andrew Lock and Charles R. Peters. Oxford: Clarendon Press. Pp. 793–858.

Bauman, Richard. 1977. *Verbal Art as Performance.* Prospect Heights, Ill.: Waveland Press.

———. 1986. *Story, Performance, and Event: Contextual Studies of Oral Narrative.* Cambridge: Cambridge University Press.

———. 1992. *Folklore, Cultural Performances, and Popular Entertainments.* New York: Oxford University Press.

———, and Donald Braid. 1998. "The Ethnography of Performance in the Study of Oral Traditions." In Foley 1998a: 106–22.

———, and Charles L. Briggs. 1990. "Poetics and Performance as Critical Perspectives on Language and Social Life." *Annual Review of Anthropology,* 19: 59–88.

———, and Pamela Ritch. 1994. "Informing Performance: Producing the *Coloquio* in Tierra Blanca." *Oral Tradition,* 9: 255–80.

———, and Joel Sherzer, eds. 1989. *Explorations in the Ethnography of Speaking.* 2d ed. Cambridge: Cambridge University Press.

Beissinger, Margaret H., Jane Tylus, and Susanne Lindgren Wofford, eds. 1999. *Epic Traditions in the Contemporary World: The Poetics of Community.* Berkeley and Los Angeles: University of California Press.

Belcher, Stephen. 1999. *Epic Traditions of Africa.* Bloomington: Indiana University Press.

Benson, Larry D. 1966. "The Literary Character of Anglo-Saxon Narrative Poetry." *Publications of the Modern Language Association,* 49: 365–73.

Bessinger, Jess B. 1978. *A Concordance to the Anglo-Saxon Poetic Records.* Programmed by Philip H. Smith. Ithaca: Cornell University Press.

Biebuyck, Daniel, and Kahombo C. Mateene, eds. and trans. 1969. *The Mwindo Epic from the Banyanga (Congo Republic).* Berkeley and Los Angeles: University of California Press.

Bjork, Robert E. 1997. "Digressions and Episodes." In Bjork and Niles 1997: 193–212.

———, and John D. Niles, eds. 1997. *A Beowulf Handbook.* Lincoln: University of Nebraska Press.

Blackburn, Stuart H. et al., eds. 1989. *Oral Epics in India.* Berkeley and Los Angeles: University of California Press.

Bold, Valentina. 2001. "Rude Bard of the North: James Macpherson and the Folklore of Democracy." *Journal of American Folklore,* 114: 464–77.

Bonair-Agard, Roger et al. n.d. *Burning Down the House: Selected Poems from the Nuyorican Poets Café National Slam Champions.* New York: Soft Skull Press.

Bosley, Keith, trans. 1989. *The Kalevala.* New York: Oxford University Press.

Boyarin, Daniel. 1993. "Placing Reading: Ancient Israel and Medieval Europe." In J. Boyarin 1993: 10–37.

Boyarin, Jonathan. 1993. *The Ethnography of Reading.* Berkeley and Los Angeles: University of California Press.

Bradbury, Nancy Mason. 1998a. *Writing Aloud: Storytelling in Late Medieval England.* Urbana: University of Illinois Press.

———. 1998b. "Traditional Referentiality: The Aesthetic Power of Oral Traditional Structures." In Foley 1998a: 136–45.

Brault, Gerard R., ed. 1978a. *The Song of Roland: An Analytical Edition.* 2 vols. University Park: Pennsylvania State University Press.

———. 1978b. "The French Chansons de Geste." In Oinas 1978: 193–215.

———. 1984. *La Chanson de Roland: Student Edition.* University Park: Pennsylvania State University Press.

Briggs, Charles L. 1988. *Competence in Performance: The Creativity of Tradition in Mexicano Verbal Art.* Philadelphia: University of Pennsylvania Press.

Bright, William, ed. 1993. *A Coyote Reader.* Berkeley and Los Angeles: University of California Press.

Brill de Ramírez, Susan Berry. 1999. *Contemporary American Indian Literatures and the Oral Tradition.* Tucson: University of Arizona Press.

Brown, Duncan. 1998. *Voicing the Text: South African Oral Poetry and Performance.* Cape Town: Oxford University Press.

Brown, Mary Ellen. 1996. "The Mechanism of the Ancient Ballad: William Motherwell's Explanation." *Oral Tradition,* 11: 175–89.

Burgess, Glyn. 1990. *The Song of Roland.* New York: Penguin.

Canales, Maria Cristina, and Jane Frances Morrissey, eds. and trans. 1996. *Gracias, Matiox, Thanks, Hermano Pedro: A Trilingual Anthology of Guatemalan Oral Tradition.* New York: Garland.

Canfora, Luciano. 1990. *The Vanished Library: A Wonder of the Ancient World.* Berkeley and Los Angeles: University of California Press.

Cavallo, Guglielmo, and Roger Chartier, eds. 1999. *A History of Reading in the West.* Trans. Lydia G. Cochrane. Amherst: University of Massachusetts Press. Orig. publ. as *Histoire de la lecture dans le monde occidental.* Rome-Bari: Giuseppe Laterza & Figli Spa, 1997, and Paris: Editions de Seuil, 1995.

Chantraine, Pierre. 1950. "Les verbes grecs signifiant 'lire'." In *Mélanges Henri Grégoire,* Annuaires de l'Institute de Philologie et d'Histoire Orientales et Slaves, 10. Brussels: Secrétariat des Editions de l'Institut. Vol. 2, pp. 115–26.

Chao Gejin. 1997. "Mongolian Oral Epic Poetry: An Overview." *Oral Tradition,* 12: 322–36.

Clanchy, M. T. 1979. *From Memory to Written Record: England, 1066–1307.* London and Cambridge, Mass.: Arnold and Harvard University Press.

Collins, William A., ed. and trans. 1998. *The Guritan of Radin Suane: A Study of the Besemah Oral Epic from South Sumatra.* Leiden: KITLV Press.

Conrad, Joseph L. 1983. "Magic Charms and Healing Rituals in Contemporary Yugoslavia." *Southeastern Europe,* 10: 99–120.

Coote, Mary P. 1978. "Serbocroatian Heroic Songs." In Oinas 1978: 257–85.

―――. 1992. "On the Composition of Women's Songs." *Oral Tradition,* 7: 332–48.

Coplan, David B. 1994. *In the Time of the Cannibals: The Word Music of South Africa's Basotho Migrants.* Chicago: Aldine.

Creed, Robert P. 1975. "Widsith's Journey through Germanic Tradition." In *Anglo-Saxon Poetry: Essays in Appreciation for John C. McGalliard,* ed. Lewis E. Nicholson and Dolores Warwick Frese. Notre Dame: University of Notre Dame Press. Pp. 376–87.

Daniels, Peter D., and William Bright, eds. 1996. *The World's Writing Systems.* New York: Oxford University Press.

Davidson, Olga M. 1994. *Poet and Hero in the Persian Book of Kings.* Ithaca: Cornell University Press.

Davies, Sioned. 1992. "Storytelling in Medieval Wales." *Oral Tradition,* 7: 231–57.

de Vet, Thérèse. 1996. "The Joint Role of Orality and Literacy in the Composition, Transmission, and Performance of the Homeric Texts: A Comparative View." *Transactions of the American Philological Association,* 126: 43–76.

Devlin, Paul. 1998. *Slamnation.* New York: The Cinema Guild. 91 mins. (<http://www.slamnation.com>)

Digges, Diana, and Joanne Rappaport. 1993. "Literacy, Orality, and Ritual Practice in Highland Colombia." In J. Boyarin 1993: 139–55.

Doane, A. N. 1994. "The Ethnography of Scribal Writing and Anglo-Saxon Poetry: Scribe as Performer." *Oral Tradition,* 9: 420–39.

DuBois, Thomas A. 1995. *Finnish Folk Poetry and the* Kalevala. New York: Garland.

―――. 1998. "Ethnopoetics." In Foley 1998a: 123–35.

Duggan, Joseph J. 1969. *A Concordance to the Chanson de Roland.* Columbus: Ohio State University Press.

———. 1973. *The Song of Roland: Formulaic Style and Poetic Craft.* Berkeley and Los Angeles: University of California Press.

———. 1974. "Formulaic Diction in the *Cantar de mio Cid* and the Old French Epic." *Forum for Modern Language Studies,* 10: 260–69. Rpt. in Joseph J. Duggan, ed., *Oral Literature: Seven Essays.* Edinburgh: Scottish Academic Press, 1975. Pp. 74–83.

———. 1989. *The* Cantar de mio Cid: *Poetic Creation in Its Economic and Social Contexts.* Cambridge: Cambridge University Press.

Dundes, Alan, Jerry W. Leach, and Bora Özkök. 1972. "The Strategy of Turkish Boys' Verbal Dueling Rhymes." In *Directions in Sociolinguistics: The Ethnography of Communication,* ed. John J. Gumperz and Dell Hymes. New York: Holt, Rinehart, and Winston. Pp. 130–60.

Eades, Caroline, and Françoise Létoublon. 1999. "From Film Analysis to Oral-Formulaic Theory: The Case of the Yellow Oilskins." In *Contextualizing Classics: Ideology, Performance, Dialogue,* ed. Thomas M. Falkner, Nancy Felson, and David Konstan. Lanham, Md.: Rowman & Littlefield. Pp. 301–16.

Edwards, Mark W. 1986. "Homer and Oral Tradition: The Formula, Part I." *Oral Tradition,* 1: 171–230.

———. 1988. "Homer and Oral Tradition: The Formula, Part II." *Oral Tradition,* 3: 11–60.

———. 1992. "Homer and Oral Tradition: The Type-Scene." *Oral Tradition,* 7: 284–330.

Eisenstein, Elizabeth L. 1968. "Some Conjectures about the Impact of Printing on Western Society and Thought." *Journal of Modern History,* 40: 1–56.

———. 1979. *The Printing Press as an Agent of Change: Communications and Cultural Transformations in Early-Modern Europe.* 2 vols. Cambridge: Cambridge University Press.

———. 1980. "The Emergence of Print Culture in the West." *Journal of Communication,* 30, i: 99–106.

Erdely, Stephen. 1995. *Music of Southslavic Epics from the Bihać Region of Bosnia.* New York: Garland.

Erzgräber, Willi, and Sabine Volk, eds. 1988. *Mündlichkeit und Schriftlichkeit im englischen Mittelalter.* ScriptOralia, 5. Tübingen: Gunter Narr.

Evers, Larry, and Barre Toelken, eds. 2001. *Native American Oral Traditions: Collaboration and Interpretation.* Logan: Utah State University Press. Orig. publ. as a special issue of *Oral Tradition,* 13, i (1998).

Fine, Elizabeth C. 1994. *The Folklore Text: From Performance to Print.* Bloomington: Indiana University Press. Orig. ed. 1984.

Finnegan, Ruth. 1970. *Oral Literature in Africa.* Oxford: Oxford University Press.

———. 1977. *Oral Poetry: Its Nature, Significance, and Social Context.* Cambridge: Cambridge University Press. Rpt. Bloomington: Indiana University Press, 1992.

———. 1988. *Literacy and Orality: Studies in the Technology of Communication.* Oxford: Basil Blackwell.

————, and Margaret Orbell, eds. 1995. *South Pacific Oral Traditions.* Voices in Performance and Text. Bloomington: Indiana University Press.

Foley, John Miles. 1985. *Oral-Formulaic Theory and Research: An Introduction and Annotated Bibliography.* New York: Garland. Rpt. 1988, 1992. Updated electronic version at <http://www.oraltradition.org>.

————, ed. 1986. *Oral Tradition in Literature: Interpretation in Context.* Columbia: University of Missouri Press.

————. 1988. *The Theory of Oral Composition: History and Methodology.* Bloomington: Indiana University Press. Rpt. 1992.

————. 1990. *Traditional Oral Epic: The* Odyssey, Beowulf, *and the Serbo-Croatian Return Song.* Berkeley and Los Angeles: University of California Press. Rpt. 1993.

————. 1991. *Immanent Art: From Structure to Meaning in Traditional Oral Epic.* Bloomington: Indiana University Press.

————. 1992. "Word-Power, Performance, and Tradition." *Journal of American Folklore,* 105: 275–301.

————. 1994. "Proverbs and Proverbial Function in South Slavic and Comparative Epic." *Proverbium,* 11: 77–92.

————. 1995a. *The Singer of Tales in Performance.* Bloomington: Indiana University Press.

————. 1995b. "Folk Literature." In Greetham 1995: 600–26.

————. 1997. "Oral Tradition and Its Implications." In Morris and Powell 1997: 146–73.

————, ed. 1998a. *Teaching Oral Traditions.* New York: Modern Language Association.

————. 1998b. "The Impossibility of Canon." In Foley 1998a: 13–33.

————. 1999. *Homer's Traditional Art.* University Park: Pennsylvania State University Press.

————. 2002. "Macpherson's Ossian: Trying to Hit a Moving Target." *Journal of American Folklore,* 115: 99–106.

————, ed. and trans. 2003. *Halil Bajgorić's The Wedding of Mustajbey's Son Bećirbey.* Folklore Fellows Communications. Suomalainen Tiedeakatemia. Forthcoming.

————, and Barbara Kerewsky-Halpern. 1976. "'Udovica Jana': A Case Study of an Oral Performance." *Slavonic and East European Review,* 54: 11–23.

————. 1978. "*Bajanje:* Healing Magic in Rural Serbia." In *Culture and Curing: Anthropological Perspectives on Traditional Medical Beliefs and Practices,* ed. Peter Morley and Roy Wallis. London: Peter Owen. Pp. 40–56.

Gaskill, Howard, ed. 1996. *The Poems of Ossian and Related Works (The Ossianic Works of James Macpherson).* Edinburgh: Edinburgh University Press.

Glazner, Gary Mex, ed. 2000. *Poetry Slam: The Competitive Art of Performance Poetry.* San Francisco: Manic D Press.

Goetsch, Paul, ed. 1990. *Mündliches Wissen in neuzeitlicher Literatur.* Tübingen: Gunter Narr.

Goldin, Frederick, trans. 1978. *The Song of Roland.* New York: Norton.

Goody, Jack. 1987. *The Interface between the Written and the Oral.* Cambridge: Cambridge University Press.

———. 2000. *The Power of the Written Tradition.* Washington, D.C.: Smithsonian Institution Press.

Gordy, Eric D. 1999. *The Culture of Power in Serbia: Nationalism and the Destruction of Alternatives.* University Park: Pennsylvania State University Press.

Gossen, Gary H. 1974. *Chamulas in the World of the Sun: Time and Space in a Maya Oral Tradition.* Cambridge, Mass.: Harvard University Press.

Graff, Harvey J. 1987. *The Legacies of Literacy: Continuities and Contradictions in Western Culture and Society.* Bloomington: Indiana University Press.

Greenberg, Robert D. 2000. "Language Politics in the Federal Republic of Yugoslavia: The Crisis over the Future of Serbian." *Slavic Review,* 59: 625–40.

Greetham, David C., ed. 1995. *Scholarly Editing: A Guide to Research.* New York: Modern Language Association.

Gunner, Liz. Forthcoming. "Frozen Assets? Orality and the Public Space in Kwa-Zulu Natal: *Izibongo* and *Isicathamiya.*" In *Script, Subjugation, and Subversion: Essays in Orality, Literacy, and Colonialism,* ed. Jonathan A. Draper. Durban: University of Natal Press.

Habermalz, Sabine. 1998. "'Signs on a White Field': A Look at Orality *in* Literacy and James Joyce's *Ulysses.*" *Oral Tradition,* 13: 285–305.

Hale, Thomas A. 1998. *Griots and Griottes: Masters of Words and Music.* Bloomington: Indiana University Press.

Halpern, Joel M., Barbara Kerewsky-Halpern, and John Miles Foley. 1983. "Oral Genealogies and Official Records: A Comparative Approach Using Serbian Data." *Southeastern Europe,* 10: 150–74.

Hanks, W. F. 1989. "Text and Textuality." *Annual Review of Anthropology,* 18: 95–127.

Haring, Lee, ed. 1994. *African Oral Traditions.* A special issue of *Oral Tradition,* 9, i.

Harris, William V. 1989. *Ancient Literacy.* Cambridge, Mass.: Harvard University Press.

Harrison, Robert, trans. 1970. *The Song of Roland.* New York: Mentor.

Haslam, Michael. 1997. "Homeric Papyri and Transmission of the Text." In Morris and Powell 1997: 55–100.

Hatto, Arthur T., ed. and trans. 1990. *The Manas of Wilhelm Radloff.* Wiesbaden: Otto Harrassowitz.

Havelock, Eric A. 1963. *Preface to Plato.* Cambridge, Mass.: Harvard University Press. Rpt. 1982.

———. 1986. *The Muse Learns to Write: Reflections on Orality and Literacy from Antiquity to the Present.* New Haven: Yale University Press.

Heaney, Seamus, trans. 2000. *Beowulf.* New York: Farrar, Straus, and Giroux.

Heath, Shirley Brice. 1982. "What No Bedtime Story Means: Narrative Skills at Home and School." *Language in Society,* 11: 49–76.

———. 1988. "Protean Shapes in Literary Events: Ever-Shifting Oral and Literate Traditions." In Kintgen et al. 1988: 348–70.

Heissig, Walther. 1996. "The Present State of the Mongolian Epic and Some Topics for Future Research." *Oral Tradition,* 11: 85–98.

Hemstreet, Keith et al. 2000. *nycSLAMS,* New York: Zoom Culture. (<http://www.zoomculture.com>)

Hirsch, Edward. 1999. *How to Read a Poem, and Fall in Love with Poetry.* New York: Harcourt.

Hladczuk, John, William Eller, and Sharon Hladczuk, comps. 1989. *Literacy/Illiteracy in the World: A Bibliography.* New York: Greenwood Press.

Hobart, Michael E., and Zachary S. Schiffman. 1998. *Information Ages: Literacy, Numeracy, and the Computer Revolution.* Baltimore: Johns Hopkins University Press.

Holton, Milne, and Vasa D. Mihailovich, trans. 1997. *Songs of the Serbian People: From the Collections of Vuk Karadžić.* Pittsburgh: University of Pittsburgh Press.

Honko, Lauri. 1998. *Textualising the Siri Epic.* Folklore Fellows Communications, 264. Helsinki: Suomalainen Tiedeakatemia.

———, ed. 2000a. *Textualization of Oral Epics.* Berlin: Mouton de Gruyter.

———. 2000b. "Text as Process and Practice: The Textualization of Oral Epics." In Honko 2000a: 3–54.

———, with Chinnappa Gowda, Anneli Honko, and Viveka Rai, eds. and trans. 1998a. *The Siri Epic as Performed by Gopala Naika.* Part 1. Folklore Fellows Communications, 265. Helsinki: Suomalainen Tiedeakatemia.

———, eds. and trans. 1998b. *The Siri Epic as Performed by Gopala Naika.* Part 2. Folklore Fellows Communications, 266. Helsinki: Suomalainen Tiedeakatemia.

———, and Anneli Honko. 2000. "Variation and Textuality in Oral Epics: A South Indian Instance." In *Thick Corpus, Organic Variation, and Textuality in Oral Tradition,* ed. Lauri Honko. Helsinki: Finnish Literature Society. Pp. 351–72.

———, Senni Timonen, and Michael Branch, eds. 1993. *The Great Bear: A Thematic Anthology of Oral Poetry in the Finno-Ugrian Languages.* Poems trans. by Keith Bosley. Helsinki: Finnish Literature Society.

Horsley, Richard A., with Jonathan A. Draper. 1999. *Whoever Hears You Hears Me: Prophets, Performance, and Tradition in Q.* Harrisburg, Pa.: Trinity Press International.

Howe, Nicholas. 1993. "The Cultural Construction of Reading in Anglo-Saxon England." In J. Boyarin 1993: 58–79.

Hudson, Nicholas. 1994. *Writing and European Thought.* Cambridge: Cambridge University Press.

Hymes, Dell. 1977. "Discovering Oral Performance and Measured Verse in American Indian Narrative." *New Literary History,* 7: 431–57. Rev. in Hymes 1981: 79–141.

———. 1981. *"In Vain I Tried to Tell You": Essays in Native American Ethnopoetics.* Philadelphia: University of Pennsylvania Press.

———. 1989. "Ways of Speaking." In Bauman and Sherzer 1989: 433–51, 473–74.

———. 1994. "Ethnopoetics, Oral-Formulaic Theory, and Editing Texts." *Oral Tradition,* 9: 330–70.

Irwin, Bonnie D. 1995. "What's in a Frame? The Medieval Textualization of Traditional Storytelling." *Oral Tradition,* 10: 27–53.

———. 1998. "The Frame Tale East and West." In Foley 1998a: 391–99.

Jaffee, Martin S. 1998. "The Hebrew Scriptures." In Foley 1998a: 321–29.

———. 1999. "Oral Tradition in the Writings of Rabbinic Oral Torah: On Theorizing Rabbinic Orality." *Oral Tradition,* 14: 3–32.

———. 2001. *Torah in the Mouth: Writing and Oral Tradition in Palestinian Judaism 200 B.C.E.–400 C.E.* Oxford: Oxford University Press.

Janko, Richard. 1990. "The *Iliad* and Its Editors: Dictation and Redaction." *Classical Antiquity,* 9: 326–34.

Jensen, Minna Skafte. 2000. "The Writing of the *Iliad* and the *Odyssey.*" In Honko 2000a: 57–70.

Johns, Adrian. 1998. *The Nature of the Book: Print and Knowledge in the Making.* Chicago: University of Chicago Press.

Johnson, John William. 1980. "Yes, Virginia, There Is an Epic in Africa." *Review of African Literatures,* 11: 308–26.

———. 1992. *The Epic of Son-Jara: A West African Tradition.* Text by Fa-Digi Sisòkò. Bloomington: Indiana University Press. Orig. ed. 1986.

———. 2000. "Authenticity and Oral Performance: Textualizing the Epics of Africa for Western Audiences." In Honko 2000a: 237–46.

——— et al. 1997. *Oral Epics from Africa: Vibrant Voices from a Vast Continent.* Bloomington: Indiana University Press.

Kaschula, Russell H. 1995. "Mandela Comes Home: The Poets' Perspective." *Oral Tradition,* 10: 91–110.

———. 2000. *The Bones of the Ancestors Are Shaking: Xhosa Oral Poetry in Context.* Cape Town: Juta Press.

Kay, Matthew. 1995. *The Index of the Milman Parry Collection 1933–1935: Heroic Songs, Conversations, and Stories.* New York: Garland.

Keeling, Richard. 1992. *Cry for Luck: Sacred Song and Speech among the Yurok, Hupa, and Karok Indians of Northwestern California.* Berkeley and Los Angeles: University of California Press.

Kelber, Werner H. 1997. *The Oral and the Written Gospel: The Hermeneutics of Speaking and Writing in the Synoptic Tradition, Mark, Paul, and Q.* Voices in Performance and Text. Bloomington: Indiana University Press. Orig. ed. Philadelphia: Fortress Press, 1983.

Kent, George P. 1983. "The Poetic Order of Healing in a Czech Incantation against Erysipelas." *Southeastern Europe,* 10: 121–49.

Kerewsky-Halpern, Barbara. 1980. "Genealogy as Oral Genre in a Serbian Village." In *Oral Traditional Literature: A Festschrift for Albert Bates Lord,* ed. John Miles Foley. Columbus, Ohio: Slavica. Pp. 301–21.

———. 1981. "Text and Context in Serbian Ritual Lament." *Canadian-American Slavic Studies,* 15: 52–60.

———, and John Miles Foley. 1978. "The Power of the Word: Healing Charms as an Oral Genre." *Journal of American Folklore,* 91: 903–24.

Kernan, Alvin. 1987. *Printing Technology, Letters, and Samuel Johnson.* Princeton: Princeton University Press.

Kintgen, Eugene R., Barry M. Kroll, and Mike Rose. 1988. *Perspectives on Literacy.* Carbondale and Edwardsville: Southern Illinois University Press.

Klaeber, Frederick, ed. 1950. *Beowulf and the Fight at Finnsburg.* 3d ed. with 1st and 2d supplements. Boston: D. C. Heath.

Klein, Anne Carolyn. 1994. "Oral Genres and the Art of Reading in Tibet." *Oral Tradition,* 9: 281–314.

Koljević, Svetozar. 1980. *The Epic in the Making.* Oxford: Clarendon Press.

Kolsti, John S. 1990. *The Bilingual Singer: A Study in Albanian and Serbo-Croatian Oral Epic Poetry.* New York: Garland.

Krupat, Arnold. 1989. *The Voice in the Margin: Native American Literature and the Canon.* Berkeley and Los Angeles: University of California Press.

———, ed. 1993. *New Voices in Native American Literary Criticism.* Washington, D.C.: Smithsonian Institution Press.

Labov, William. 1972. *Language in the Inner City: Studies in the Black English Vernacular.* Philadelphia: University of Pennsylvania Press.

Lattimore, Richmond. 1951. *The Iliad of Homer.* Chicago: University of Chicago Press.

Lee, Nancy C. 2002. *The Singers of Lamentations: Cities under Siege from Ur to Jerusalem to Sarajevo. . . .* Leiden: Brill.

Leslau, Charlotte, and Wolf Leslau, eds. 1962. *African Proverbs.* With decorations by Jeff Hill. White Plains, N.Y.: Peter Pauper Press. Rpt. 1985.

Levin, Marc. 1998. *Slam.* Offline Entertainment Group.

Lord, Albert B. 1960. *The Singer of Tales.* Cambridge, Mass.: Harvard University Press. 2d ed. by Stephen A. Mitchell and Gregory Nagy, 2000, with audio and video CD.

———. 1986. "The Merging of Two Worlds: Oral and Written Poetry as Carriers of Ancient Values." In Foley 1986: 19–64.

———. 1989. "Theories of Oral Literature and the Latvian *Dainas.*" In Vikis-Freibergs 1989a: 35–48.

———. 1991. *Epic Singers and Oral Tradition.* Ithaca: Cornell University Press.

———. 1995. *The Singer Resumes the Tale.* Ed. Mary Louise Lord. Ithaca: Cornell University Press.

———, and Béla Bartók, eds. and trans. 1951. *Serbo-Croatian Folk Songs.* New York: Columbia University Press.

MacCoull, Leslie. 1999. "Oral-Formulaic Approaches to Coptic Hymnography." *Oral Tradition,* 14: 354–400.

Magner, Thomas F. 1972. *Introduction to the Croatian and Serbian Language.* State College, Pa.: Singidunum Press. Rev. ed. University Park: Pennsylvania State University Press, 1997.

Magoun, Francis P., Jr. 1953. "The Oral-Formulaic Character of Anglo-Saxon Narrative Poetry." *Speculum,* 28: 446–67.

Malone, Kemp, ed. 1962. *Widsith.* Copenhagen: Rosenkilde and Bagger.

Manguel, Alberto. 1996. *A History of Reading.* New York: Penguin.

Martin, Henri-Jean. 1994. *The History and Power of Writing.* Chicago: University of Chicago Press. Orig. publ. as *L'histoire et pouvoirs d'écrit.* Librairie Académique Perrin, 1988.

Martin, Richard P. 1989. *The Language of Heroes: Speech and Performance in the* Iliad. Ithaca: Cornell University Press.

———. 1998. "Homer's *Iliad* and *Odyssey.*" In Foley 1998a: 339–50.

Mason, Bruce Lionel. 1998. "E-Texts: The Orality and Literacy Issue Revisited." *Oral Tradition*, 13: 306–29.

Matthias, John, and Vladeta Vučković, trans. 1987. *The Battle of Kosovo*. Athens, Ohio: Swallow Press / Ohio University Press.

McCarthy, William B. 1990. *The Ballad Matrix*. Bloomington: Indiana University Press.

——, ed. 1994. *Jack in Two Worlds: Contemporary North American Tellers and Their Tales*. Chapel Hill: University of North Carolina Press.

——. 2001. "Oral Theory and Epic Studies." *Choice*, 39, 1 (September): 61–75.

McDowell, John Holmes. 1989. *Sayings of the Ancestors: The Spiritual Life of the Sibundoy Indians*. Lexington: University Press of Kentucky.

——. 1998. "Native American Traditions (South)." In Foley 1998a: 162–73.

McKean, Thomas A. 2001. "The Fieldwork Legacy of James Macpherson." *Journal of American Folklore*, 114: 447–63.

McKitterick, Rosamond, ed. 1990. *The Uses of Literacy in Early Mediaeval Europe*. Cambridge: Cambridge University Press.

McLean, Mervyn, and Margaret Orbell. 1975. *Traditional Songs of the Maori*. Wellington: Reed.

Mieder, Wolfgang. 1982. *International Proverb Scholarship: An Annotated Bibliography*. New York: Garland.

——, and Alan Dundes, eds. 1981. *The Wisdom of Many: Essays on the Proverb*. New York: Garland.

Mihailovich, Vasa D., ed. and trans. 1986. *The Mountain Wreath, by P. P. Njegoš*. Irvine, Calif.: Charles Schlacks.

Miletich, John S. 1978a. "Oral-Traditional Style and Learned Literature: A New Perspective." *Poetics and the Theory of Literature*, 3: 345–56.

——. 1978b. "Elaborate Style in South Slavic Oral Narrative and in Kačić-Miošić's *Razgovor*." In *American Contributions to the Eighth International Conference of Slavists (Zagreb and Ljubljana, September 3–9, 1978)*. Vol. 1: Linguistics and Poetics, ed. Henrik Birnbaum. Columbus, Ohio: Slavica. Pp. 522–31.

——, ed. 1991. *Serbo-Croatian Oral Traditions*. A special issue of *Oral Tradition*, 6, ii–iii.

Miner, Earl. 1993. "Poetic Contests." In *The New Princeton Encyclopedia of Poetry and Poetics*, ed. Alex Preminger and T. V. F. Brogan. Princeton: Princeton University Press. Pp. 927–29.

Morris, Ian, and Barry Powell, eds. 1997. *A New Companion to Homer*. Leiden: Brill.

Murko, Matija. 1990. "The Singers and Their Epic Songs." Trans. J. M. Foley. *Oral Tradition*, 5: 107–30.

Nagy, Gregory. 1996a. *Homeric Questions*. Austin: University of Texas Press.

——. 1996b. *Poetry as Performance: Homer and Beyond*. Cambridge: Cambridge University Press.

Nagy, Joseph Falaky. 2001. "Observations on the Ossianesque in Medieval Irish Literature and Modern Irish Folklore." *Journal of American Folklore*, 114: 436–46.

Nettle, Daniel, and Suzanne Romaine. 2000. *Vanishing Voices: The Extinction of the World's Languages*. Oxford: Oxford University Press.

Niditch, Susan. 1995. "Oral Register in the Biblical Libretto: Towards a Biblical Poetic." *Oral Tradition,* 10: 387–408.

———. 1996. *Oral World and Written Word: Ancient Israelite Literature.* Louisville: Westminster John Knox Press.

Niles, John D. 1994. "Editing *Beowulf:* What Can Study of the Ballads Tell Us?" *Oral Tradition,* 9: 440–67.

———. 1998. "British American Balladry." In Foley 1998a: 280–90.

———. 1999. *Homo Narrans: The Poetics and Anthropology of Oral Literature.* Philadelphia: University of Pennsylvania Press.

Nixon, Robert. 1994. *Homelands, Harlem, and Hollywood: South African Culture and the World Beyond.* New York: Routledge.

Obiechina, Emmanuel. 1992. "Narrative Proverbs in the African Novel." *Oral Tradition,* 7: 197–230.

O'Donnell, James J. 1998. *Avatars of the Word: From Papyrus to Cyberspace.* Cambridge, Mass.: Harvard University Press.

Oesterreicher, Wulf. 1997. "Types of Orality in Text." In *Written Voices, Spoken Signs: Tradition, Performance, and the Epic Text,* ed. Egbert Bakker and Ahuvia Kahane. Cambridge, Mass.: Harvard University Press. Pp. 190–214, 257–60.

Oinas, Felix J., ed. 1978. *Heroic Epic and Saga: An Introduction to the World's Great Folk Epics.* Bloomington: Indiana University Press.

O'Keeffe, Katherine O'Brien. 1990. *Visible Song: Transitional Literacy in Old English Verse.* Cambridge: Cambridge University Press.

———. 1997. "Diction, Variation, the Formula." In Bjork and Niles 1997: 85–104.

Okpewho, Isidore. 1992. *African Oral Literature: Backgrounds, Character, Continuity.* Bloomington: Indiana University Press.

Olson, David R. 1994. *The World on Paper: The Conceptual and Cognitive Implications of Writing and Reading.* Cambridge: Cambridge University Press.

———, and Nancy Torrance, eds. 1991. *Literacy and Orality.* Cambridge: Cambridge University Press.

Ong, Walter J. 1981. *Fighting for Life: Contest, Sexuality, and Consciousness.* Ithaca: Cornell University Press.

———. 1982. *Orality and Literacy: The Technologizing of the Word.* New York and London: Methuen.

Opland, Jeff. 1980. *Anglo-Saxon Oral Poetry: A Study of the Traditions.* New Haven: Yale University Press.

———. 1983. *Xhosa Oral Poetry: Aspects of a Black South African Tradition.* Cambridge: Cambridge University Press.

———. 1998. *Xhosa Oral Poets and Poetry.* Cape Town: David Philip.

Oral Tradition. 1986–. A journal devoted to the world's oral traditions and related forms. Searchable index at <http://www.oraltradition.org>.

Parks, Ward. 1990. *Verbal Dueling in Heroic Narrative: The Homeric and Old English Traditions.* Princeton: Princeton University Press.

Parry, Milman. 1971. *The Making of Homeric Verse: The Collected Papers of Milman Parry.* Oxford: Oxford University Press. Rpt. 1987.

Parthasarathy, R., trans. 1993. *The Cilappatikaram of Ilanko Atikal: An Epic of South India.* New York: Columbia University Press.

Pennington, Anne, and Peter Levi. 1984. *Marko the Prince.* New York: St. Martin's Press.

People's Poetry Gathering: March 30–April 1, 2001. New York: City Lore and Poets House.

Pihel, Erik. 1996. "A Furified Freestyle: Homer and Hip Hop." *Oral Tradition,* 11: 249–69.

Pinsky, Robert. 1998. *The Sounds of Poetry: A Brief Guide.* New York: Farrar, Straus, and Giroux.

Popović, Tatyana. 1988. *Prince Marko: The Hero of South Slavic Epics.* Syracuse: Syracuse University Press.

Porter, James. 2001. "'Bring Me the Head of James Macpherson': The Execution of Ossian and the Wellsprings of Folkloristic Discourse." *Journal of American Folklore,* 114: 396–435.

Powell, Barry B. 1991. *Homer and the Origin of the Greek Alphabet.* Cambridge: Cambridge University Press.

Prendergast, Guy L. 1971 [1875]. *A Complete Concordance to the Iliad of Homer.* Rev. by Benedetto Marzullo. Hildesheim: Georg Olms.

Raffel, Burton, trans. 1963. *Beowulf.* New York: Mentor. Rpt. 1999.

———, trans. 1998. *Poems and Prose from the Old English.* New Haven: Yale University Press.

Raheja, Gloria Goodwin, ed. 1997. *South Asian Oral Traditions.* A special issue of *Oral Tradition,* 12, i.

Rai, B. A. Viveka. 1996. "Epics in the Oral Genre System of Tulunadu." *Oral Tradition,* 11: 163–72.

Ramsey, Jarold. 1999. *Reading the Fire: The Traditional Indian Literatures of America.* Rev. ed. Seattle: University of Washington Press.

Reichl, Karl. 1992. *Turkic Oral Epic Poetry: Traditions, Forms, Poetic Structures.* Albert Bates Lord Studies in Oral Literature, 7. New York: Garland.

———. 2000. *Singing the Past: Turkic and Medieval Heroic Poetry.* Ithaca: Cornell University Press.

Roach, Keith, ed. 2000. *Nuyorican Poets Cafe Slambook: Grand Slam Finale 2000.* New York: Clare Ultimo.

Rosenberg, Bruce A. 1988. *Can These Bones Live? The Art of the American Folk Preacher.* Urbana: University of Illinois Press.

———. 1994. "Forrest Spirits: Oral Echoes in Leon Forrest's Prose." *Oral Tradition,* 9: 315–27.

Roy, Arundhati. 1997. *The God of Small Things.* New York: Random House.

Rubin, David C. 1995. *Memory in Oral Traditions: The Cognitive Psychology of Epic, Ballads, and Counting-Out Rhymes.* New York: Oxford University Press.

Rychner, Jean. 1955. *La Chanson de geste: Essai sur l'art épique des jongleurs.* Geneva and Lille: Droz and Giard.

———. 1958. "La Chanson de geste, épopée vivante." *La Table ronde,* 132: 152–67.

Saenger, Paul. 1997. *Space between Words: The Origins of Silent Reading.* Stanford: Stanford University Press.

Sale, Merritt. 1999. "Virgil's Formularity and *Pius Aeneas.*" In *Signs of Orality: The Oral Tradition and Its Influence in the Greek and Roman World,* ed. E. A. Mackay. Leiden: Brill. Pp. 199–220.

Sargent, Stuart H. 1994. "Context of the Song Lyric in Sung Times: Communication Technology, Social Change, Morality." In *Voices of the Song Lyric in China,* ed. Pauline Yu. Berkeley and Los Angeles: University of California Press. Pp. 226–56.

Schaefer, Ursula. 1992. *Vokalität: Altenglische Dichtung zwischen Mündlichkeit und Schriftlichkeit.* ScriptOralia, 39. Tübingen: Gunter Narr.

———. 1993. "Alterities: On Methodology in Medieval Literary Studies." *Oral Tradition,* 8: 187–214.

Schmandt-Besserat, Denise. 1992. *Before Writing.* Vol. 1: *From Counting to Cuneiform.* Austin: University of Texas Press.

SCHS. 1953–. *Serbocroatian Heroic Songs* (*Srpskohrvatske junačke pjesme*). Cambridge, Mass., and Belgrade: Harvard University Press and the Serbian Academy of Sciences.

Seeger, Judith. 1990. *Count Claros: Study of a Ballad Tradition.* New York: Garland.

Sherzer, Joel. 1998. *Verbal Art in San Blas: Kuna Culture through Its Discourse.* Albuquerque: University of New Mexico Press. Orig. ed. Cambridge: Cambridge University Press, 1990.

Shuman, Amy. 1986. *Storytelling Rights: The Uses of Oral and Written Texts by Urban Adolescents.* Cambridge: Cambridge University Press.

Small, Jocelyn Penny. 1997. *Wax Tablets of the Mind: Cognitive Studies of Memory and Literacy in Classical Antiquity.* New York: Routledge.

Smith, Colin, ed. 1964. *Spanish Ballads.* Oxford: Pergamon Press.

Smith, John D., ed. and trans. 1991. *The Epic of Pabuji: A Study, Transcription, and Translation.* Cambridge: Cambridge University Press.

Stock, Brian. 1983. *The Implications of Literacy: Written Language and Models of Interpretation in the Eleventh and Twelfth Centuries.* Princeton: Princeton University Press.

———. 1990. *Listening for the Text: On the Uses of the Past.* Baltimore: Johns Hopkins University Press.

Stratton, Richard, and Kim Wozencraft, eds. 1998. *Slam: The Screenplay and Filmmakers' Journals.* New York: Grove Press.

Street, Brian V. 1984. *Literacy in Theory and Practice.* Cambridge: Cambridge University Press.

———. 1993. *Cross-cultural Approaches to Literacy.* Cambridge: Cambridge University Press.

———. 1995. *Social Literacies: Critical Approaches to Literacy in Development, Ethnography, and Education.* London and New York: Longman.

Svenbro, Jesper. 1999. "Archaic and Classical Greece: The Invention of Silent Reading." In Cavallo and Chartier 1999: 37–63.

Swann, Brian, ed. 1983. *Smoothing the Ground: Essays on Native American Oral Literature.* Berkeley and Los Angeles: University of California Press.

————, ed. 1992. *On the Translation of Native American Literatures.* Washington, D.C.: Smithsonian University Press.

Swann, Brian, and Arnold Krupat, eds. 1987. *Recovering the Word: Essays on Native American Literature.* Berkeley and Los Angeles: University of California Press.

Swiderski, Richard M. 1988. "Oral Text: A South Indian Instance." *Oral Tradition,* 3: 122–37.

Tanselle, G. Thomas. 1995. "The Varieties of Textual Editing." In Greetham 1995: 9–32.

Taylor, Andrew. 2001. "Was There a Song of Roland?" *Speculum,* 76: 28–65.

Tedlock, Dennis, trans. 1972. *Finding the Center: Narrative Poetry of the Zuni Indians.* New York: Dial Press, 1972. Rpt. Lincoln: University of Nebraska Press, 1978.

————. 1983. *The Spoken Word and the Work of Interpretation.* Philadelphia: University of Pennsylvania Press.

————. 1990. "From Voice and Ear to Hand and Eye." *Journal of American Folklore,* 103: 133–56.

————. 1993. *Breath on the Mirror: Mythic Voices and Visions of the Living Maya.* New York: HarperCollins.

————, trans. 1996. *Popol Vuh: The Mayan Book of the Dawn of Life.* Rev. ed. New York: Simon & Schuster.

————, trans. 1999. *Finding the Center: The Art of the Zuni Storyteller.* 2d ed. Lincoln: University of Nebraska Press. Orig. ed. 1972.

Temple, Robert. 1986. *The Genius of China: Three Thousand Years of Science, Discovery, and Invention.* New York: Simon & Schuster.

Thomas, Rosalind. 1989. *Oral Tradition and Written Record in Classical Athens.* Cambridge: Cambridge University Press.

Titon, Jeff Todd. 1988. *Powerhouse for God: Speech, Chant, and Song in an Appalachian Baptist Church.* Austin: University of Texas Press.

————. 1994. *Early Downhome Blues: A Musical and Cultural Analysis.* 2d ed. Chapel Hill: University of North Carolina Press. Orig. ed. Urbana: University of Illinois Press, 1977.

Toelken, Barre. 1998. "Native American Traditions (North)." In Foley 1998a: 151–61.

Urban, Greg. 1991. *A Discourse-Centered Approach to Culture: Native South American Myths and Rituals.* Austin: University of Texas Press.

Vikis-Freibergs, Vaira, ed. 1989a. *Linguistics and Poetics of Latvian Folk Songs.* Kingston and Montreal: McGill-Queen's University Press.

————. 1989b. "Text Variants in the Latvian Folk-Song Corpus: Theoretical and Practical Problems." In Vikis-Freibergs 1989a: 49–72.

Vitz, Evelyn Birge. 1998. "Old French Literature." In Foley 1998a: 373–81.

Wagner, Richard A. 1983. "Different Views of Historical Reality: Oral and Written Recollections in a Serbian Village." *Southeastern Europe,* 10: 175–88.

Warner, Elizabeth A. 1974. "Pushkin in the Russian Folk-Plays." In *Oral Literature: Seven Essays,* ed. Joseph J. Duggan. Edinburgh and New York: Scottish Academic Press and Barnes and Noble. Pp. 101–7.

Webber, Ruth H. 1986a. "The *Cantar de Mio Cid:* Problems of Interpretation." In Foley 1986: 65–88.

———. 1986b. "Hispanic Oral Literature: Accomplishments and Perspectives." *Oral Tradition,* 1: 344–80.

Wehmeyer-Shaw, Debra. 1993. "Rap Music: An Interview with DJ Romeo." *Oral Tradition,* 8: 225–46.

Wiget, Andrew, ed. 1996. *Handbook of Native American Literature.* New York: Garland.

Wilson, Duncan. 1986. *The Life and Times of Vuk Stefanović Karadžić, 1787–1864.* Ann Arbor: University of Michigan. Orig. ed. Oxford: Clarendon Press, 1970.

Words on Fire. 2000. Providence, R.I.: n.p.

Yang Enhong. 1998. "A Comparative Study of the Singing Styles of Mongolian and Tibetan Geser/Gesar Artists." *Oral Tradition,* 13: 422–34.

Zemke, John. 1998. "General Hispanic Traditions." In Foley 1998a: 202–15.

Zumthor, Paul. 1987. *La Lettre et la voix: De la "littérature" médiévale.* Paris: Editions du Seuil.

———. 1990. *Oral Poetry: An Introduction.* Trans. Kathryn Murphy-Judy. Minneapolis: University of Minnesota Press. Orig. publ. as *Introduction à la poésie orale.* Paris: Editions du Seuil, 1983.

Zumwalt, Rosemary Lévy. 1998. "A Historical Glossary of Critical Approaches." In Foley 1998a: 75–94.

Index

John Miles Foley is Curators' Professor of Classical Studies and English and Byler Endowed Chair in the Humanities at the University of Missouri–Columbia, where he teaches ancient Greek, medieval English, and South Slavic language and literature. Among his recent books are *Traditional Oral Epic, Immanent Art, The Singer of Tales in Performance,* and *Homer's Traditional Art.* Foley serves as director of the Center for Studies in Oral Tradition at the University of Missouri and is the founding editor of the journal *Oral Tradition.*

The University of Illinois Press
is a founding member of the
Association of American University Presses.

Composed in 10.5/13 Minion
with Minion display
by Jim Proefrock
at the University of Illinois Press
Designed by Dennis Roberts
Manufactured by Thomson-Shore, Inc.

University of Illinois Press
1325 South Oak Street
Champaign, IL 61820-6903
www.press.uillinois.edu